ink & wash
wildflowers

25 Watercolor & Ink Projects to Bring Native Flowers to Life

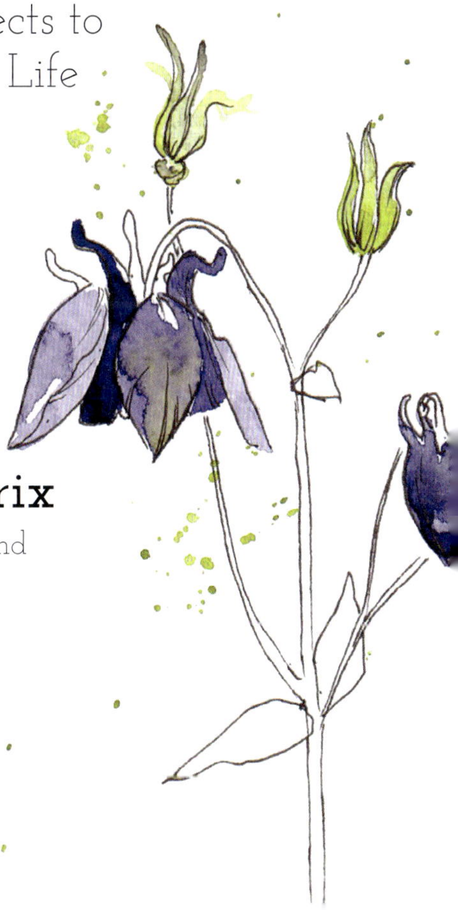

camilla damsbo brix

author of *Ink & Wash Florals* and
Ink & Wash in the Garden

PAGE STREET
PUBLISHING CO.

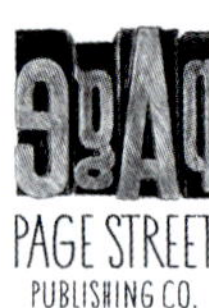

PAGE STREET
PUBLISHING CO.

Copyright © 2025 Camilla Damsbo Brix

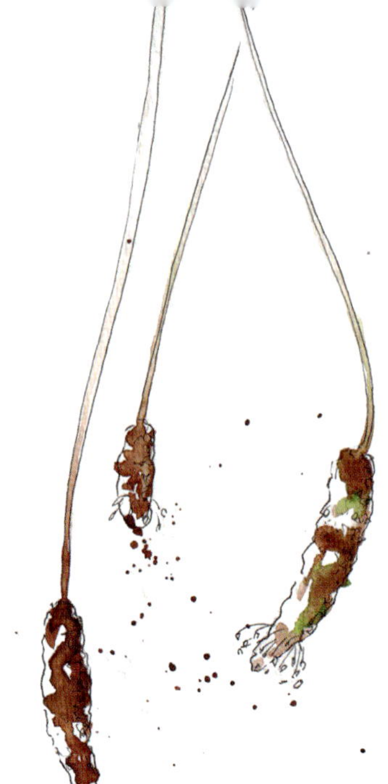

First published in 2025 by

Page Street Publishing Co.

27 Congress Street, Suite 1511

Salem, MA 01970

www.pagestreetpublishing.com

Distributed by Macmillan, sales in Canada by The Canadian Manda Group.

29 28 27 26 25   1 2 3 4 5

ISBN-13: 979-8-89003-349-9

Library of Congress Control Number: 2025942708

Edited by Sadie Hofmeester

Cover and book design by Emma Hardy for Page Street Publishing Co.

Photography by Camilla Damsbo Brix and Jess Lycoops

Artwork by Camilla Damsbo Brix

Printed and bound in the United States of America

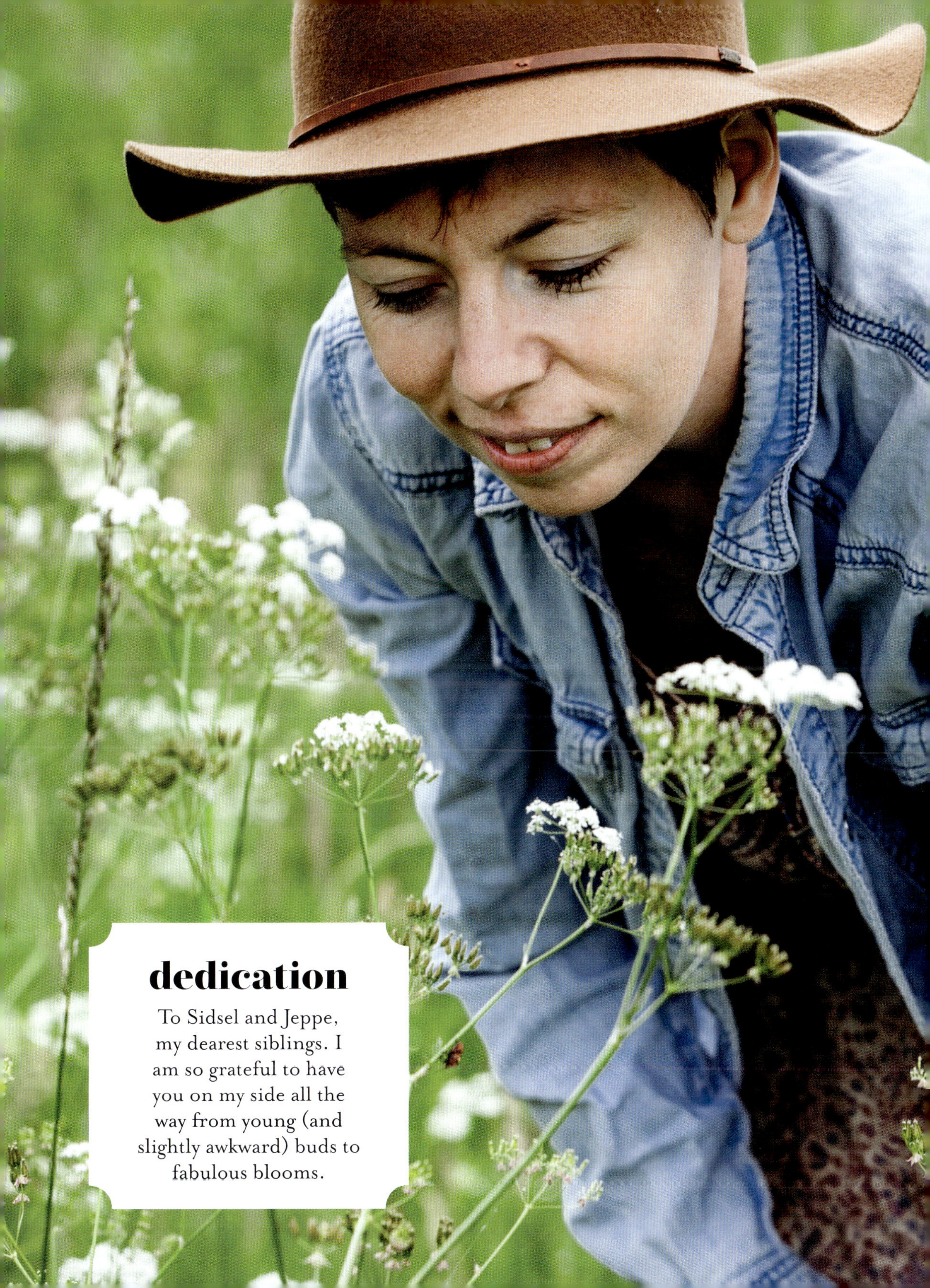

dedication

To Sidsel and Jeppe,
my dearest siblings. I
am so grateful to have
you on my side all the
way from young (and
slightly awkward) buds to
fabulous blooms.

contents

part III
Five Dancing Grasses   105

part IV
Four Dreamy Meadow Compositions   125

part V
Wildflowers Are a Love Story   151

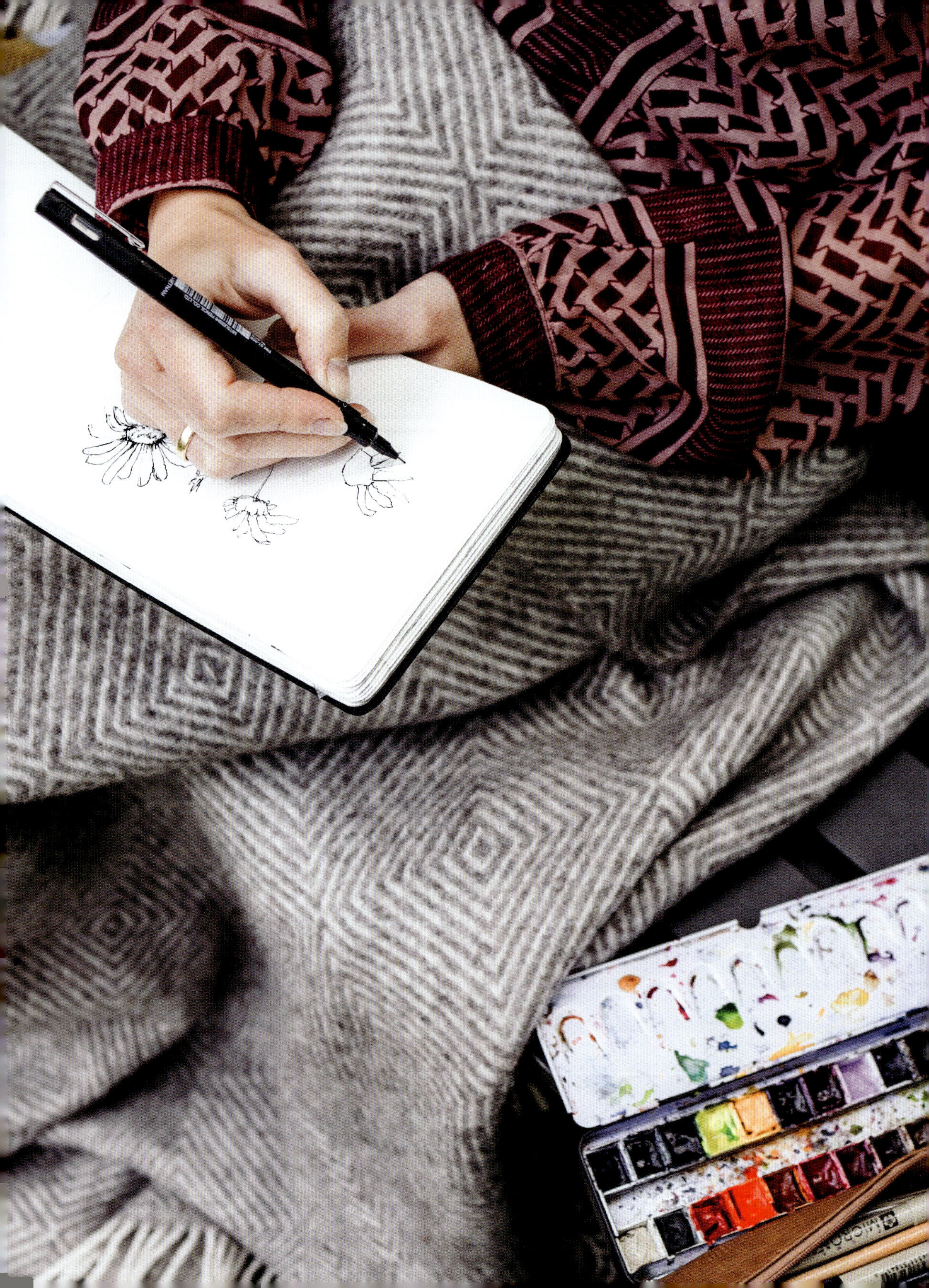

welcome!

I want to welcome you with open arms! This is my third book, and I have to say that this book has been on my mind for many years . . . almost writing itself in my head. Every time I went for a walk and saw a wildflower on the side of the road, I made mental notes and sketches. I observed how it changed through the seasons and enjoyed every bit of the journey. From the fragrant wild roses to the whimsical dandelions, they all had a mystical beauty to them.

At some point I realized that the flowers changed incredibly fast and if I wanted to capture this, I needed a unique style. I wanted a style that was quick, dynamic and fun. This is when I noticed how great ink and wash, also known as line and wash, is. The sketches are fast, light and filled with lots of movement—just like the flowers. And as a bonus, this technique does not require many supplies, so I could just have a grab-and-go set for every time I went outside.

My hope is that this book will inspire you to go outside as well to observe, explore and sketch. The wildflowers out there are stunning, especially when we start to look further than just the perfect, full blooms. There is beauty in the young buds in the spring, the fading colors at the end of season and the flowers surviving against heavy rain and slug attacks.

Before we dive into the good stuff, I would love to give you a guided tour of the book so you know what to expect. We start by diving into the basics that are great to know for when you first get started. Here, I try to remove the myth that it is expensive to create art by focusing on how few supplies and techniques you actually need to get started.

Then, I take you through a few techniques I use specifically when creating wildflowers in different growth stages and in different lighting and settings. I want to show you that you never run out of motifs if you are open to everything that nature provides. It is quite magical.

After the techniques, you are taken through sixteen step-by-step wildflower tutorials followed by five tutorials of simple grasses. I thought it was really fun to include grasses because they are a super simple element to add to your floral drawing to give it movement and texture. When you feel like you are ready to put everything together, you can jump to the next section where you will meet four floral compositions. These are all quite different, showing the variety of ways you can combine the flowers you just learned to sketch in larger compositions and landscapes.

Finally, you are ready to be sent out into the flower field with a sketchbook in hand. In the final section, I talk about floral artist goggles and why you don't want to leave them at home, how you avoid overwhelm at floral peak season and also about the incredible love story sketching wildflowers really is.

I would absolutely love to see what you create! So, share your sketches on Instagram and tag me. I'm @camilla_damsbo_art over there. You are making the world a brighter and happier place every time you observe and sketch a flower, and I would love to be a small part of that.

Camilla Damsbo Brix

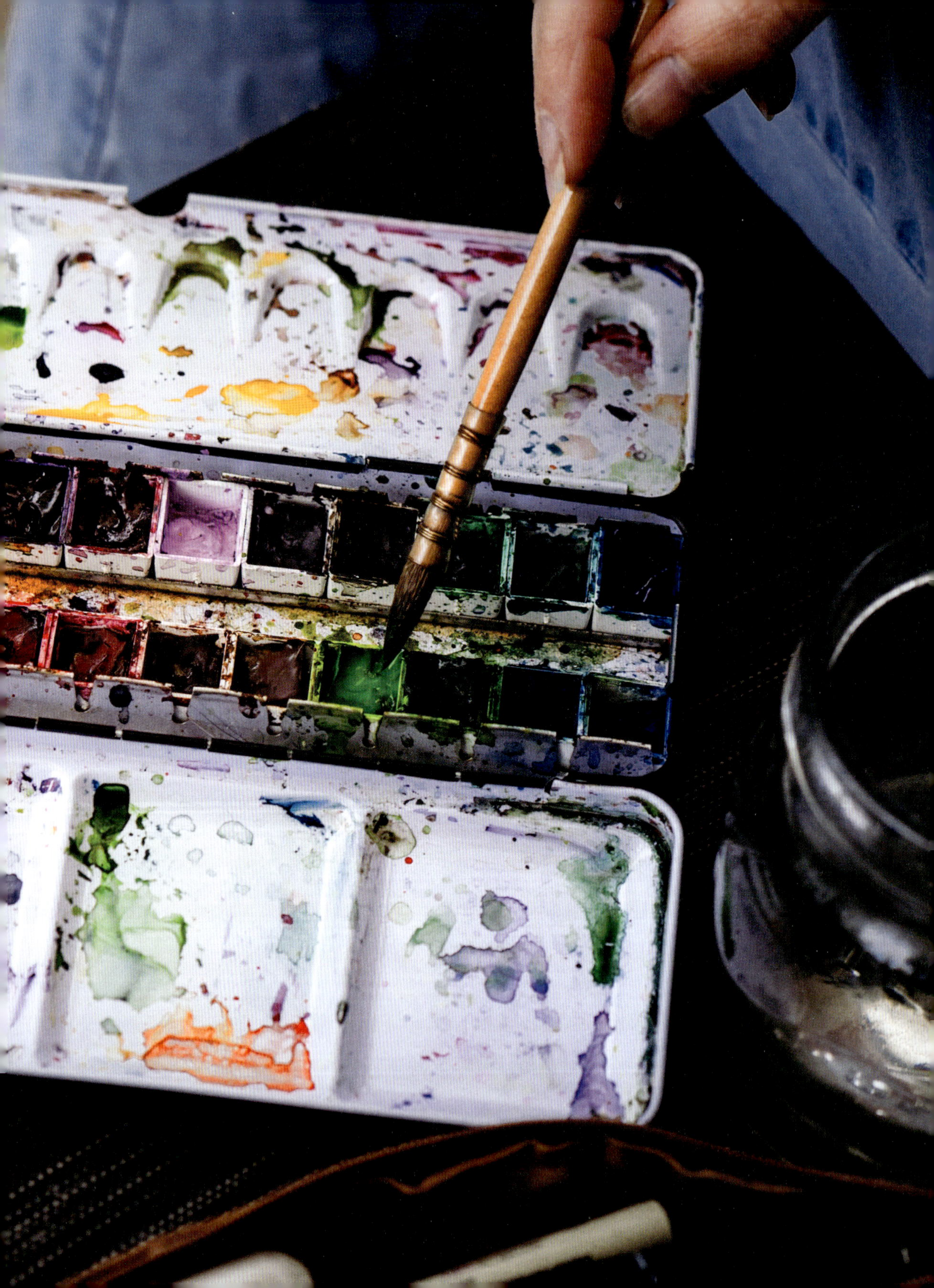

part I
all you need to get started

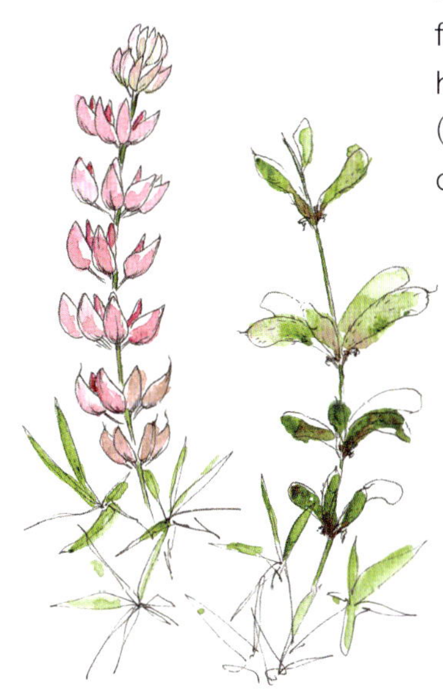

It's tempting to think you need a lot of supplies to get started—especially when you tackle a technique that includes drawing as well as painting. But here in the first chapter, I want to tackle that art myth and show how little you actually need. With just a few materials (and a couple of techniques) you'll be ready to make art in no time at all!

supplies

To make beautiful ink and wash wildflowers, you don't need to invest in a lot of expensive supplies. With only a few materials, you'll be ready to venture into your neighborhood meadow and bring it home with you in your sketchbook!

Brushes

In the twenty-five tutorials in this book, I only use four different brushes. And one of them, the fan brush used in Feather Grass (page 121), is experimental and not necessary if you don't have one in your stash just yet. For the most part, I use a medium size 4 brush. For very thin lines, I use a small size 1 brush and for bigger washes, a size 8. A small, medium and big brush are all you need to get variation in your lines.

> **Pro Tip:** When you dip a brush (especially a small brush) in water, you can sometimes get water droplets on the handle. At some point, gravity will take that bad boy droplet down and there is a risk of ruining your drawing. So, make sure to be aware of droplets and remove them with a paper towel.

My brushes are all synthetic round brushes. I love these brushes so much. They hold just the right amount of water without getting so wet that you can't control it. Also, no squirrels were harmed making them, which is a pretty big thing, too.

Fineliners

In this book, I only use fineliners in sizes 01 and 005. The 01 is for the outlines and the 005 fineliner for all the texture, direction lines and details. My go-to brand is Pigma Micron®, because they just have a nice flow to them that I enjoy a lot. Usually, I only go for black fineliners and you can start there too. But after you are done with the book I strongly recommend experimenting with other colors because that is super fun, too.

You don't need to use the same brand as I do, but make sure your fineliners are waterproof and lightfast. That way they won't smear in water or be ruined by the sun, almost like waterproof mascara with SPF 50.

Paper

With these small line and wash sketches, you don't need super fancy or expensive cotton paper. We use very little water in these sketches compared to big watercolor paintings, so cellulose paper works perfectly. And because you don't have to worry about costly paper, you can be freer and a lot more experimental in your art. I use Canson Montval® 300gsm (140lb) cold press cellulose paper in this book.

Make sure your paper is 300gsm (140lb) watercolor paper, though, so that it doesn't buckle right away when water hits it. That is just annoying, and you risk getting holes in your paper. Unless you are going for the Swiss cheese look, I would steer far away from copy paper—just saying. Don't go there.

Paint

For the tutorials in the book, I use my regular Daniel Smith set and try to keep a minimal color palette of just ten colors. I do this in order to make it super easy to create compositions that work well together.

> **Pro Tip:** My paints are all tube paints that I squeeze into pans. I let them dry for 48 hours and they work just as well as prefilled pans. The only difference is the price, which in my opinion is a game-changer. Having more money to buy supplies will never be a bad thing, right?

Colors I Used	Alternative Colors
Prussian Blue (cool blue)	Winsor Blue or Ultramarine Blue
Payne's Gray (gray with a blue tone)	Mix this by using Ultramarine Blue and Burnt Sienna or by using Lamp Black with a bit of blue.
Dioxazine Violet (cool violet)	Mix this by using Phthalo Blue and slowly adding a cool red until you get the shade you like.
Sap Green (warm, earthy green)	Olive Green, or mix this using Hooker's Green and a bit of red.
Green Gold (cool green)	Mix this by using a warm green like Sap Green and a cool yellow like Hansa Yellow Light.
Quinacridone Rose (cool red)	Permanent Rose, Carmine or Rose Madder
Hansa Yellow Light (cool yellow)	Lemon Yellow or Winsor Yellow
New Gamboge (warm yellow)	Cadmium Yellow Deep, Sunflower Yellow or other warm yellows
Burnt Umber (warm brown)	Sepia or Burnt Sienna
Van Dyke Brown (cool brown)	Mix this by using brown and a bit of Lamp Black.

Other Things You Are Going to Love Having Around

With all that paint, you will need a small ceramic palette for mixing. If you don't have one, just grab a white plate in the kitchen and you are all set.

Another essential that is used in a lot of the tutorials is, of course, a pencil. And with that come its best friends: The sharpener and the eraser. Together, those three things can make the drawing process easier and so much more fun.

Finally, you will of course need a jar of water and a cloth to dry off your brush. Nothing fancy is needed here. My water jar is actually an old jam jar and my cloth is cotton, so I can wash it once in a while and make it last for many, many years.

Experiment: Mist Spray Bottle, Fan Brushes and More

It's always fun to experiment. And you can do that with so many things. Here in the book, I use a mist spray bottle to spread the water on the Forget-Me-Not flowers (page 37) and a fan brush to create the flowy Feather Grass (page 121). When you feel comfortable with the simple supplies you need in the book, go crazy and try something new. Trust me, it's so much fun and suddenly you will start looking at everything as a potential painting tool. Just imagine what you could do with beautiful lace from an old tablecloth or a twig from the forest.

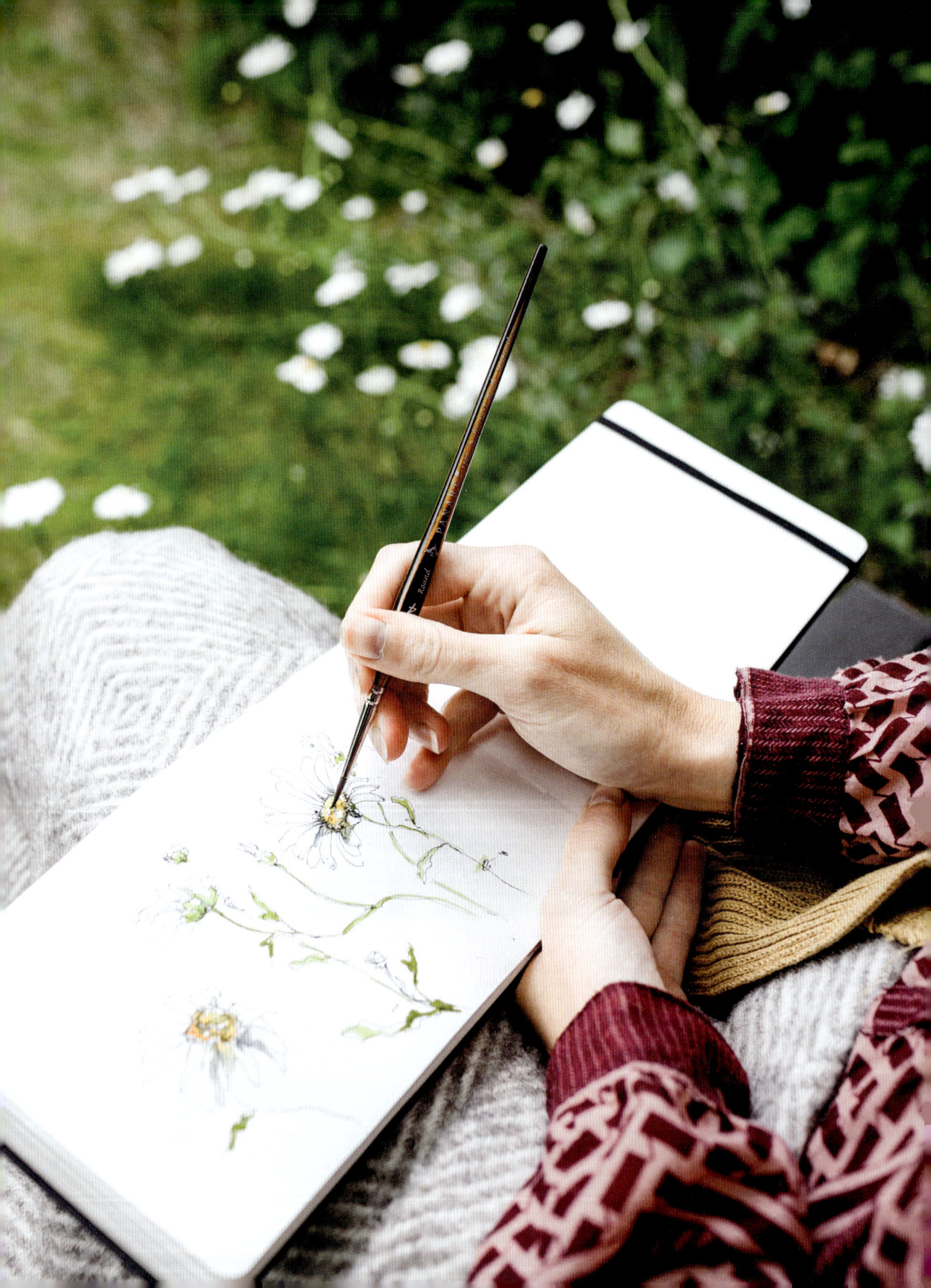

fundamental watercolor techniques

The native plants you will find in this book are all made with simple painting and drawing techniques. To give you an overview and prepare you for what's to come, I've listed them here below.

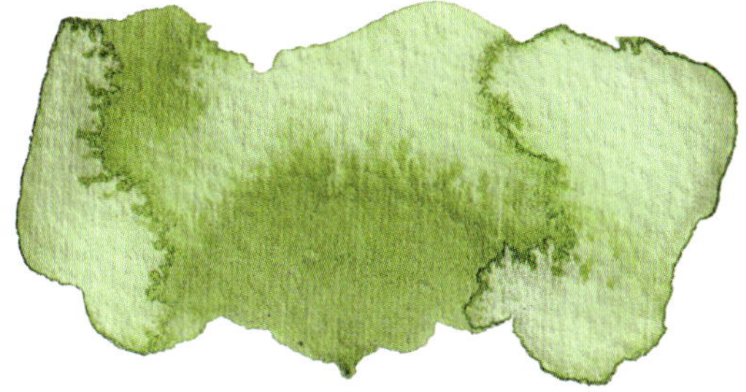

Wet-on-Dry

When you paint with the wet-on-dry technique, it's almost like drawing with a pencil. You start by wetting your brush in water and then loading it with paint. Then, you paint directly on the dry paper. This technique gives you a lot of control in contrast to the wet-on-wet technique. You can create several layers of wet-on-dry paint that will make your colors vibrant and strong. Be sure to let the first layer dry completely before doing the next one.

Wet-on-Wet

To create the ethereal watercolor look, you start by wetting the paper with clean water. When the page is glossy, but without puddles of water, load your brush with paint. Then softly let the brush touch the water and the color will burst into the water like fireworks. It can be tempting to help the paint flow in the water but try to pace yourself. Let the water do the work because it is pretty good at it. I know letting go of control can be challenging, but trust me, you will create magic if you do.

If the paint is not flowing, it might be because you need more water. Drip in a bit more water to get it to flow.

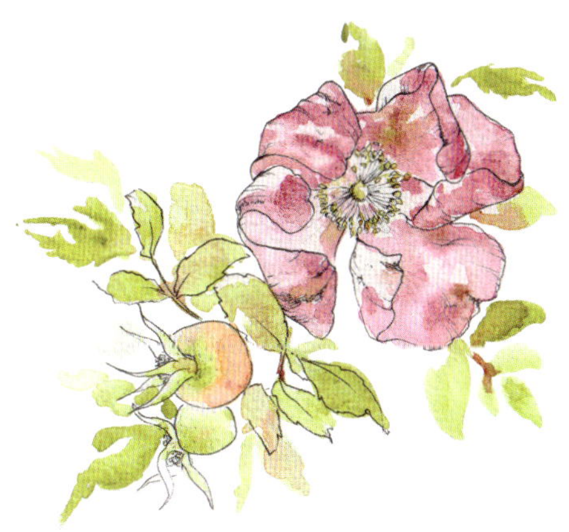

Charging

As long as your paper is wet, you can keep adding more color to make it even more vibrant. You can also add other colors to get a color variation in your paint. At some point, the paper will start to dry of course and then you risk getting water blooms, those darker lines in the middle of the paint that show the drying edge. It's a matter of taste if you like that or not. Personally, I think they are super pretty and a big part of the natural watercolor look.

Charging the colors is not always easy to control because you have to look out for the drying areas. You can deal with this in two ways: Either practice it a few times beforehand or you can just trust the process and paint like there is no tomorrow. It's all up to you.

Underpainting

When you want to set the mood for a painting, you can do something really cool called under-painting. You take one color and paint either the entire paper or just the part you want to modify before adding the paint you would normally use. It won't be the white paper setting the mood, but the color of the underpainting. An example of this could be a pink rose sketch. Instead of starting with pink, you would paint the entire area in warm yellow first. After the underpainting has dried, you paint the rose like you would otherwise have done. The yellow will shine through the pink layer and give it a beautiful, warm glow.

I know what you are thinking, and YES! We are going to play with this technique on page 127 to set a sunrise mood.

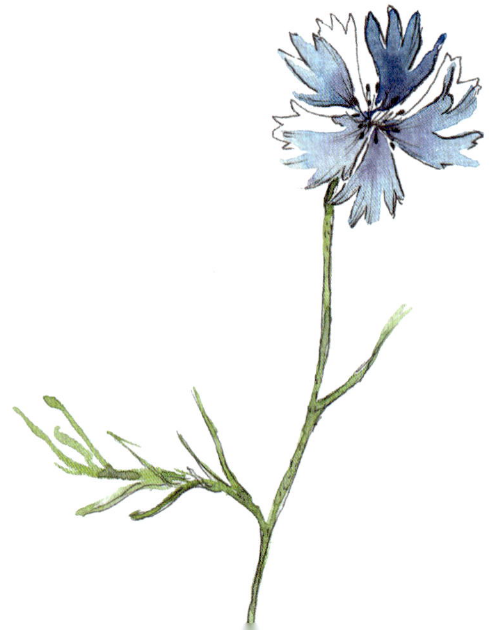

basic fineliner techniques

Outlines and Direction Lines

Outlines are always done first and usually I use my 01 fineliner for these. The outlines are a quick sketch of the outer shape of, for example, a flower or a leaf. I often leave white space in my outlines to avoid it looking too heavy or cartoony. The outline will give us a flat shape that we can build from.

Direction or shaping lines help us make curves in the flat shapes we created with the outline. You can say that the direction lines help us shape things. To create a hierarchy in the lines, I always use a smaller 005 fineliner for the direction lines. Start from the outline and work your way in following the shape. You don't need many lines to suggest the curve, so be careful not to overdo it. Less is usually more.

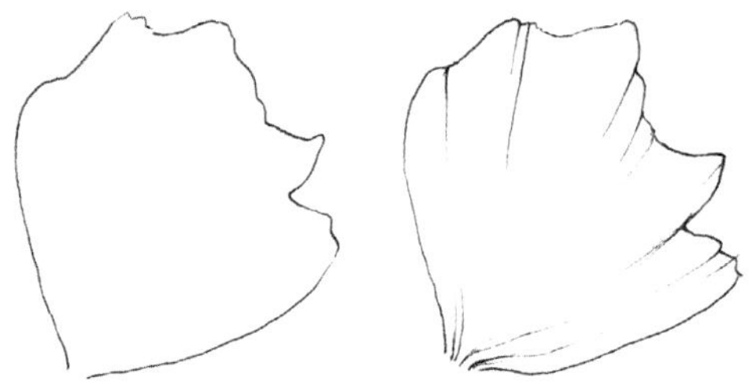

How to Hold Your Fineliner

When you hold your fineliner, remember that the ink comes out of the tip and not the sides like a pencil. This can be a bit annoying at the beginning, so it's good to practice drawing with it a few times before getting started.

You can decide the level of control by choosing how to hold the fineliner. When you hold close to the tip, you have a lot of control, and this is great for finer details. When you move your hand up the handle, you lose a bit of control over the lines. This can sound scary, but it is great for quicker sketches of leaves and details we want to keep in the back with less focus.

Drying Times (or When to Take a Break)

One of the beautiful things about ink and wash is the built-in breaks. Since we are working with two different mediums, it is super important to wait for either the paint or the fineliner to dry 100% before continuing to the next.

The fineliners often dry fast and will only take seconds before you can erase the pencil guidelines or apply the watercolor. But when you do watercolor first, you might want to go for a walk or make a slow cup of tea before you can continue to add the dark lines.

floral shapes

As kids we learn the basic flower shape is a circle with petals around like a daisy. But when we dive a bit deeper, there are actually a lot more shapes and this can open our eyes to a ton of possibilities.

First of all, there are (at least) 9 different flower shapes. Flowers also vary in shape when we see them from different angles. Furthermore, the shape of each flower will change through the seasons as it moves from bud to bloom to wilted beauty. When we start to see all this variation, it opens us up to endless possibilities of flower sketching and that is . . . incredible.

9 Different Floral Shapes

As mentioned above, there are at least nine distinct flower shapes. I made a list here below with examples of flowers with each shape.

1. **Daisy Shape:** This is the traditional, round flower with petals around the center. An example of this shape is, of course, the daisy.

2. **Cup Shape:** These flowers have petals that fold up like a cup. You can see this shape with tulips, poppies and many more.

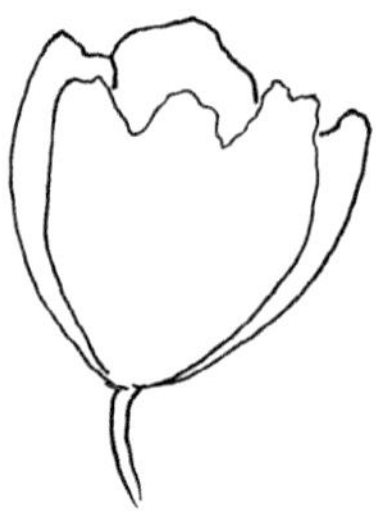

3. **Spike Shape:** These tall blooms tower over the flower field, almost like a spear. An example from the book of this spike shape is the beautiful fireweed.

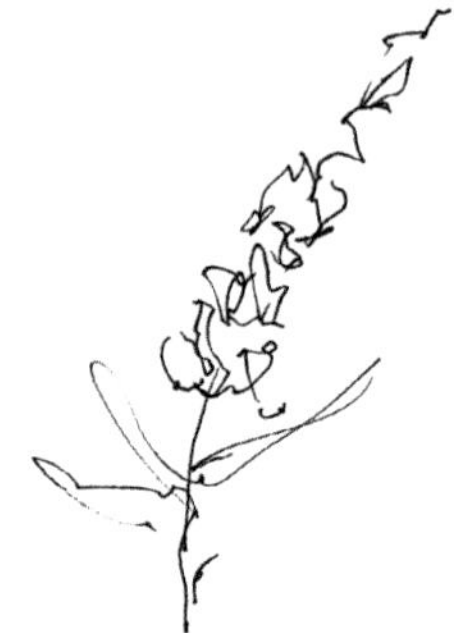

4. **Cluster Shape:** These complex cluster flowers are flowers with a lot of small blooms gathered in clusters. A great example of this flower is the hydrangea.

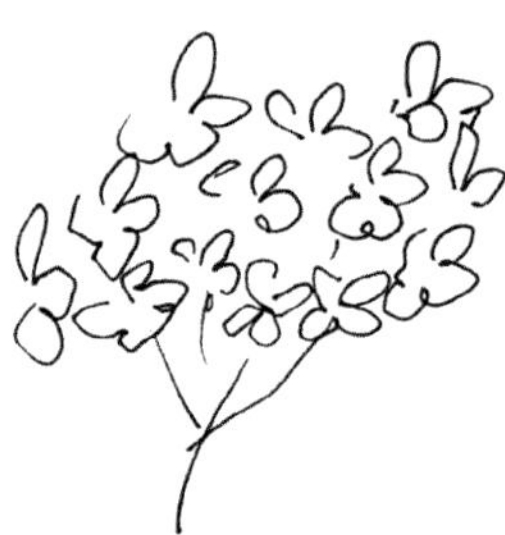

5. **Globe Shape:** This flower has a big, round flower head, like a globe on a stick, and has a bold appearance. In this category, you will find allium and agapanthus.

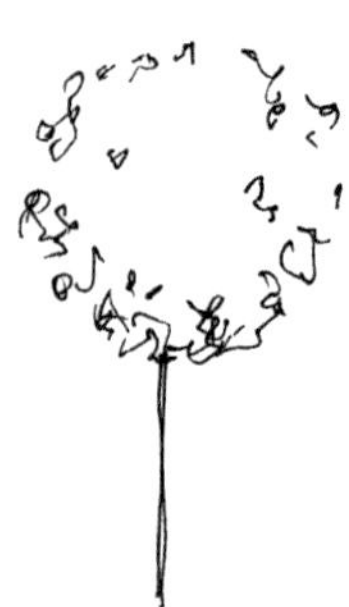

6. **Flathead Shape:** These flowers have a big, flat and horizontal head like the Queen Anne's lace.

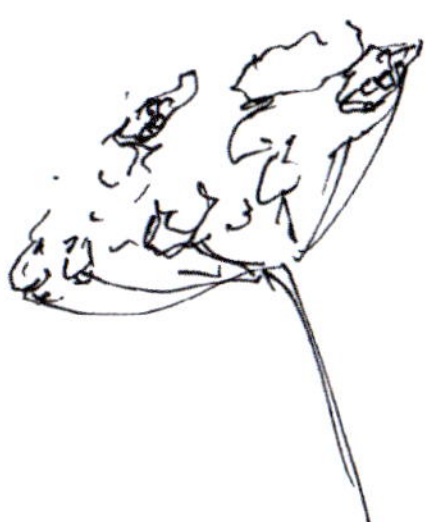

7. **Filler Shape:** These are small blooms that fill up space, making them a great companion to almost all flowers in a composition. Very often you see filler flowers with a central stalk and then lots of small blooms branching from it. An example of this could be the cute baby's breath or forget-me-not flowers.

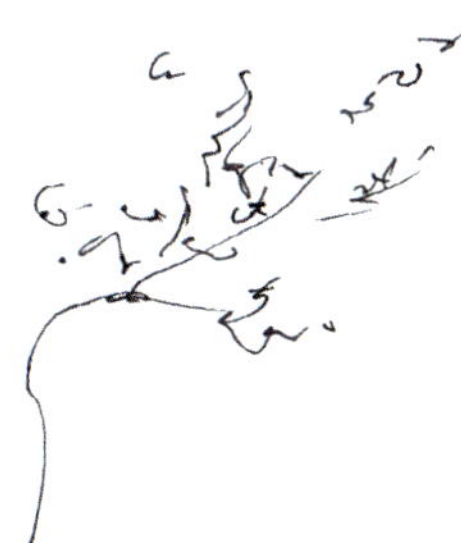

8. **Plume Shape:** Often the plume-shaped flowers are tall, like the spikes, but they are also fluffy and have a lot of nice texture. An example is the astilbe or meadowsweet.

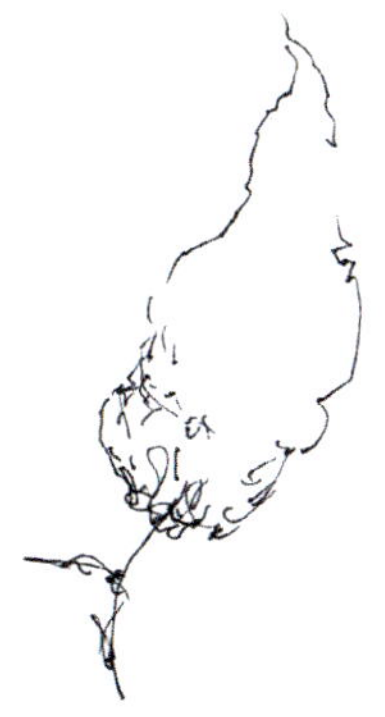

9. **Trumpet Shape:** This unusual shape looks like . . . well . . . a trumpet. Daffodils and lilies spring to mind.

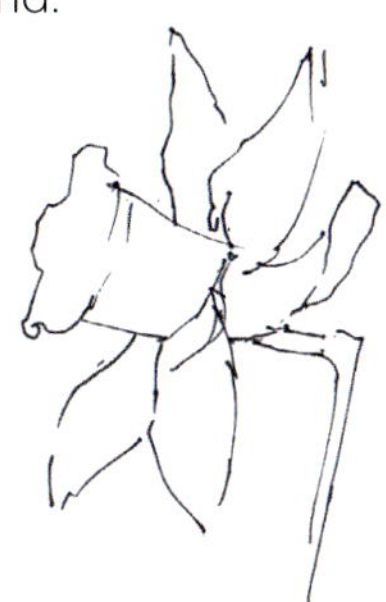

Often, we gravitate toward the easy ones we know well, but next time you need a challenge you can try picking a new shape because they all bring something exciting to the table. In this book, we are going to tackle most of them but there will still be plenty left for you to explore after you finish the last page.

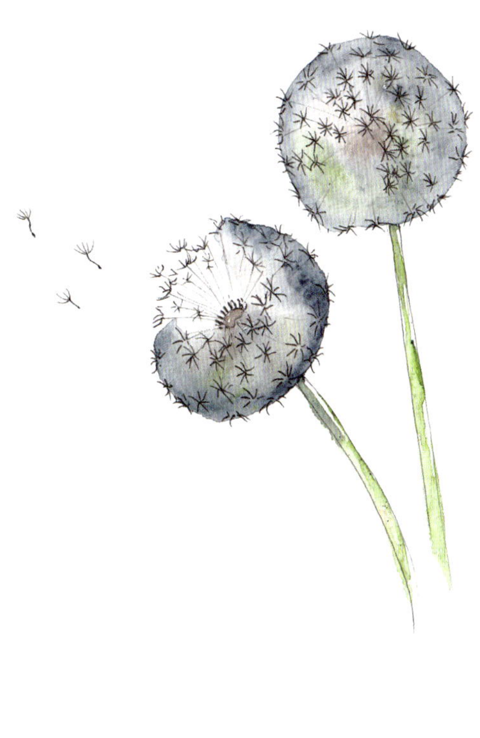

drawing flowers at an angle

As mentioned earlier, we often learn as kids to sketch a daisy in full bloom seen from above. But in real life, it's actually very rare that we see flowers like this. We tend to see flowers from some kind of angle. It can seem tricky at first, but it all comes down to observation. And trust me, it's worth it because you get more realistic flower sketches when you practice this technique.

You start with the main shape. As an example, here is a simple, round daisy shape. If the flower is round like this, the shape will become oval when viewed from the side. Then you have flower petals in the front that are foreshortened, which just means you can't see the entirety of each petal; by making your petals shorter in length but still wide, you create the illusion that they are in front of the center of the flower. There is also a good chance that some petals are folding up, hugging the flower center.

Then you have petals on the sides. Because of the angle they are viewed at, these petals appear longer and leaner.

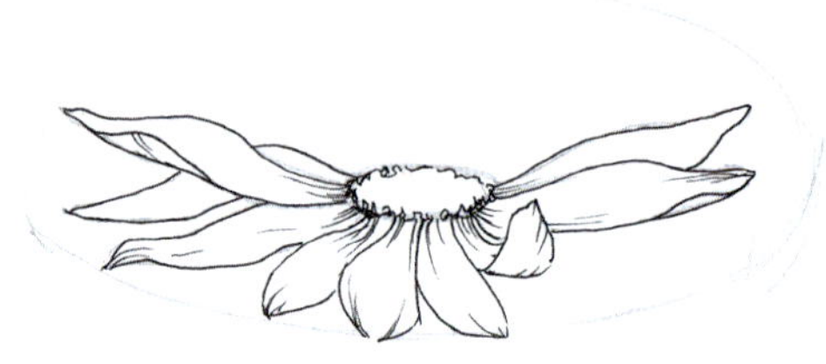

The petals in the back can be folded backward, making them look short. They can also be folded inward, giving them a bend.

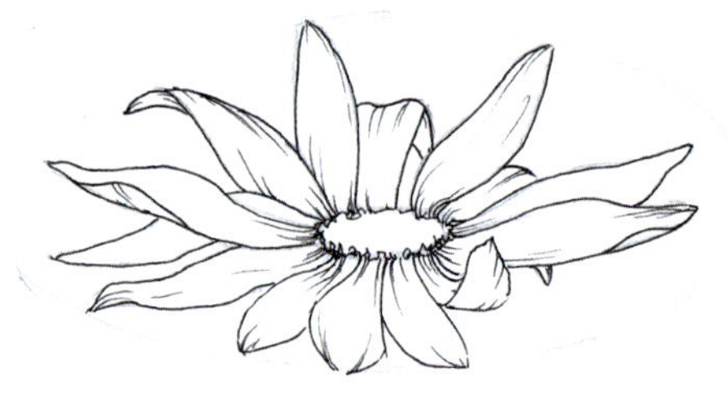

All nine of the flower shapes look different when seen from an angle. So, start by observing and do quick sketches to slowly teach your hand the shapes.

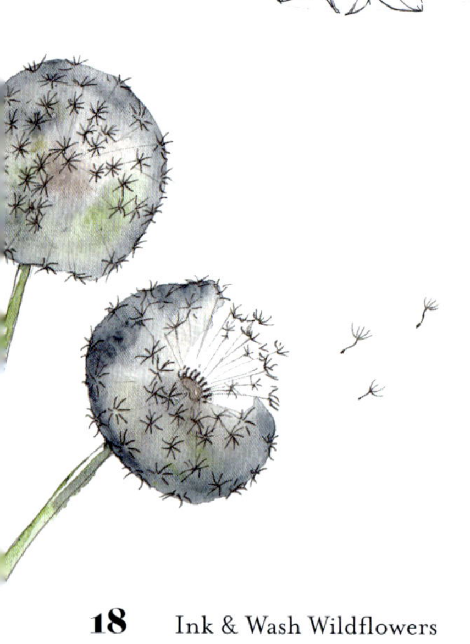

from bud to bloom to faded beauty

Have you ever had a bouquet of very early tulips buds on your table? Have you enjoyed the buds unfolding and revealing their colors and shapes? And then at some point, the blooms become drier and more curled. At that point, most of us throw out the bouquet . . . but try not to. The bouquet's life is far from over. In its last days and weeks, the bouquet shows us new colors and so much beautiful texture. It's a whole new phase of life and it is beautiful.

Transitioning Colors

When you study a bud and see it change over time, the first thing you might notice is that the color changes. In the very beginning, the buds are wrapped in green protective leaves and the bud itself has a lot of that same green color. It's young, naïve and fresh.

When it grows, it slowly loses the green color, changing into its full bloom in its main color. This is the color most of us remember, like the red of a rose or the yellow of a daffodil. But very often we can still see a bit of green if it's a younger bloom or a bit of the colors it will change into in the final stage.

As the flower ages and dries, it becomes even more interesting in my eyes. The color in the "fading" beauty is actually very far from faded. You often see its main color but then you may also see browns, greens and other colors. As an example, a red tulip will often get purple, dark red and brown spots. This stage is super interesting, and you can often spot the flower's main color still . . . a distant memory of its bloom.

Texture Changing

Just as the colors change, so do the textures. In the early stages of the flower, the buds are often very smooth with no texture or flaws . . . like a clean canvas or the cheek of a cute baby.

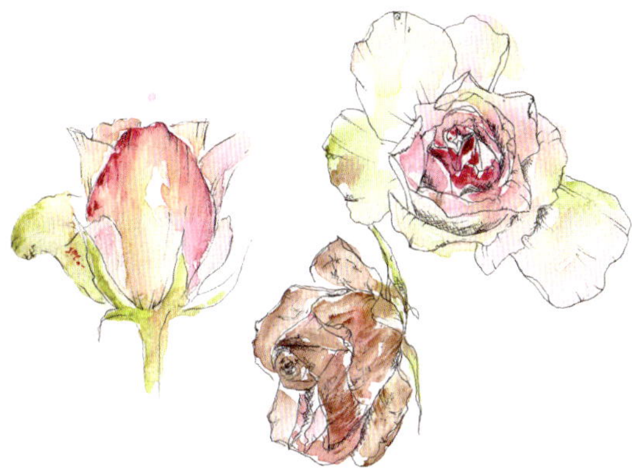

Then in full bloom, you start to see small bends and curls. The flower experiences weather, flies and other things that give it character and texture.

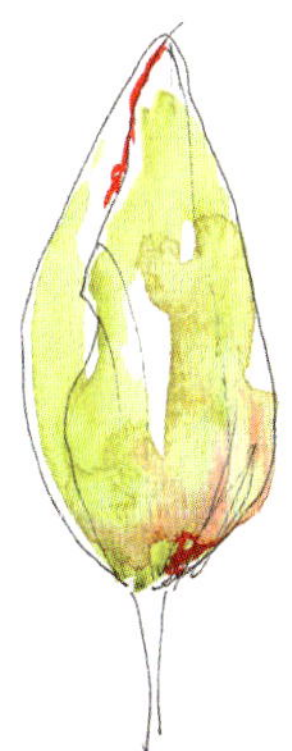

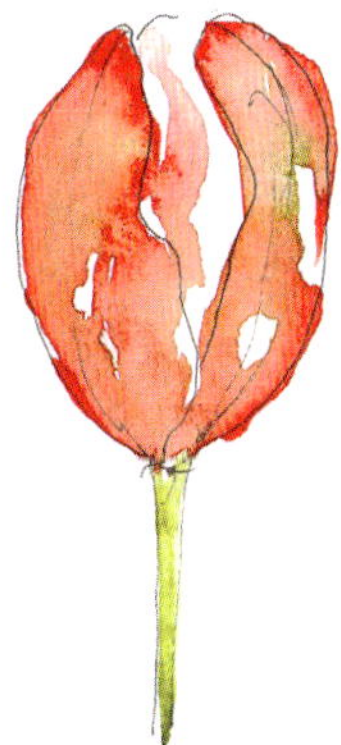

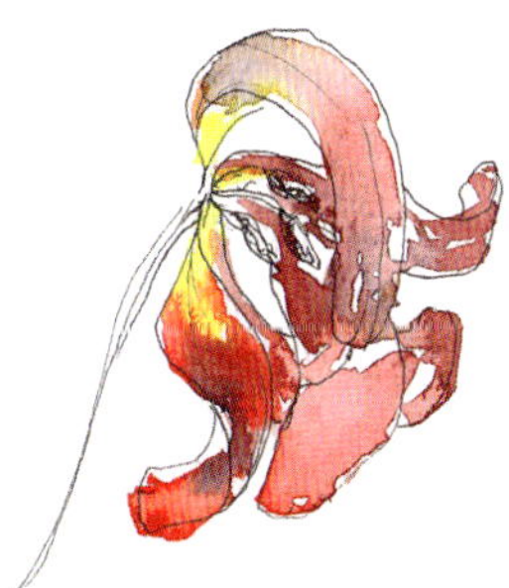

Just like with humans when we age, you will see the life a flower has lived on the skin and the petals. The flowers get more wrinkles, twists and bends. Very often, flowers also get small holes in the petals because of insects, hard rain or other challenges over the year.

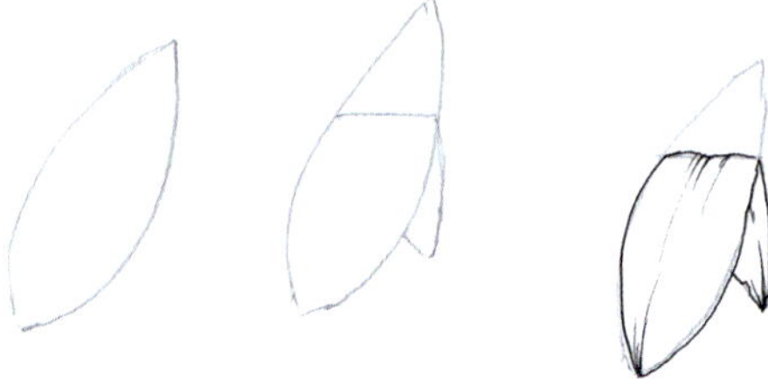

Creating Bends: As flowers make their way through life, they're faced with challenges that change them. Whether it's a storm that twists a leaf or a petal that bows as it grows heavier, to give your flowers more character, it helps to add a few bends.

To create a bent petal, start with your standard shape in pencil. Then draw a straight line where you want the bend to be. Don't forget to add the back of the bent petal peeking out from behind the front. Once you have your guidelines ready, switch to a 01 fineliner and outline the petal. The line that marks the bend should not be completely straight but should have a small dip in the middle. When you've done that, create a few shaping lines with your 005 fineliner. Let them curl in the direction of the petal, emphasizing the bend especially at the tip of the petal and the bend itself.

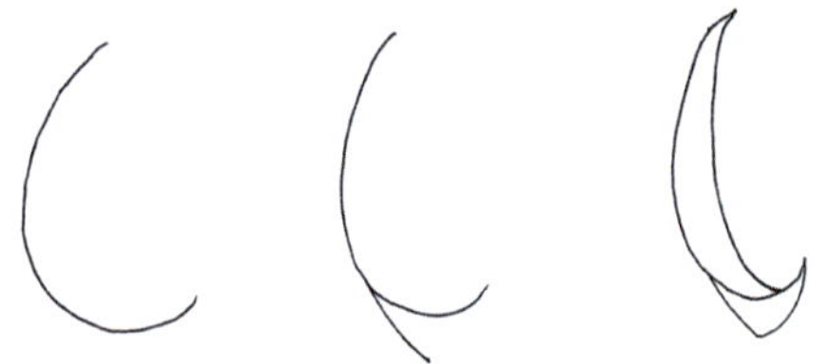

Twists: Especially as they age and grow, flowers can develop shriveled or twisted petals. To draw a twisted petal, start with a curved C-shaped line. This will be the outer edge of a petal. Then draw the bend at the bottom of the petal with a short diagonal line. This line marks the bottom of the petal and goes downward. Connect your diagonal line to the end of the original curved line to create the part of the petal that is twisting upwards. Now fill in the missing line! This will be the right side of the petal, starting where the C-shaped edge started and ending a little bit before it ends.

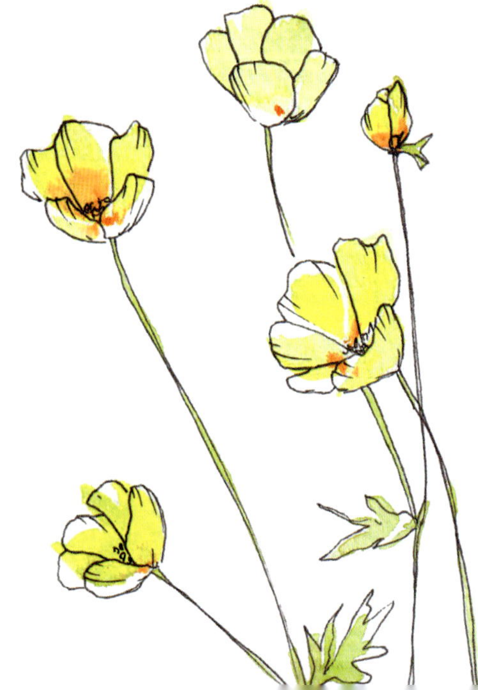

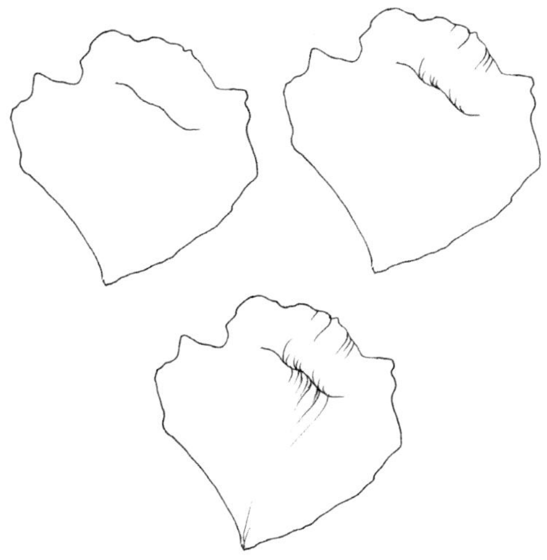

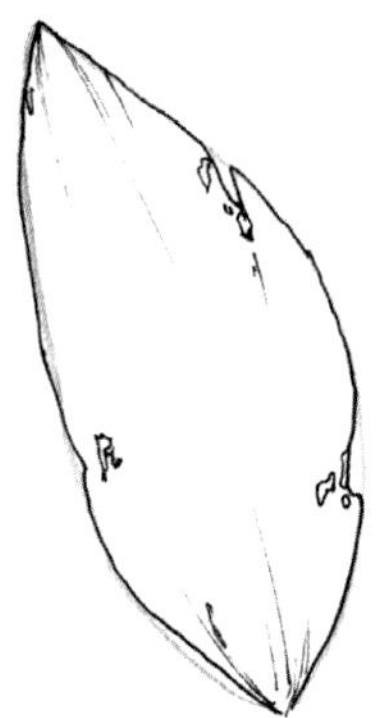

Lines and Wrinkles: We all get them as we grow older. Wrinkles show that we have lived a full life. You can easily create these badges of honor and experience for your flowers. First, draw a line with your 01 fineliner somewhere on the petal. This line should be curved and mostly parallel with the outer edge of the petal. The magic happens when you create the shaping lines with your 005 fineliner. On the side of the petal that is turning towards the center, draw shaping lines that dip into the wrinkle with a small curve towards the left. On the other side of the wrinkle, draw your shaping lines so they go up from the wrinkle in a curve towards to the right. This creates beautiful movement and can of course be switched up if you have petals moving in different directions.

Holes and Tears: Holes in a petal are one of those things you really must be careful to see. For some reason, it's one of those things our brain filters out when we see a beautiful flower. Almost like it wants us to see what we expect instead of what is actually happening. It can be annoying to realize there are holes in a petal, but they actually give it a lot of character. This petal has seen stuff. To create small holes, with your 005 fineliner, draw irregular shapes in the interior of the petal, especially close to the edges. I often draw a small shadow on one side of the shape to give it a bit of depth. Tears in the outline are created when you draw the outline in 01 fineliner. Let the line break in places to make small trianglar tears.

Flowers are so wonderful. But often when we draw flowers, we tend to leave out the "flaws." Somehow, we don't see the small imperfections. By being true to nature and honest in the way we show flowers, we create more interesting sketches with character and life. As a bonus, we become more present in our everyday lives just by noticing the beauty in all stages of life.

Maybe if we can embrace and see the beauty of a flower surviving the challenges of a season, we can start to see the beauty in our own flaws. By the way, I hate the word flaws. Instead, let's call it our uniqueness.

changing light

One thing that will always affect the colors in flowers is the changing light. It changes throughout the day from dawn to early dusk, but light also changes across the seasons. A poppy in the sun on a summer day has a very different vibe than a wilted rosehip on a frosty winter morning. The first step to sketching with light in mind is to focus on it when you are enjoying and observing blooms throughout the year. Be aware of how the colors, shadows and moods change. Light can be happy and sunny. Light can be moody in the shade, or it can be calm like the break of day. When you consider the mood of a moment, it's a lot easier to get started with your pen and paint because it will inspire your choice of colors and flowers.

Cool Light in the Shade

When the sun is out, we often seek the cooling shade to relax in. But the shade is not just lovely and refreshing; it also changes the colors of everything around. Just like we humans cool down in the shade, so do colors. It's almost like they all feel a bit blue . . . not in a sad way, but in a refreshing water kind of way. You can create shade by intentionally working with cool tones when you choose colors. That cooling feeling is exactly what we will replicate in Relaxing in the Shade (page 139).

Pro Tip: It can be a good thing to plan ahead when it comes to lighting, so you know from the beginning whether your bloom will be in shade or sun.

Hard Light in the Sun

When the sun is high in the sky, it is almost like a big spotlight. Everything turns bright and vibrant. Your colors will get a shot of extra color, your highlights will be very white and, as a result, your flowers will shine even brighter. And then . . . something funny happens. You will get the darkest and hardest cast shadows you can imagine. When the light shines the brightest, the shadows darken as well. Painting shadows in the bright sun can be tricky and a bit scary. But if you just remember to make the shadows dark and warm because they are still in the sun, then you are well on your way. I do it in A Sunlit Flower Field (page 133), so you can join me there.

Yellow Light at the Break of Dawn

In the very early morning and at dusk we experience the most beautiful phenomenon: The golden hour. This is the short period of time where the sun is low on the horizon, everything gets covered in a soothing light and nothing has hard shadows or feels cold. Instead, everything is warm. And to work with that, you can do different things. In this book, I use the underpainting technique detailed on page 14 to add warm casts to my paintings. There you learn to create a mood with my favorite color for a golden hour painting (spoiler alert: It's the wonderful new gamboge), giving everything a warm, soothing glow.

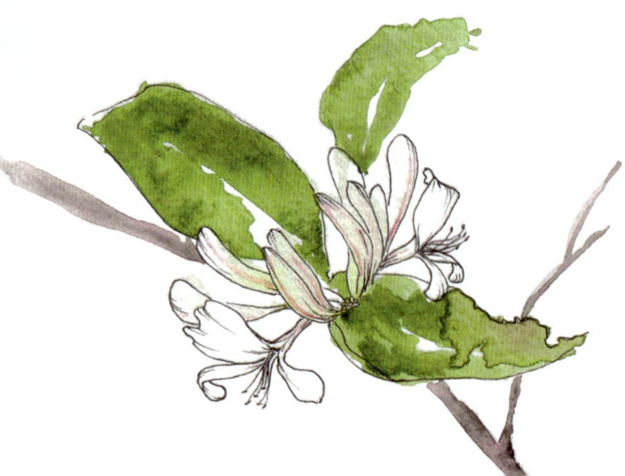

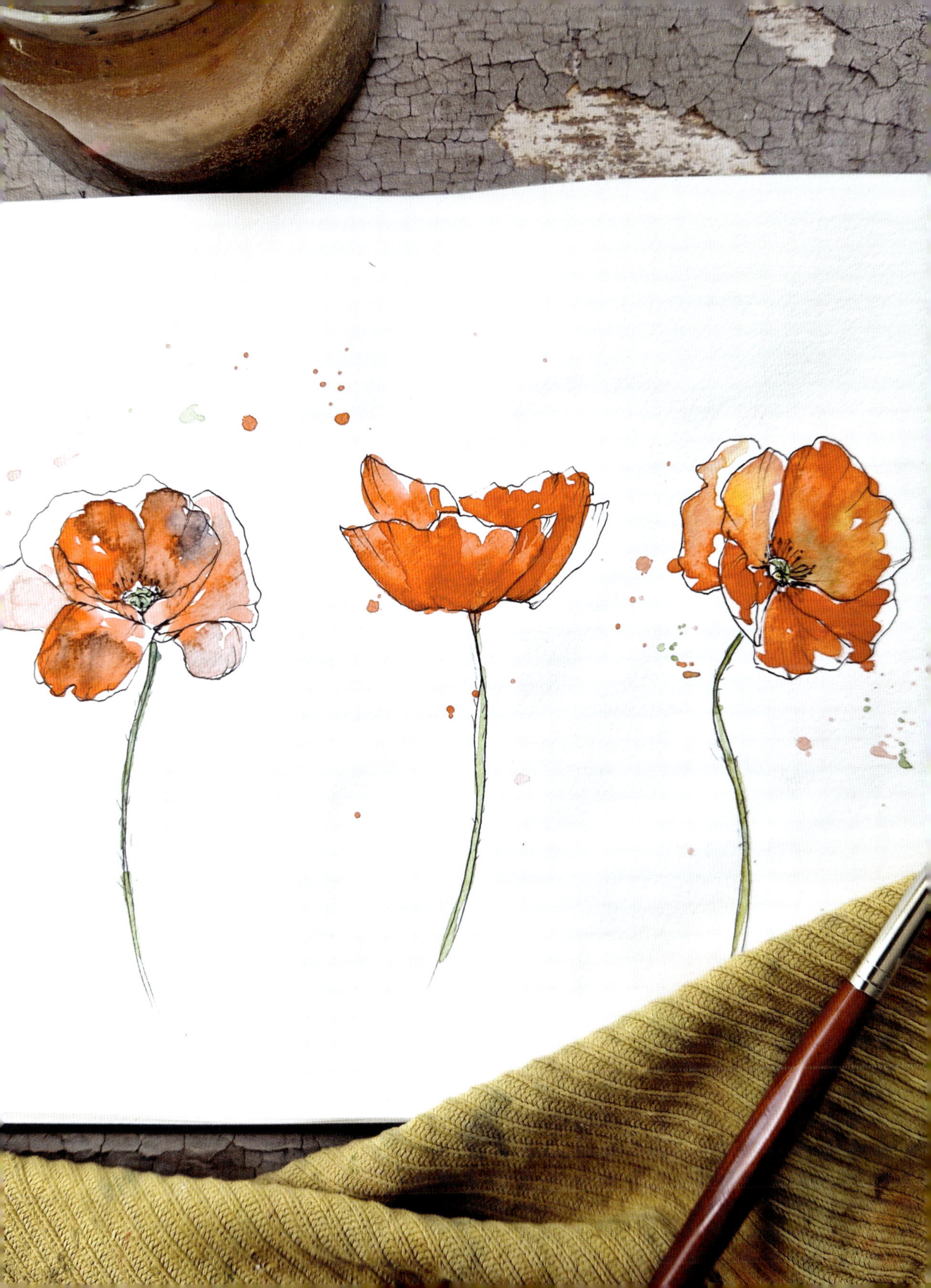

making a meadow

A sketch will be very different depending on how much of a scene you want to show. Imagine the differences between these three scenes: Painting a meadow, painting a poppy in a meadow or painting just a poppy. The story is different in each scene. Here are a few things to consider before you decide the focus of your sketch.

Foreground, Background and Middle Ground

First, you want to think about the overall scene. Do you have a foreground, background and middle ground? If you are doing an entire meadow, you will probably have all three. If you are making a sketch of a single flower among other blooms, you could have your single flower in the middle ground and other flowers in the foreground and background. You can also decide only to have a flower with an abstract background or maybe no background at all. There is no right or wrong, but it's great to give it a thought before starting.

Creating a Clear Focal Point

When you build a composition with several elements, it becomes very important to create a clear focal point so the person looking at your sketch will know where to look. You want to make sure to make the flower you are working on the star of the show. You don't want the flowers fighting for the spotlight on the paper. Creating a clear focal point can be done in several ways.

From Big to Small. The eye will usually look at the biggest flowers first, so choose flowers that complement each other when it comes to sizes. For example, if you want a peony to shine, pair it with some smaller baby's breath instead of a big red rose. It worked in *The Holiday*, but two leading ladies can be tricky.

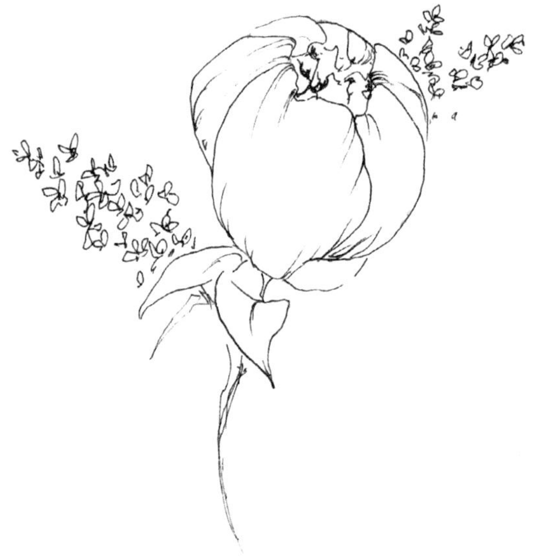

From Detailed to Less Detailed. The eye will naturally go to the area with the most detail. You can create details with a fineliner and watercolors however you like, and the area with the most detail will get the most attention.

From Saturated to Muted. People are more likely to look at areas with vibrant color than the areas with more watery mixes. So, if you want attention to flow to a bloom, make sure it's bright in color and the surrounding ones are paler and subtler.

I promise, if you follow these simple guidelines there will be no need for floral divas having tantrums and fighting for the spotlight.

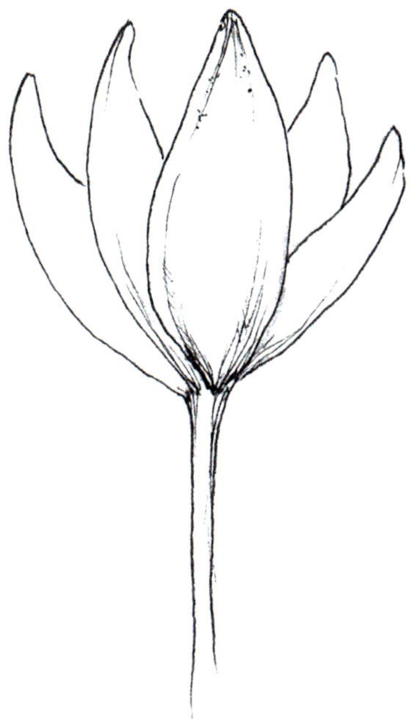

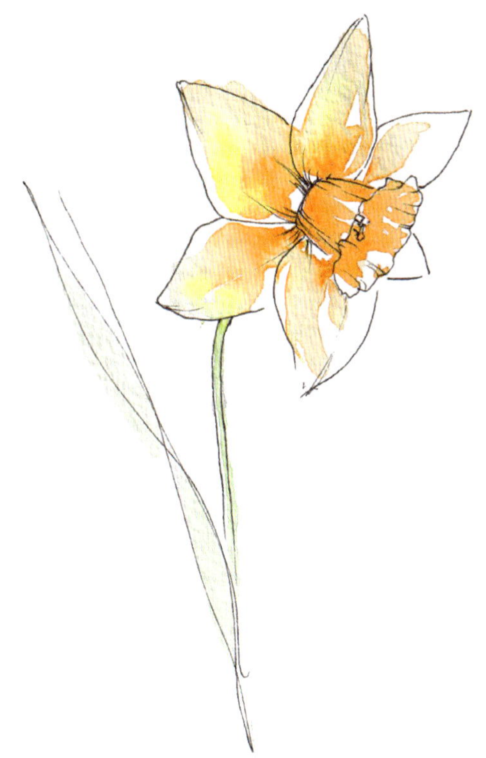

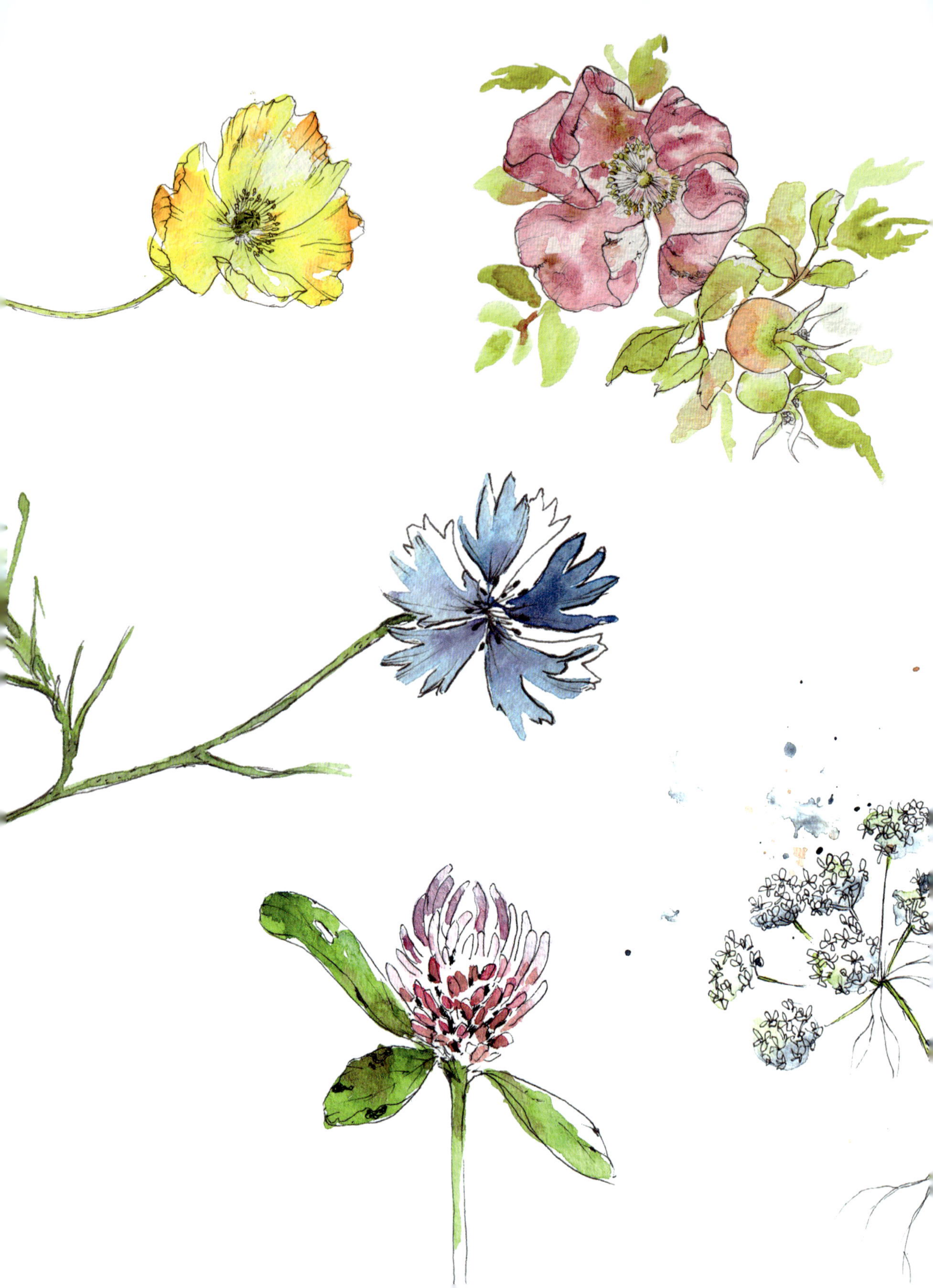

part II
sixteen blooms in the flower field

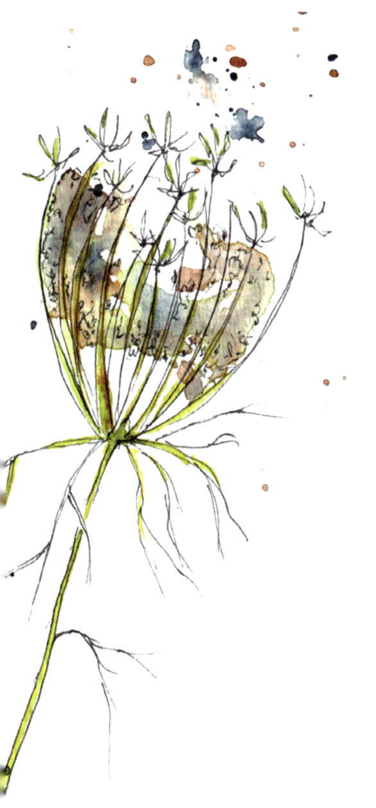

Now we are getting to the good stuff—all the beautiful wildflowers you've been waiting for. So now I will send my inner schoolteacher on lunch break and start sketching some blooms. Get out your brushes and come sketch with me, my friend.

I know that you may want to start with the project that inspires you the most. If you are new to watercolor, though, it may be helpful to work through the tutorials in order. Each painting builds upon the previous, so one way to help build your confidence is to start with buttercups (page 29), cowslips (page 33) and forget-me-nots (page 37) before working your way up to lupins (page 79), honeysuckles (page 93) and wild roses (page 97).

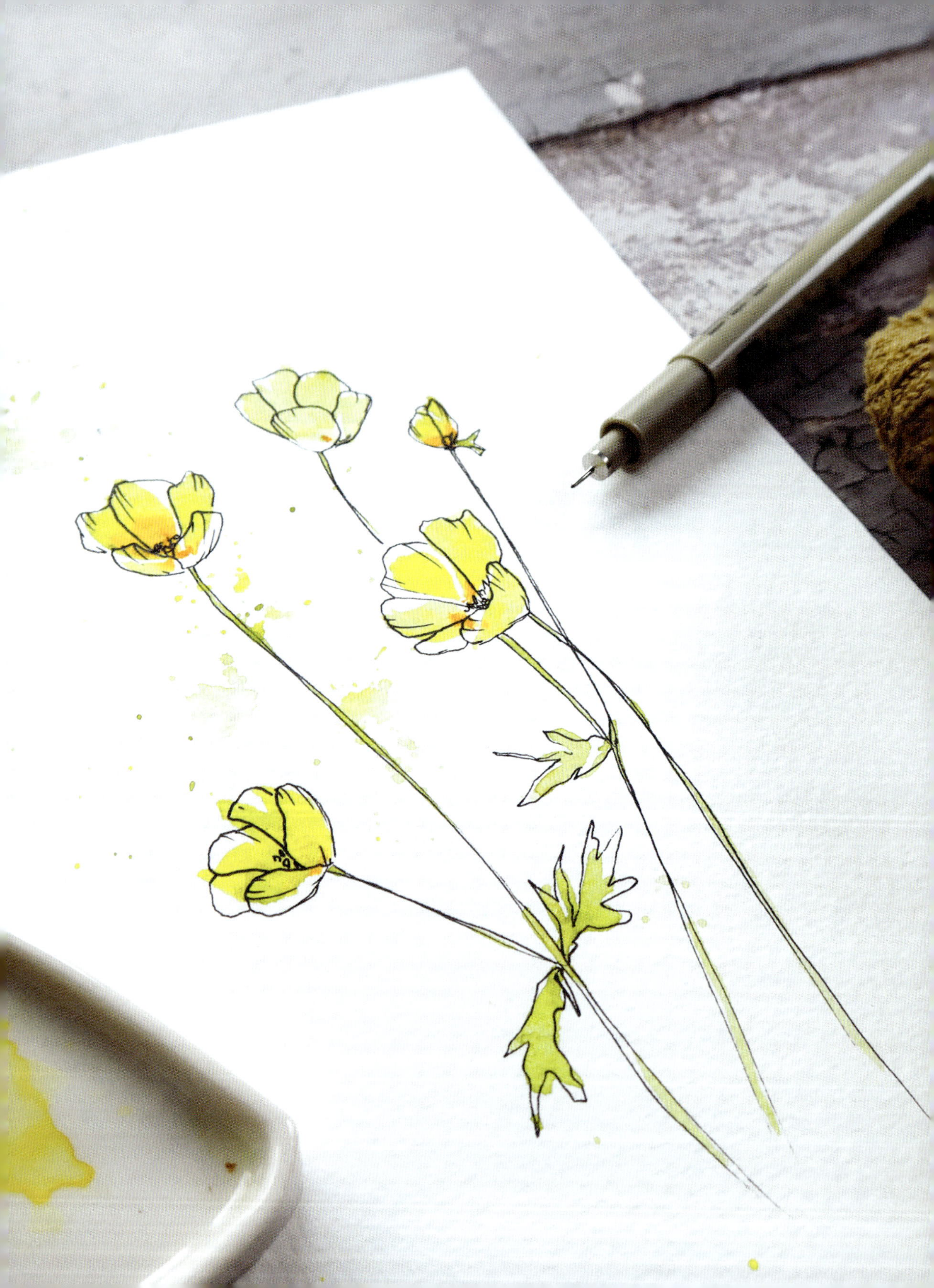

buttercup
a flower of childishness and joy

This beautiful yellow wildflower is everywhere in the springtime meadows. I totally get why they would symbolize childishness in the very best way because they look like they just wake up every day to play and enjoy life. And when us grown-ups see them, we can't help but smile and share their happiness.

Just like children, we are here to play and learn. So, what better flower than the buttercup to begin our creative journey through this book?

In this tutorial, you'll learn a classic approach to line and wash where you start the sketch with the wash and then draw all the details afterward in fineliner.

Materials

Paper: Canson Montval 300gsm (140lb) cold press

Watercolor brush size: 4

Water and cloth

Fineliner sizes: 01 and 005

Colors

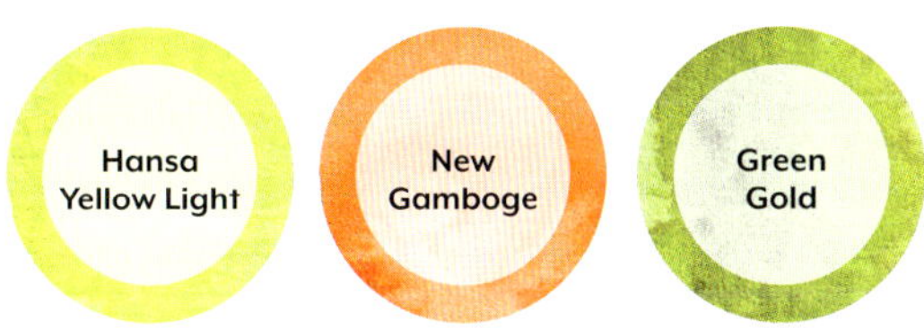

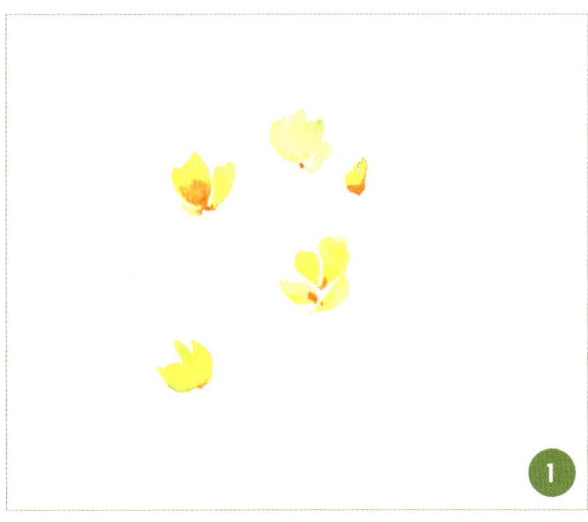

Step 1: Now it's time for paint for the first time in this book! Yay! Start with your size 4 brush and paint the flower heads loosely wet-on-dry using hansa yellow light. Let some of them have four petals, some three petals and a single flower with just one petal. Drip in a bit of new gamboge at the bottom of the flowers and a few droplets of green gold at the tip of a few of the petals.

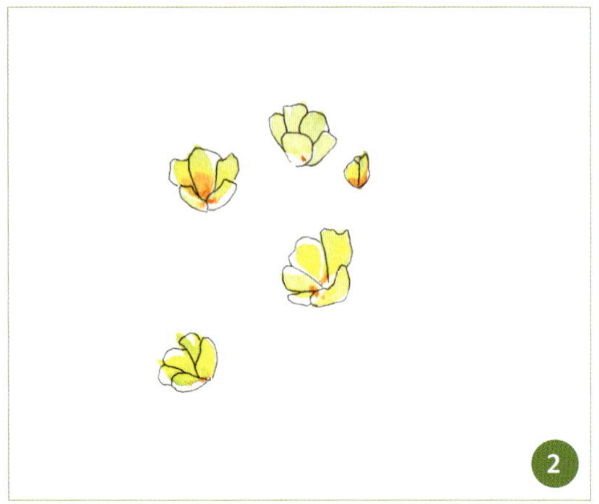

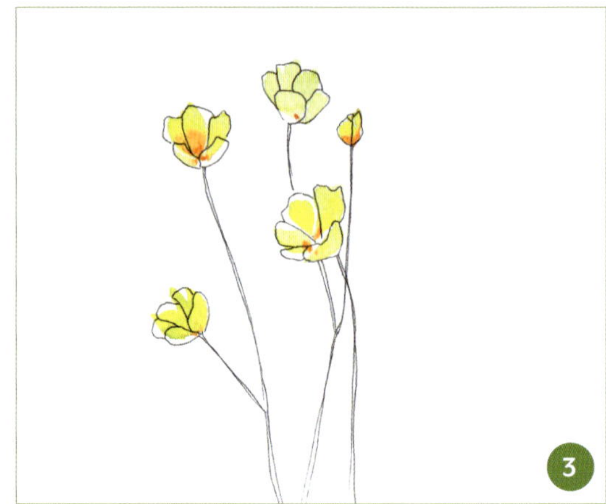

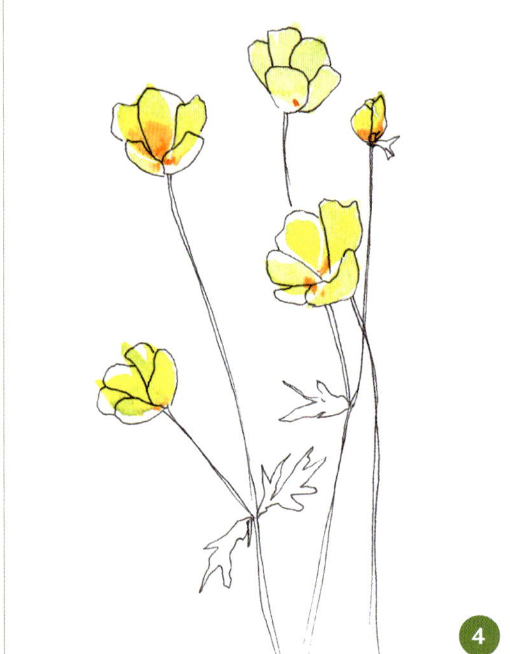

Step 2: Once the paint has dried, grab your 01 fineliner and draw a rough outline around the petals in the flower heads. Imagine that all these are seen from the side and the three lowest flowers will be a bit open toward you. Look at page 18 for a closer description of a flower with foreshortened petals.

Step 3: Still using the 01 fineliner, carefully draw the stems. Let the stems for the two flowers to the left meet up close to the bottom and also let the stems for the bud and the middle flower meet. The last flower will just have a single stem overlapping one of the others for depth.

Step 4: While you still have the 01 fineliner in hand, draw a few leaves where the stems meet. Let the leaves have a lot of points and allow them to look free.

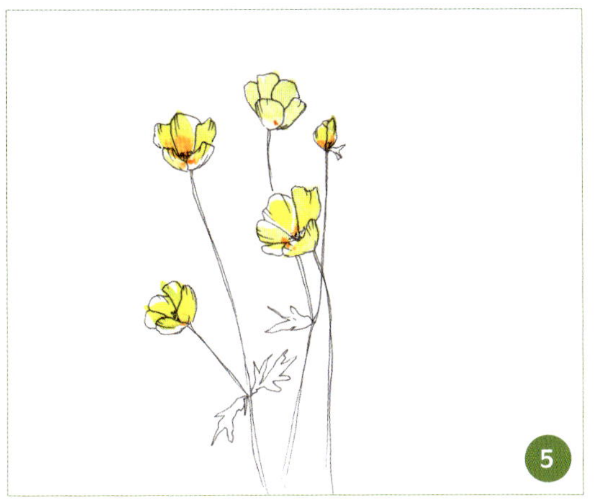

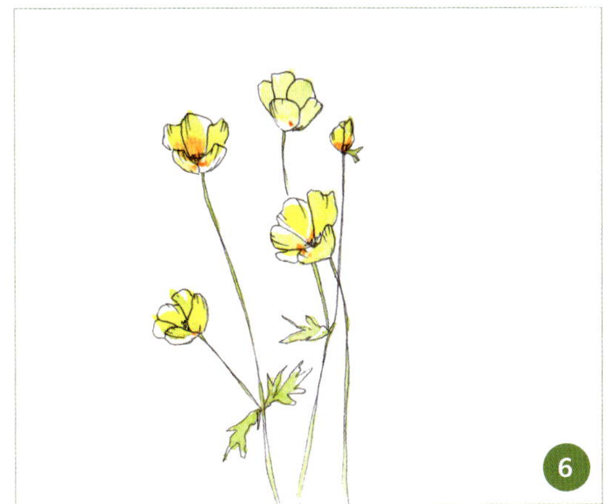

Step 5: Now use the 005 fineliner to draw direction lines on the petals. These start at the edge of the petal or from the center and curve into the petal, showing the shape. With the same fineliner, draw small doodles in the center of the open flowers. These doodles are the stamens hiding inside the flowers.

Step 6: Pick up your size 4 brush again and paint the stems with green gold and a bit of new gamboge. Leave a bit of white space on the leaves so they don't overpower the sketch.

Step 7: Finally, add that magical, artsy touch with splatter in green gold and hansa yellow light. You do this by loading your brush with one color at a time, holding it above the paper and tapping the brush handle either with your hand or another brush. Finish the splatter with water, where you only load the brush with clean water. Aim for the drops of paint when you splatter with the water to get the colors to spread a bit.

Wow, congrats! You are done with your first sketch of the book! Wait for it to dry completely and then hang it on your wall so you can admire it.

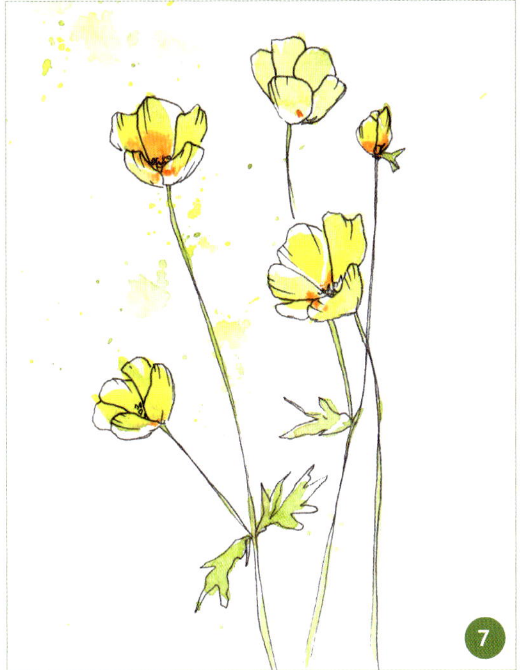

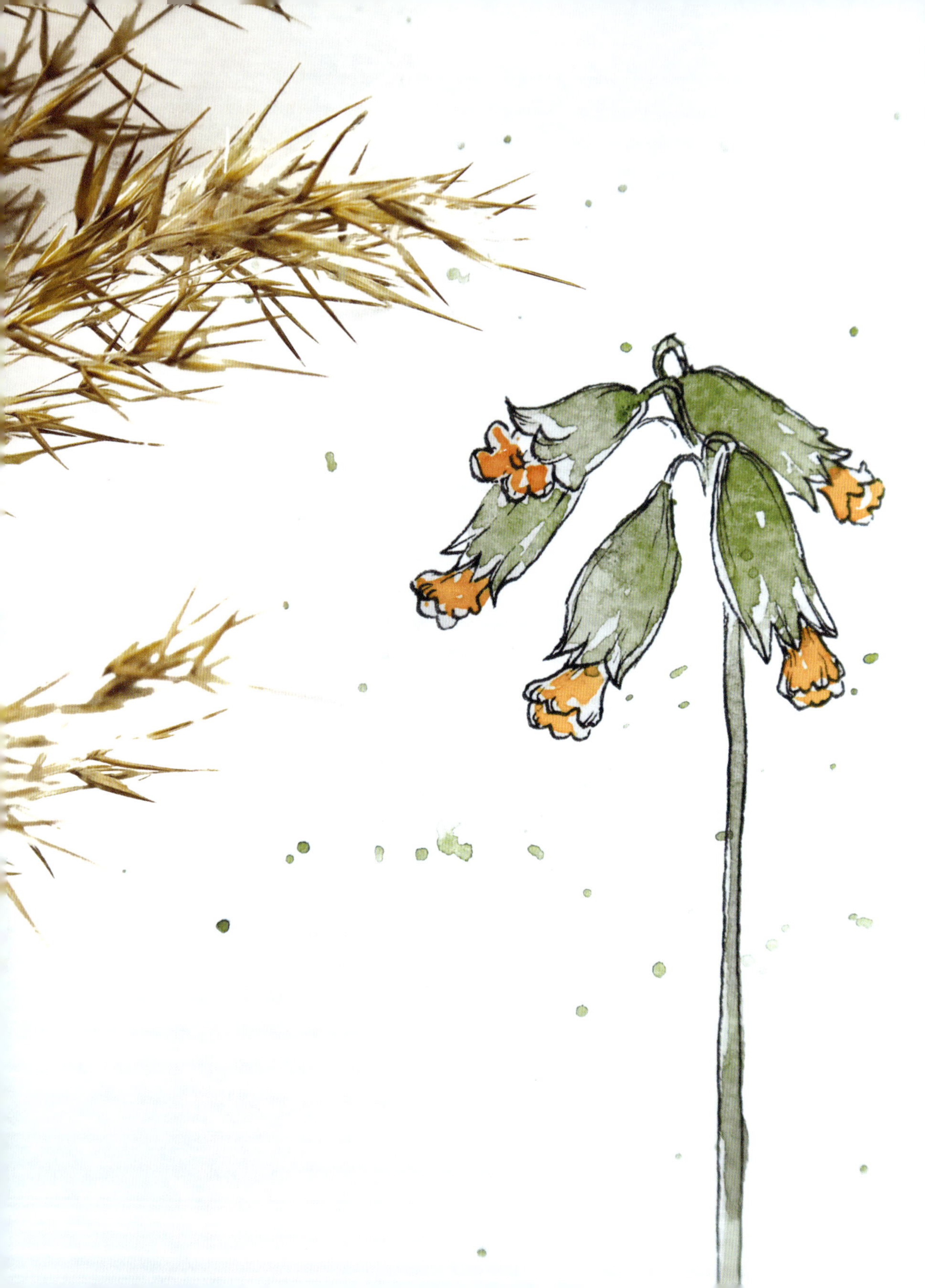

cowslip
a flower of adventure (and keys, apparently)

The cowslip is a pretty spectacular flower. When you look at it from the side (like we are going to sketch it), it looks like a bunch of keys. And it is actually said to grow where St. Peter dropped the Key of Earth. Considering how many cowslips I see in the spring, St. Peter must have had a lot of keys!

When we sketch the cowslip, we are doing a very simple design. There are no leaves; instead, we focus on mixing the colors correctly.

Materials

Paper: Canson Montval 300gsm (140lb) cold press

Pencil and eraser

Fineliner sizes: 01 and 005

Watercolor brush size: 4

Water and cloth

Palette

Colors

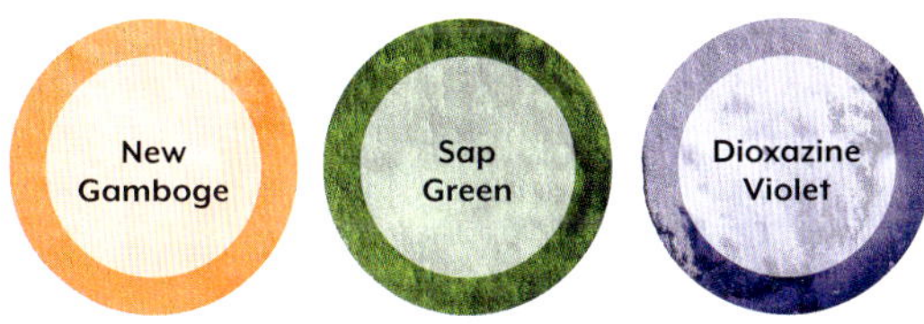

Mix

For the dusty green stem, mix sap green and dioxazine violet using 90% green and 10% violet.

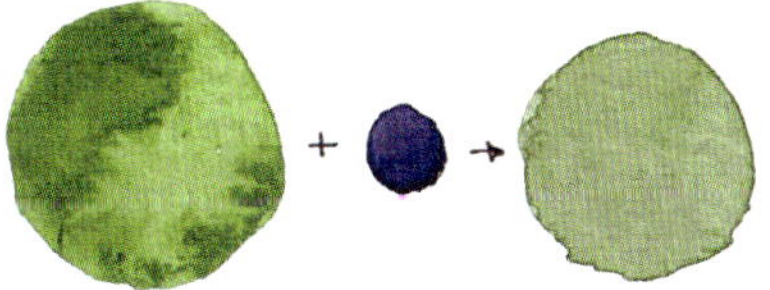

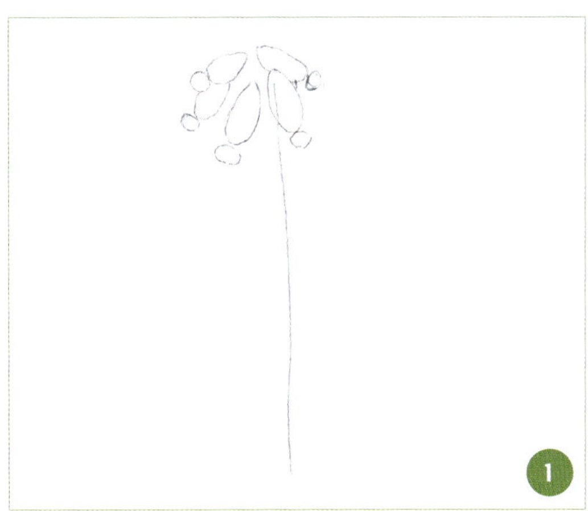

Step 1: Draw a long line in pencil with a slight curve. Then draw guides for the flowers. Let each flower be a teardrop with a flat circle underneath.

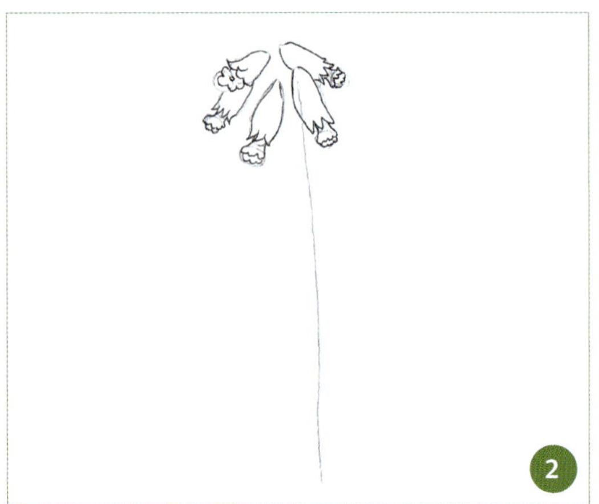

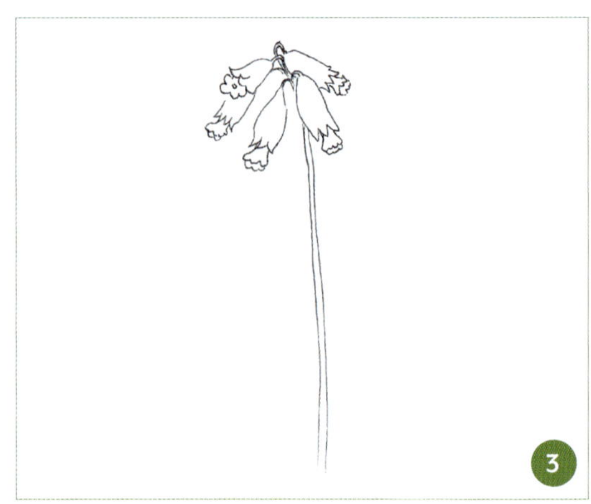

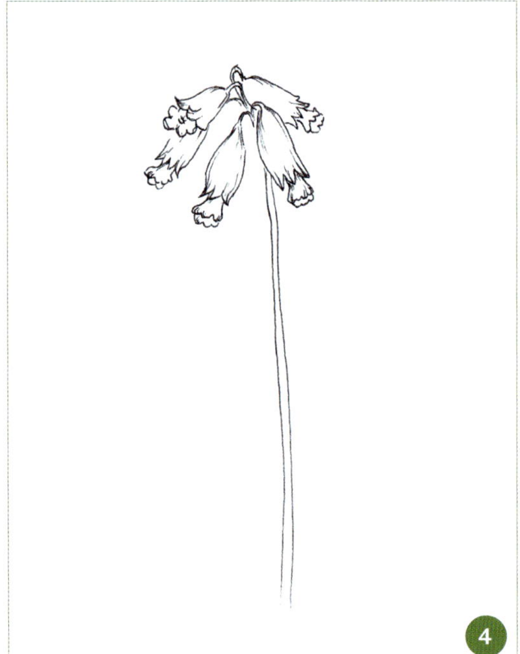

Step 2: Put down your pencil and grab the 01 fineliner. With that, draw the outline of the flowers. The bottom of the shape that faces toward the flat circle should have pointy ends, almost like the bottom of a fairy dress.

Then draw the small flowers hidden inside. Their edges are soft and have small bends like lace. You can see the backside of the flower, too. Let one of the flowers be facing you by giving it a small circle in the center.

Step 3: With the same fineliner, draw the stem. Let it curve and attach all the small flower heads with small, bent flower stems. Let them hide behind each other for depth. When you are all done with your sketch, you can erase the pencil guides.

Step 4: Get out your 005 fineliner and create direction lines in the flower heads. These are very small blooms, so don't overdo it here.

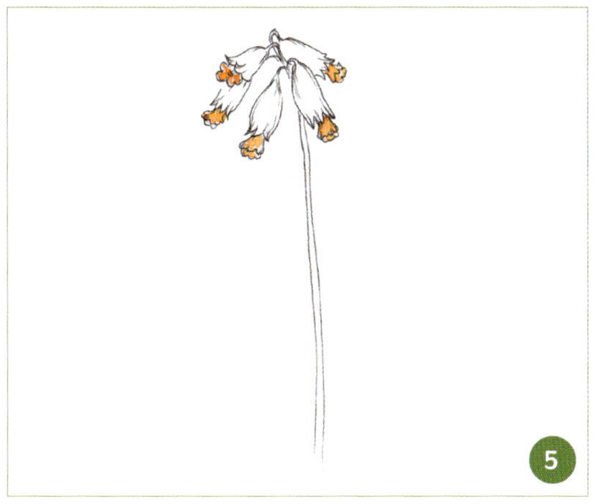

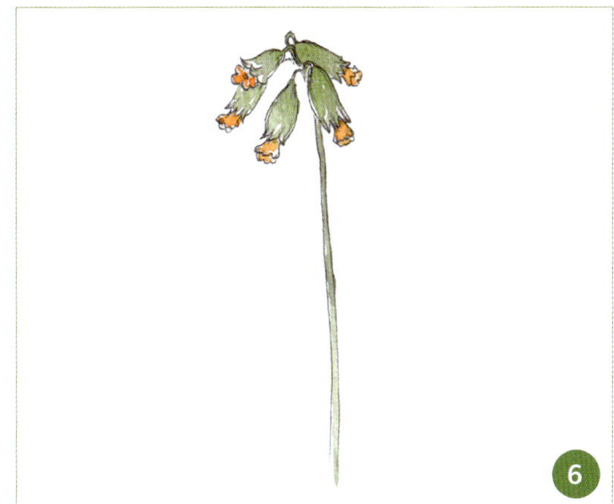

Step 5: Now it's time for some paint. Get your size 4 round brush and paint the small flowers in new gamboge. Let them dry.

Step 6: On your palette, create a mix of sap green and dioxazine violet. Paint the fairy dresses and the stem with this mix, too. While it's still wet, you can drip in a bit of vibrant violet and sap green.

Step 7: It's a simple flower, so let's give it some splatters to keep it company. Use the green mix you just painted with and then follow with clean water like we did in the Buttercup tutorial on page 29.

Well done! Now if you ever lose your keys, you can go looking for them in the flower field. Or maybe just don't lose your keys in the first place! Grab your sketchbook instead and go out to sketch the cowslips.

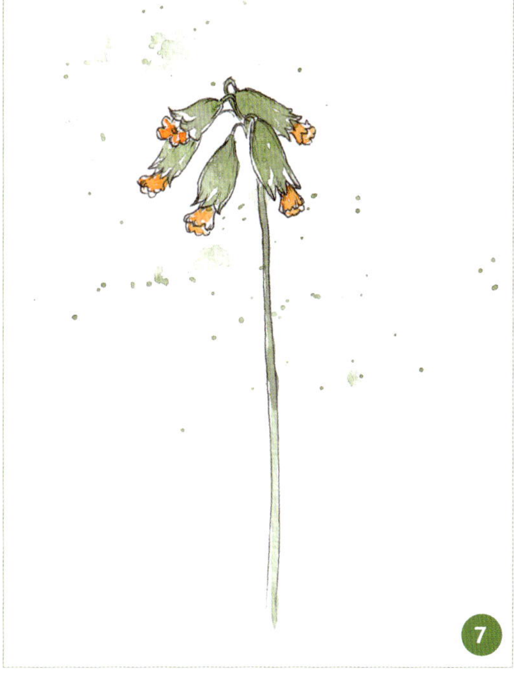

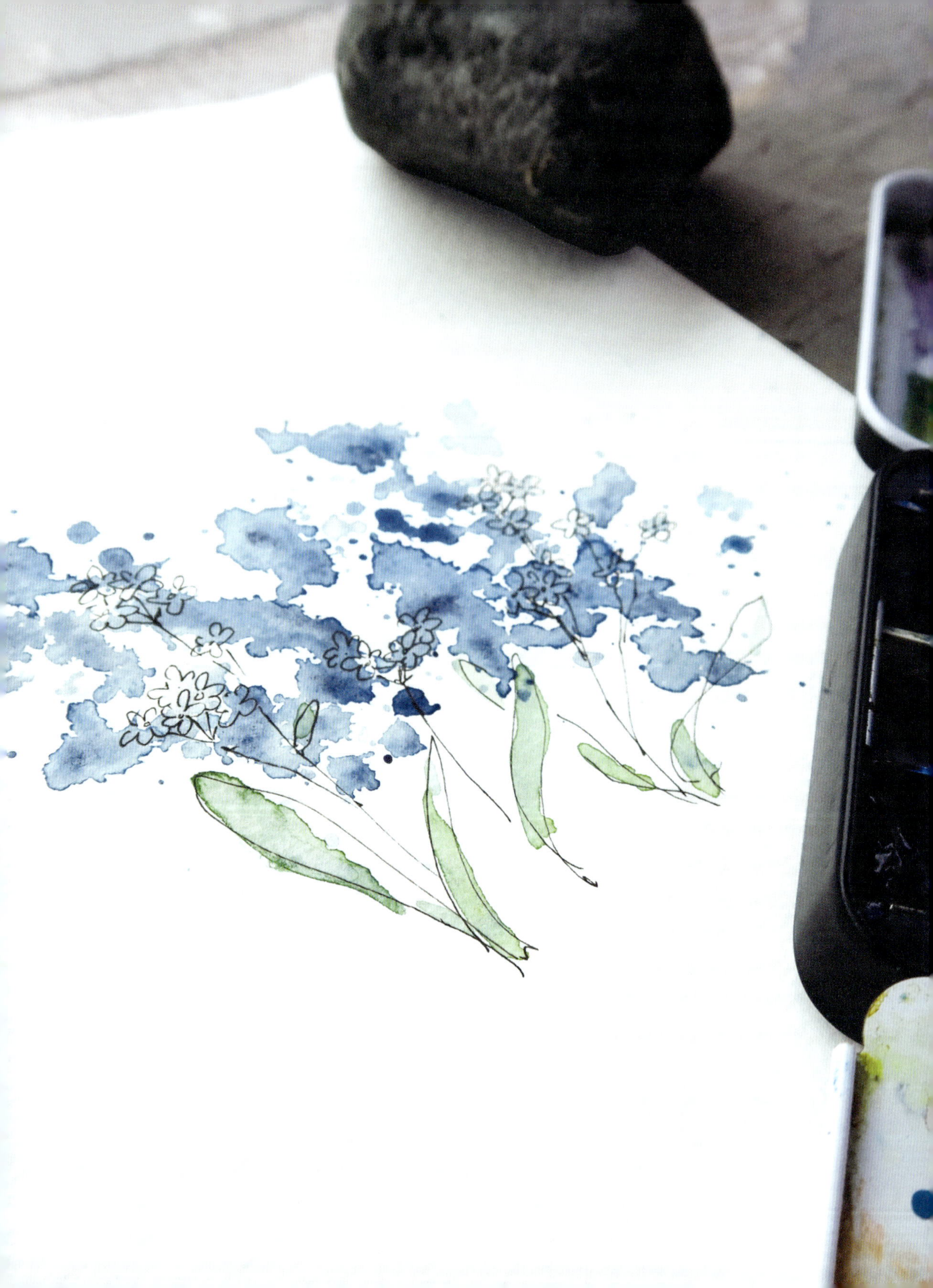

forget-me-not
a flower of true love and remembrance

The forget-me-not is a flower that always reminds me of midsummer
and collecting tiny posies of flowers for my dollhouse. As a kid, all the small
blooms made me feel so rich and lucky. And all these tiny blossoms make
forget-me-nots the perfect flower to experiment with. So, in this tutorial,
we are going to create an illusion of the abundance of flowers using splatters.
The first step before you get started is removing your laptops, cats,
boyfriends and anything else that might not enjoy paint splatters.
Trust me on this one; I speak from experience.

Materials

Paper: Canson Montval 300gsm (140lb) cold press

Watercolor brush size: 8

Water and cloth

Fineliner size: 005

Palette

Colors

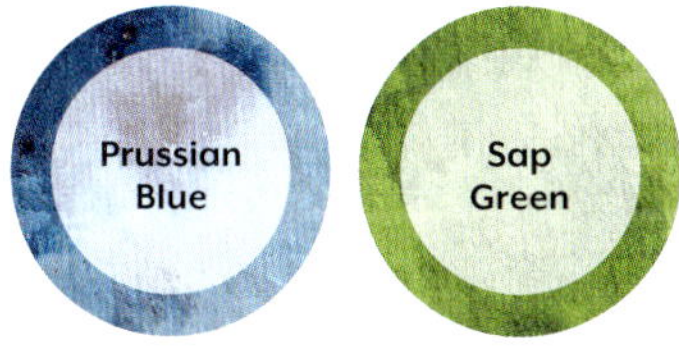

Mix

For the leaves, mix Prussian blue and sap green
in a 50% mix that will make a nice blueish green.

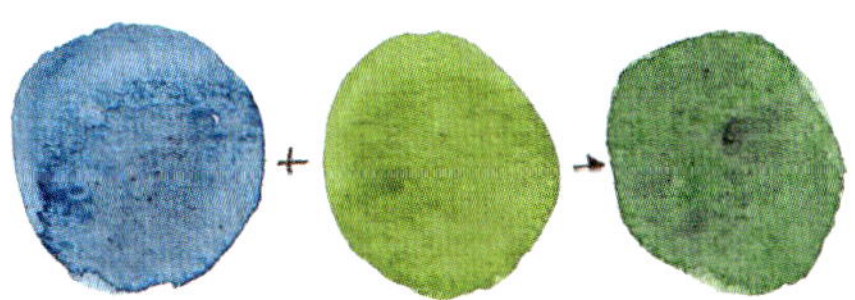

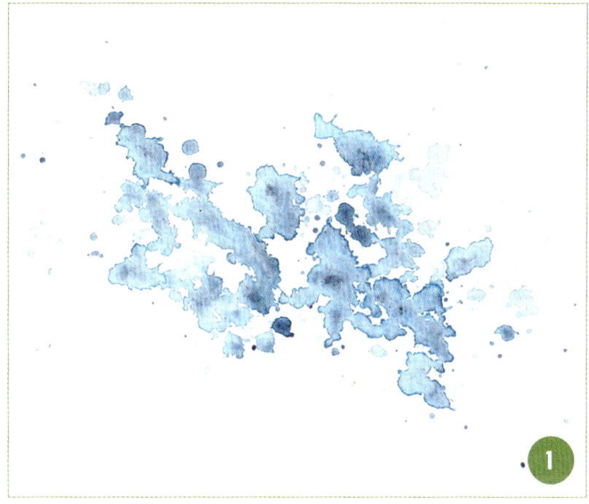

Step 1: Let's get this water game on! Start by loading your big size 8 brush with water. Hold it above the paper, take a deep breath and then tap it to splatter water in the center of the paper. Load the brush with Prussian blue and tap it again. Make sure to aim for the water droplets you created first to let it flow organically. When you are happy with your beautiful mess, leave it to dry completely. This can take a while, so maybe go for a walk or put the laundry away. Then, you have a good excuse to paint even longer afterward.

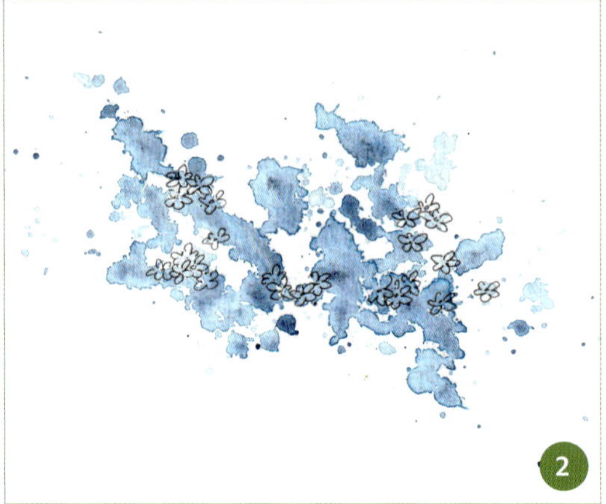

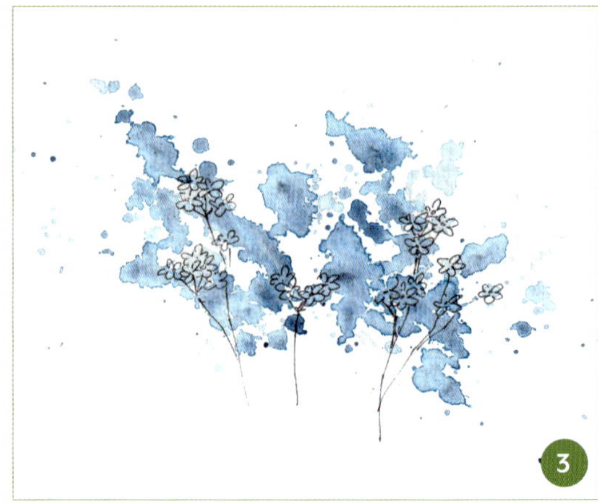

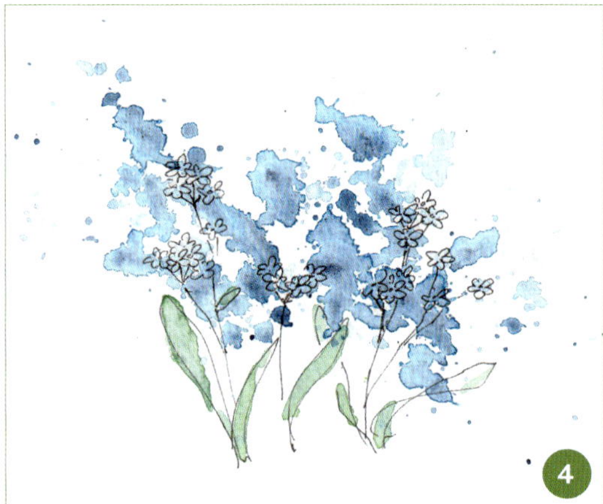

Step 2: The forget-me-not flower is actually a very simple bloom with five petals and a round center. So, take your 005 fineliner and draw a lot of small flower heads. Let some of the flowers hide behind each other for depth and gather some in clusters.

Step 3: Using the same fineliner, you can now draw the long stems. Let the stems go up to the clusters and then attach the small blooms to the stem with smaller stems.

While you are at it, draw the leaves. These are mostly at the bottom of the flowers with round edges.

Step 4: Mix Prussian blue with sap green and paint the leaves loosely wet-on-dry.

That means you just finished the shortest flower tutorial in the book! Yes, drawing flowers can sometimes take a long time; other times, they can be the perfect subject for a stolen 5-minute break.

icelandic poppy
a flower of consolation and remembrance

Since World War I, the poppy has been a symbol of hope and remembrance. And when you see an Icelandic poppy, you will know why. This flower looks like crepe paper is just floating on top of the thinnest of stems. It's like magic and gives us all hope that our stems will carry us no matter what.

With its thin, crepe-like texture, this flower is ideal for practicing wrinkles and bends in petals.

Materials

Paper: Canson Montval 300gsm (140lb) cold press
Watercolor brush sizes: 8 and 4
Water and cloth
Fineliner sizes: 005 and 01

Colors

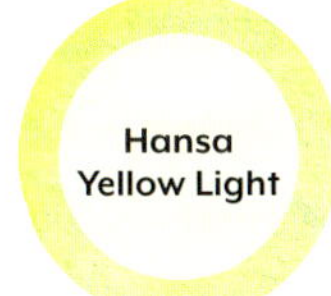

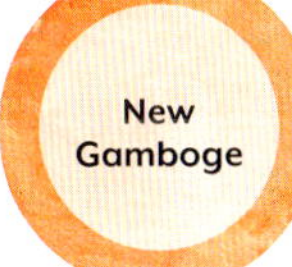

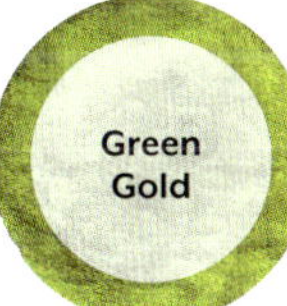

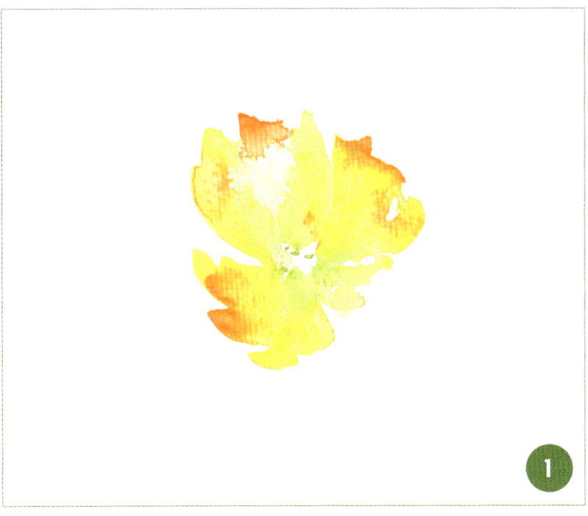

Step 1: Try to picture a poppy in your head. It is open, almost facing you. It has four petals with one of them curled in toward the center. With that in mind, paint the petals on the poppy wet-on-dry. Use hansa yellow light and a nice, big size 8 brush. While the yellow is still wet, drip in a bit of new gamboge at the edge of the petals and green gold at the center.

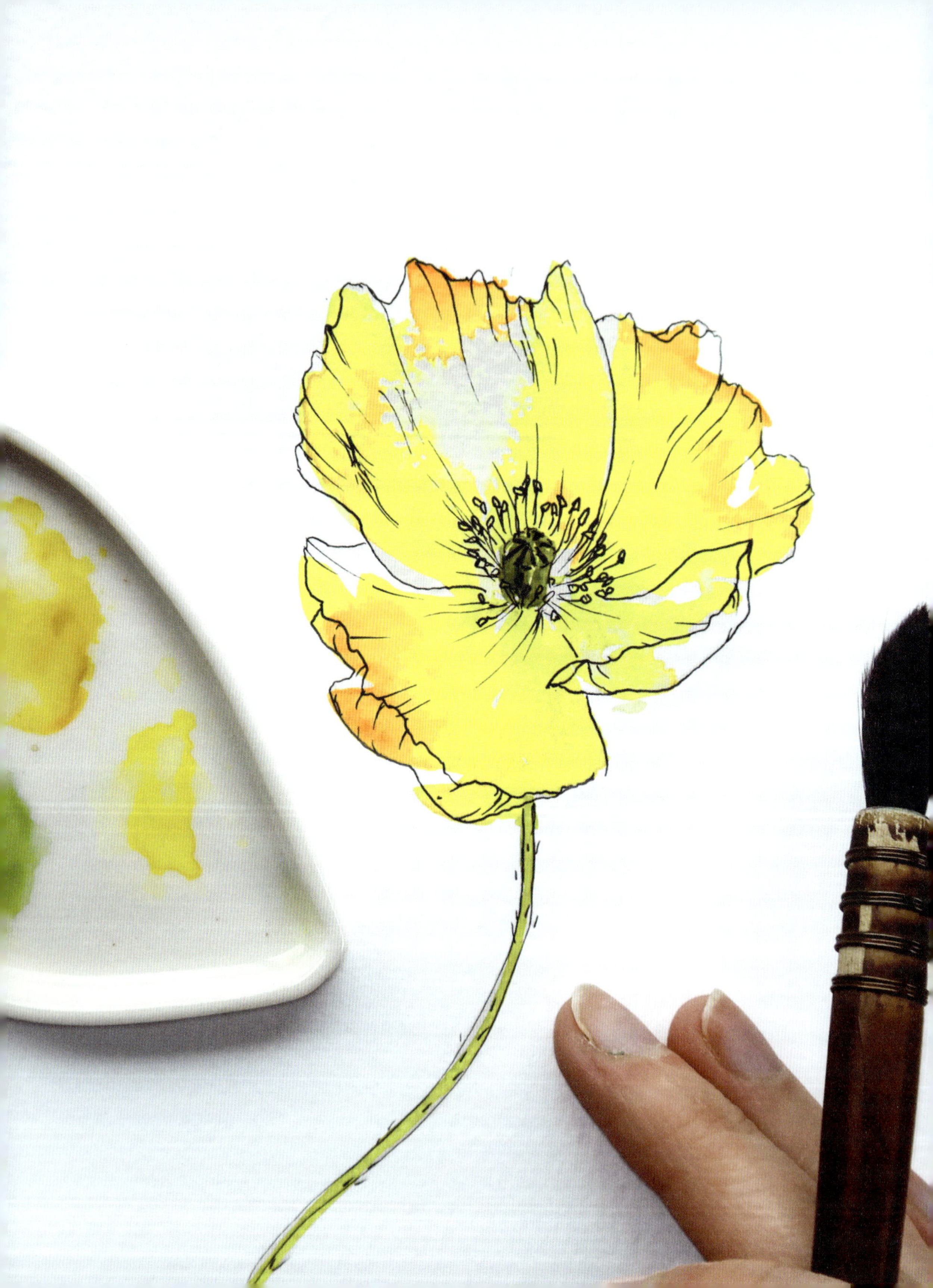

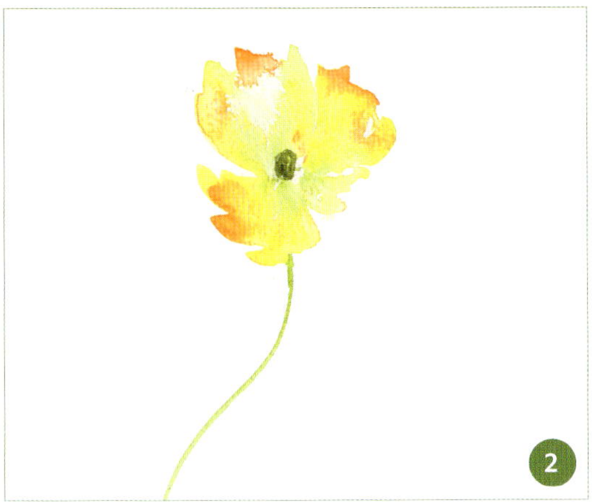

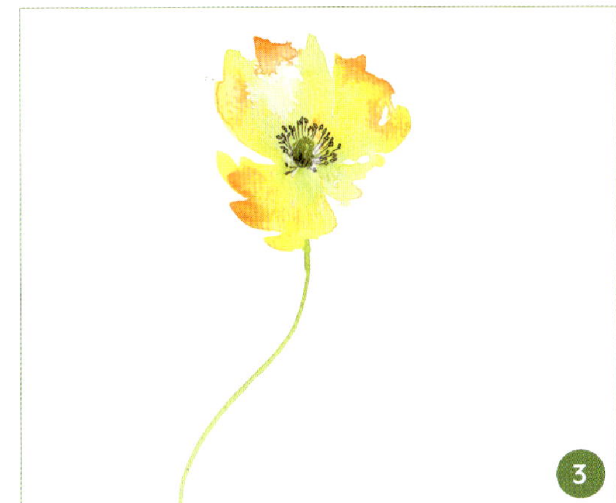

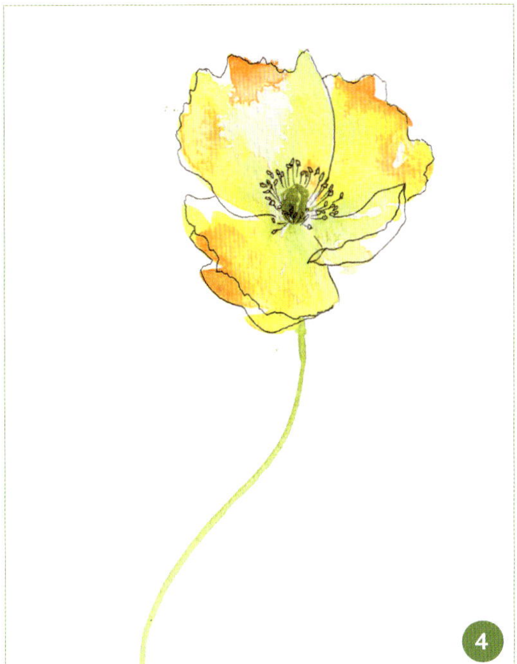

Step 2: Inside the poppy, you find a green, round center called a stigma. Use a size 4 brush to paint the stigma with green gold, and continue with the same color to paint the dancing stem.

Step 3: When the paint is dry, draw the tiny stamens with your 005 fineliner. Attach them with slightly curved lines to the center, around and behind the stigma.

Step 4: Outline the four petals with the 01 fineliner. Give the two petals closest to you a small bend and make sure the edges of the petals are super uneven.

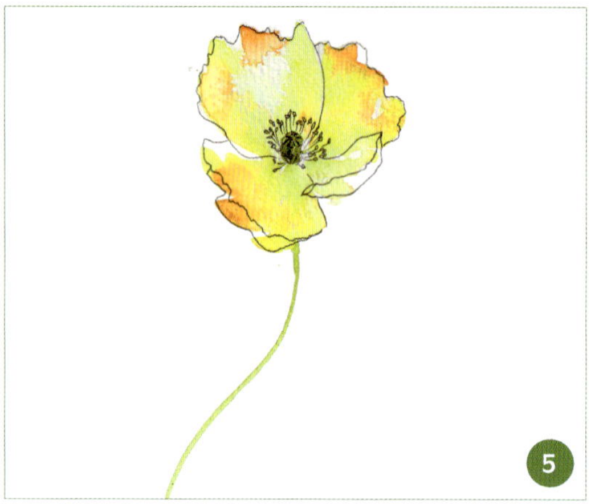

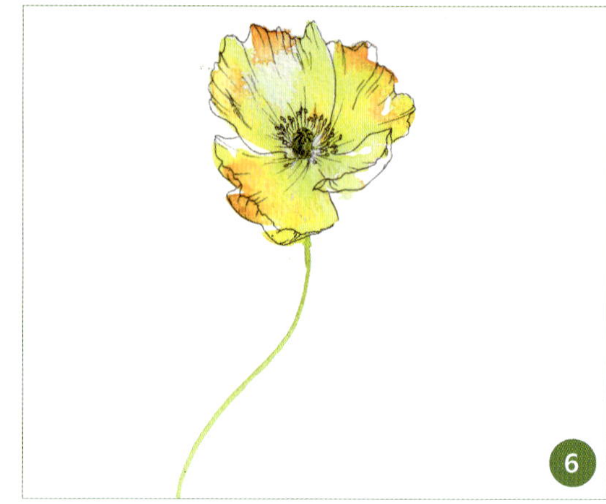

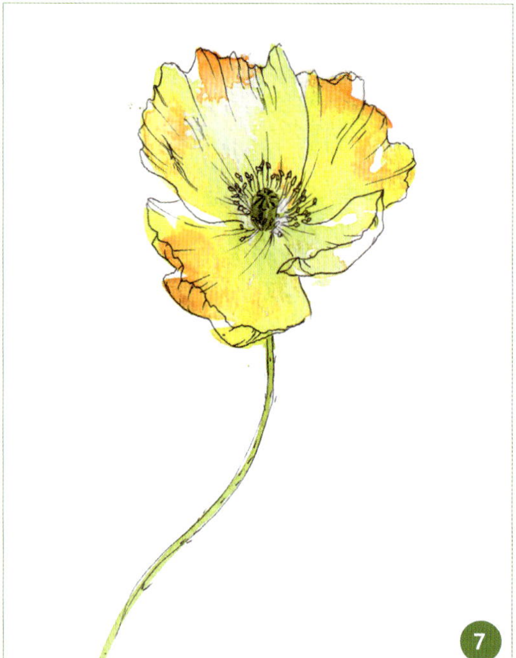

Step 5: Draw a few lines on top of the green stigma with your 01 fineliner. These lines should all point to the same spot at the top.

Step 6: Now for the crepe-like petals. Draw quite a lot of direction lines on the petals. You can bend a lot of them in different ways, creating a more curled and wrinkled look. Look at page 29 to see how I go about giving the flowers wrinkles.

Step 7: Finally, outline that thin magic stem with 005 fineliner and draw small hairs.

Well done! You can now go and do something that reminds you about how wonderful life is like calling your mom, playing with your kids or your art supplies or maybe just enjoying a cup of tea with your feet planted on grass. Doing something that grounds us in the moment will always bring us hope for the future.

clover
a flower of hope and luck

Are you also guilty of spending hours searching and hoping to find a four-leaf clover when you see a flower-filled meadow? Or maybe that's just me. It's like an instinct from childhood . . . trying to find that one special flower that brings luck. Thankfully, by now, I've realized that all flowers are special. That is why in this tutorial, you will learn to sketch a perfectly imperfect clover that is slowly starting to wilt.

Materials

Paper: Canson Montval 300gsm (140lb) cold press

Pencil and eraser

Fineliner sizes: 01 and 005

Watercolor brush size: 4

Water and cloth

Palette

Colors

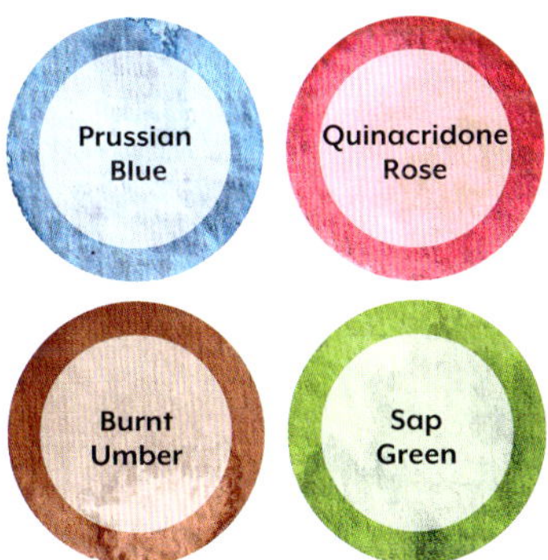

Mixes

The flower head has a blue tone because the sky is reflecting in it. So, mix your quinacridone rose with Prussian blue in a 50% mix.

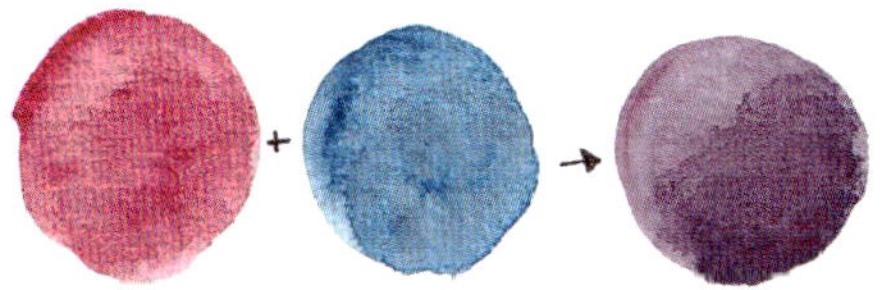

For the rest of the petals, mix 50% quinacridone rose and 50% burnt umber. When you mix it on your palette, don't combine it into one solid color; leave plenty of color variations so you have plenty of shades to choose from.

Step 1: Get a pencil out of your pencil case and draw a circle guide that is a bit uneven.

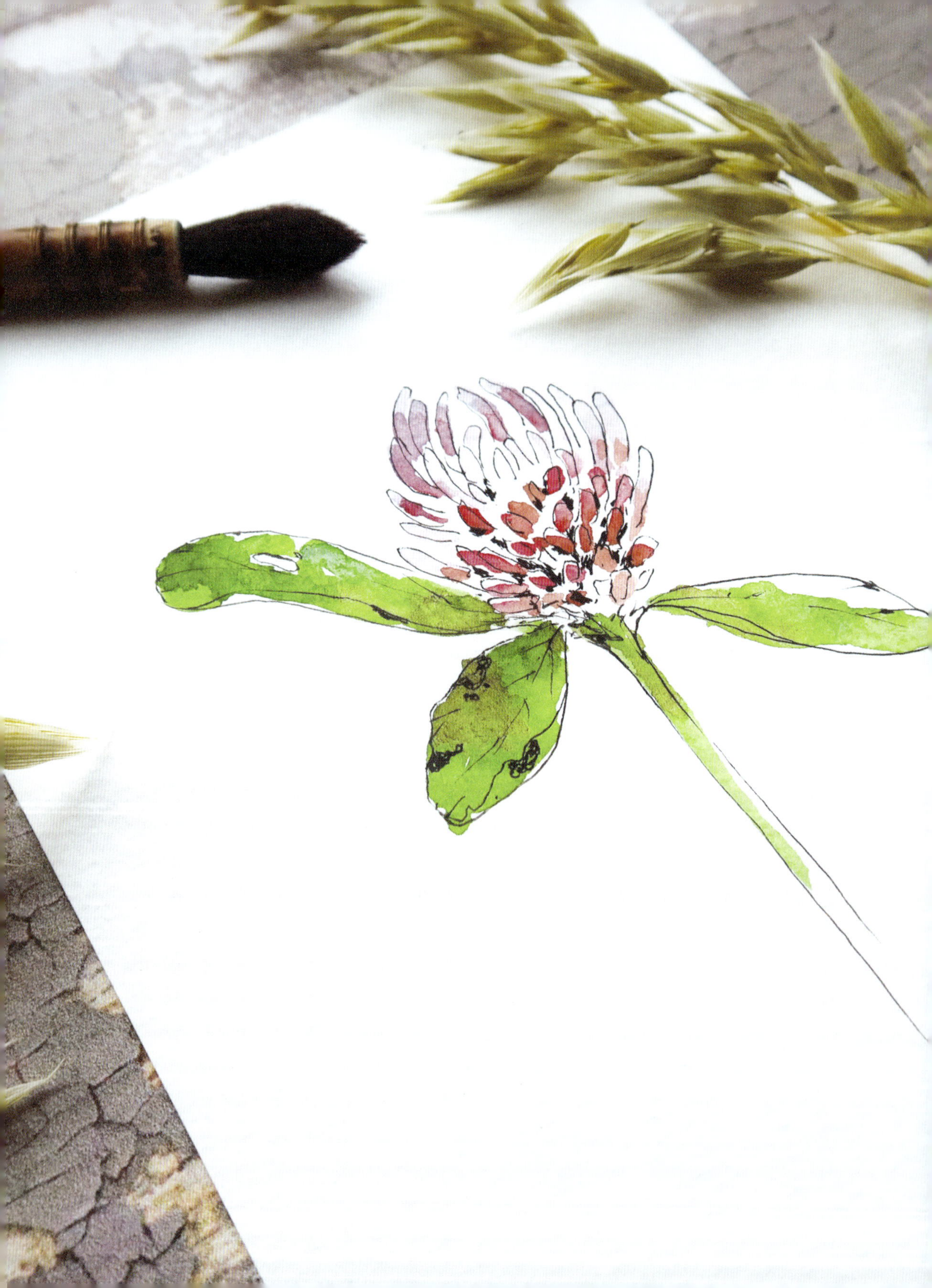

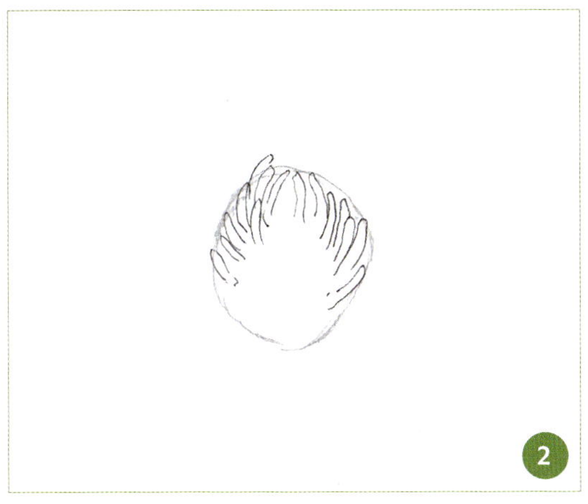

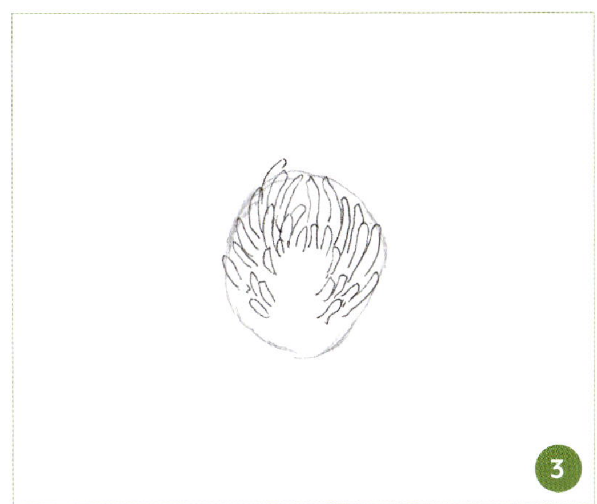

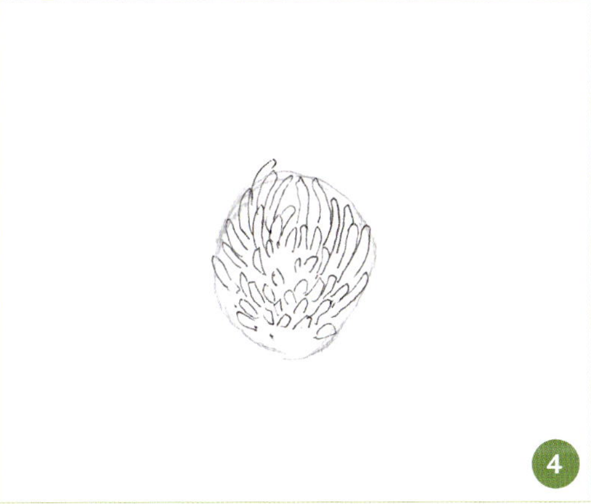

Step 2: In this tutorial, we are going to work quite a lot with banana shapes. So maybe skip this tutorial if you are super hungry, or go get something to eat. Start by drawing the outer banana-shaped petals with the 01 fineliner. They are the longest and go all the way around the circle except for the bottom. The flower head has petals that are foreshortened (page 18) so we start with the longest ones at the top.

Step 3: Fill in the next layer of petals working in toward the center and down toward the bottom. These shapes are smaller bananas.

Step 4: Now we are at the bottom of the flower head, drawing very short foreshortened banana shapes. These are like the short scales on a pine cone.

Step 5: Continue your pencil guide by drawing three leaf shapes. Place one tucked behind the clover and make that one a bit bigger than the two in front. The two in front of the clover are ovals with pointy ends where they meet the flower.

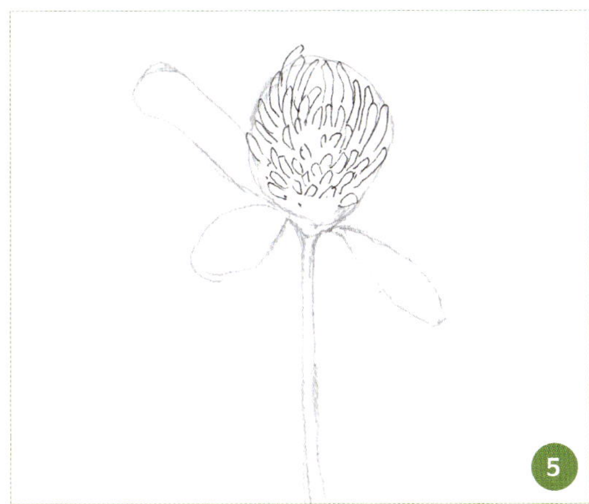

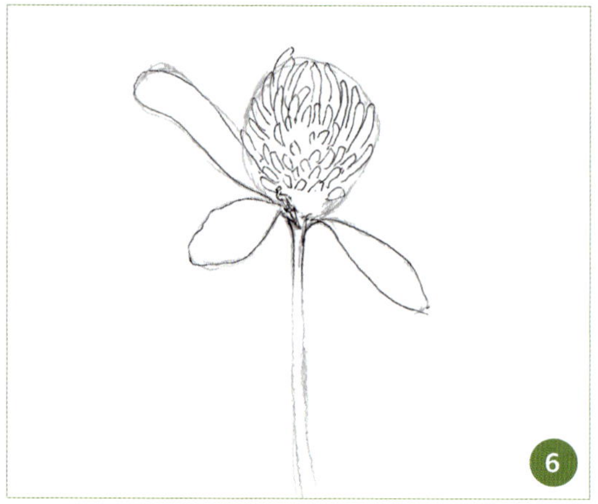

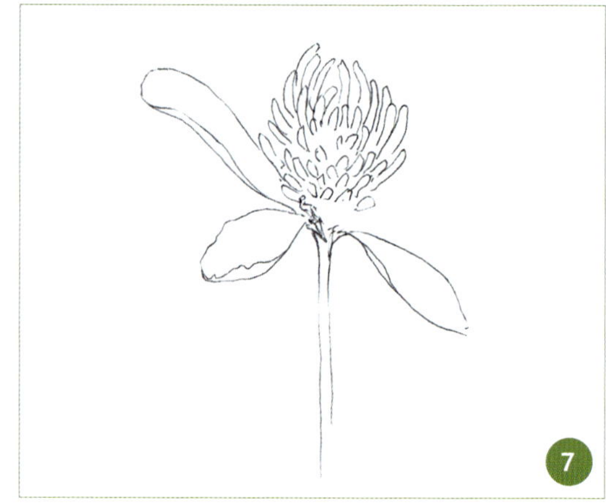

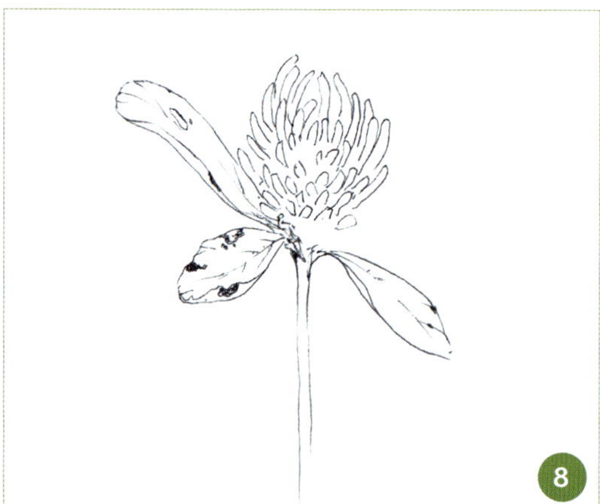

Step 6: Draw the outline on the leaves in 01 fineliner.

Step 7: To give the leaves a bit more life, draw bends on them with the 01 fineliner like on page 20. Now you can erase the pencil guide.

Step 8: It's time to put the imperfect touch on our clover. Draw small dark spots, holes and lines in the leaves with the 005 fineliner. See page 21 to see more.

Step 9: Take the 01 fineliner and draw some dark spots in the lower part of the flower head between the banana shapes for shadow.

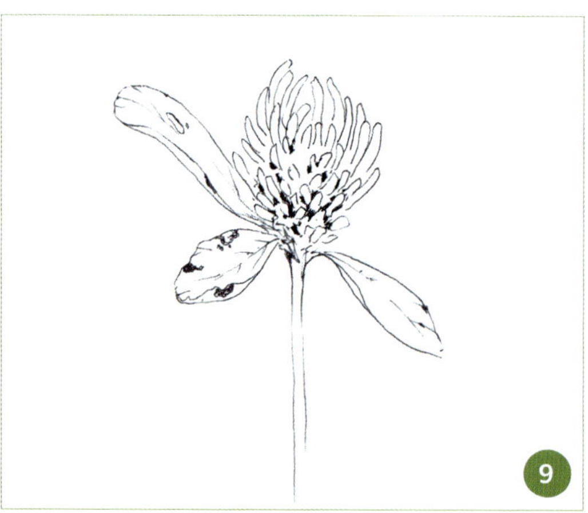

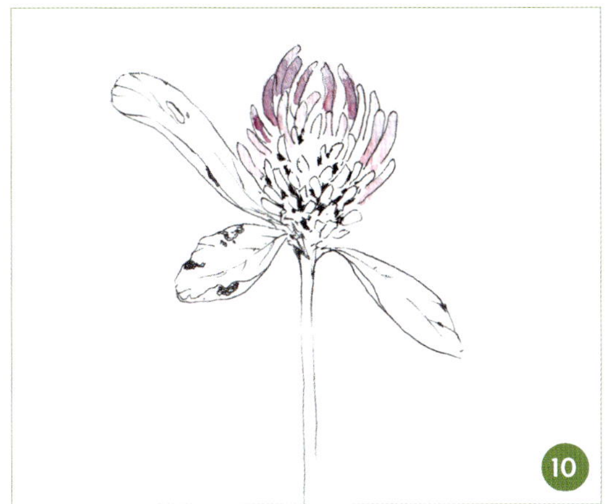

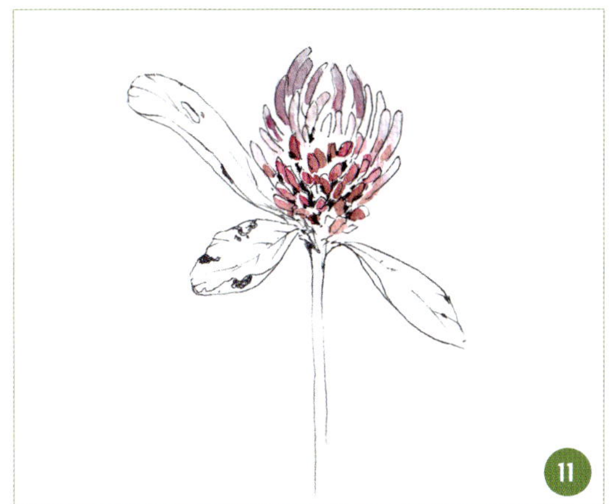

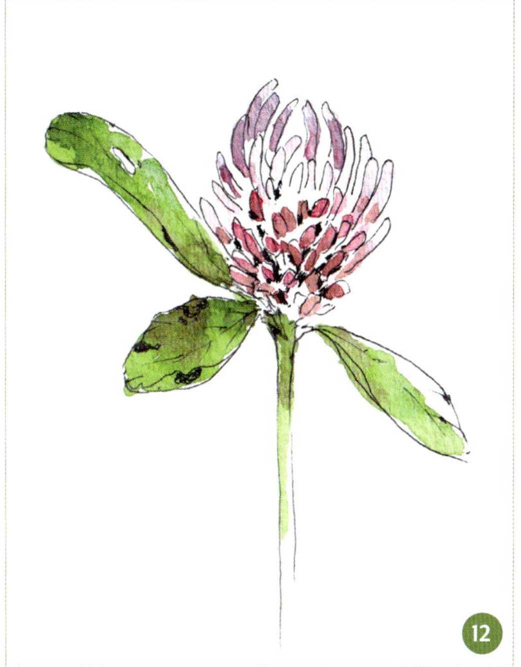

Step 10: The top petals on the flower head reflect the blue from the sky. So, paint the top of the flower head with a mix of Prussian blue and quinacridone rose using your size 4 brush.

Step 11: Paint the rest of the petals with the same brush, but this time with a mix of quinacridone rose and burnt umber. Let some of the petals be more rose and some more brown to create a nice, warm variation.

Step 12: Paint the leaves with sap green, dripping in a dash of burnt umber and quinacridone rose.

YES! You put the imperfect into perfect and that is just fabulous! I love it! Imagine how much richer our lives would be if we embraced all of life like this.

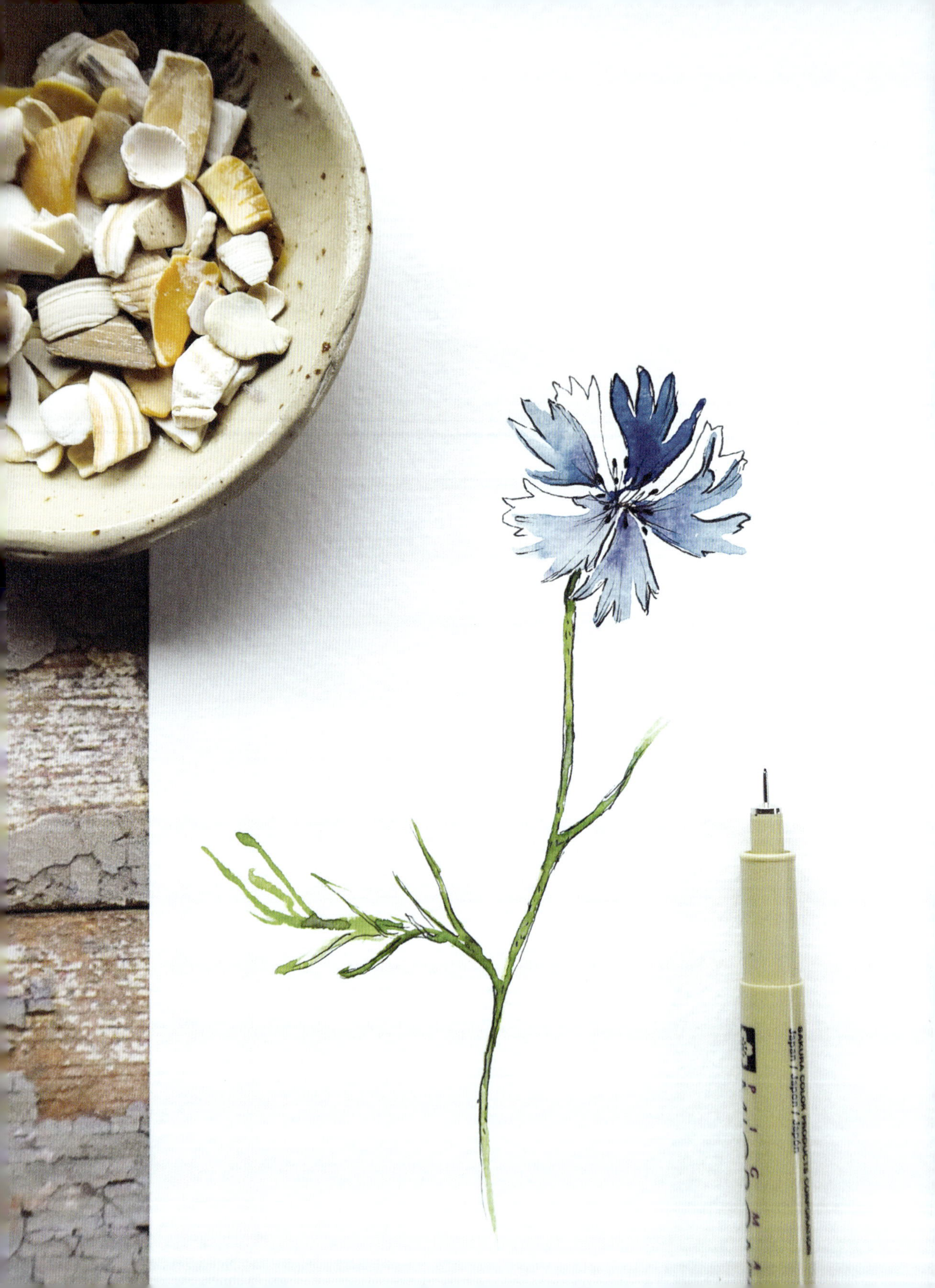

cornflower
a flower of anticipation and delicacy

Can you imagine standing in a field filled with blue cornflowers, red poppies and white oxeye daisies? Everywhere you look it's blue, red and white. Last year I got a text from a friend who found such a field! I was thrilled! I quickly picked up my babies from school and kindergarten to see this wonder. And it was magical!

To me, the cornflower is the sum of summer: Blue like the summer sky and delicate like the grasses on a beach. In this tutorial, we create depth in a new way by mixing it up and leaving part of the cornflowers unpainted.

Materials

Paper: Canson Montval 300gsm (140lb) cold press
Watercolor brush size: 4
Water and cloth
Fineliner sizes: 01 and 005

Colors

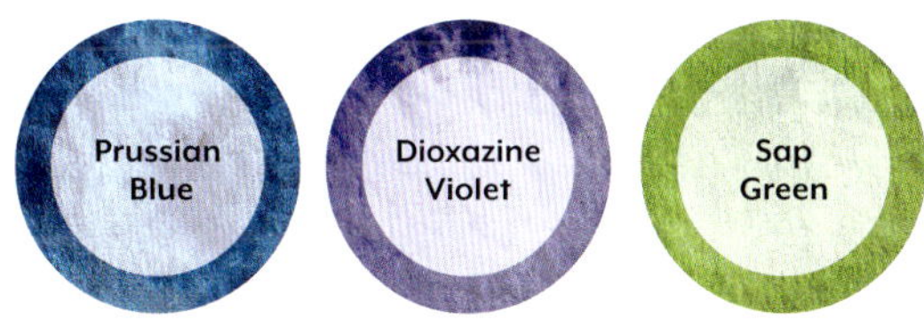

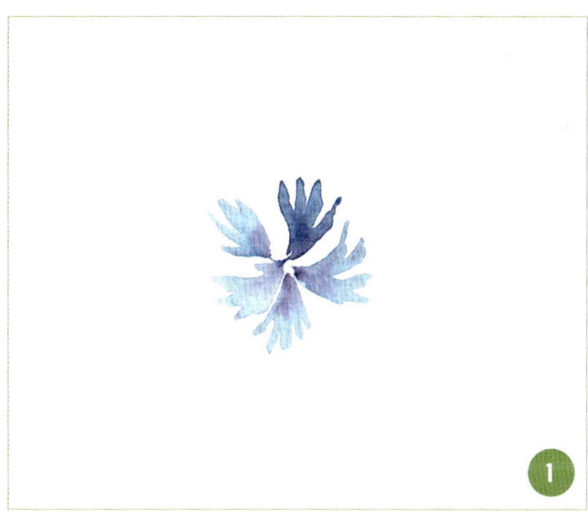

Step 1: This time we start with watercolor, so get your size 4 brush and paint five petals on dry paper. Each petal will consist of long, pointy shapes held together at the center of the flower. Paint them one at a time. Use Prussian blue and then drip in a bit of dioxazine violet where the petals meet in the center of the flower.

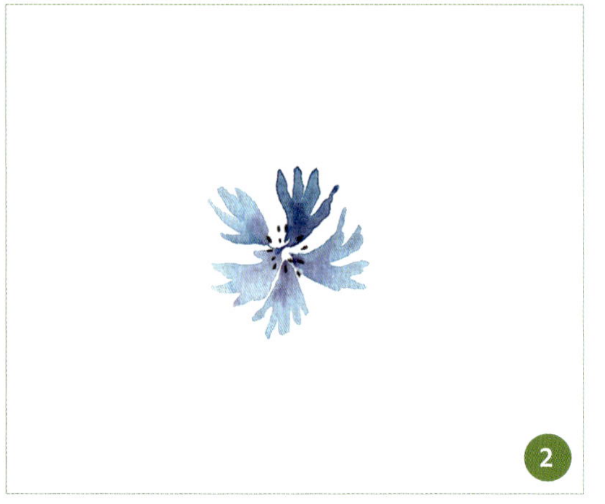

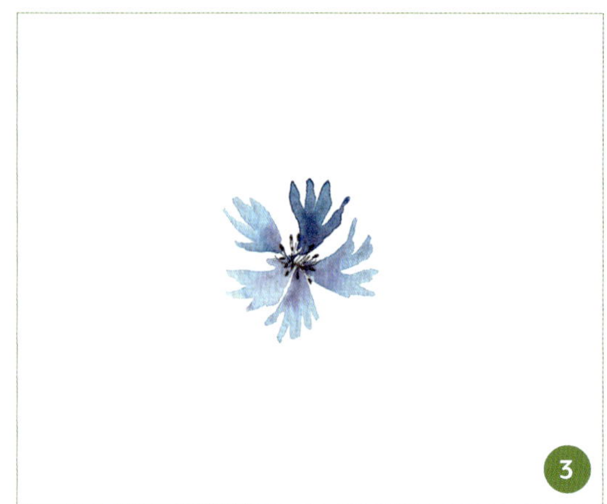

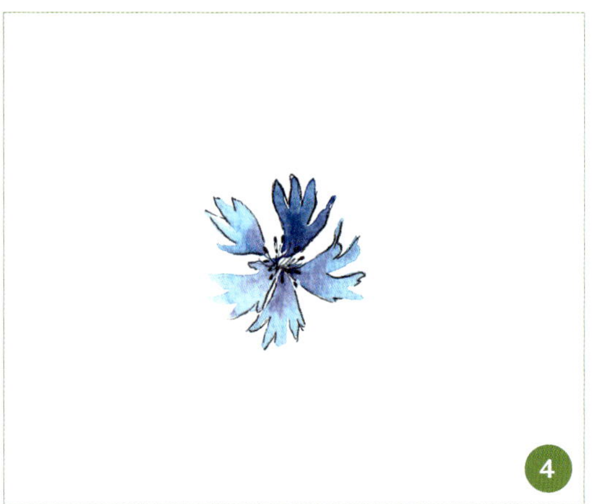

Step 2: When the paint is completely dry, draw small, oval seeds in the center of the flower with your 01 fineliner.

Step 3: Add small stamens with the 005 fineliner from the center of the flower to the seeds. The lines should not be completely straight but more of a flat, C-shaped curve. Let there be a few lines that don't meet a seed but just stand on their own.

Step 4: Take your 01 fineliner again and draw a rough outline around the petals. You want to draw only where you feel like the shape needs to be strengthened and leave holes in the line.

Step 5: Take your 005 fineliner and draw a few more petals behind the painted ones.

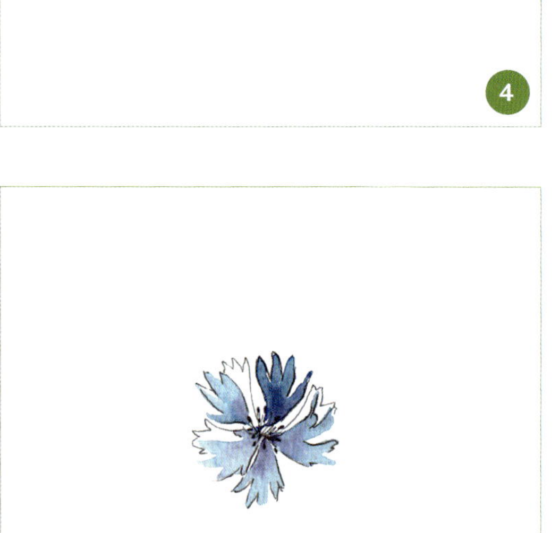

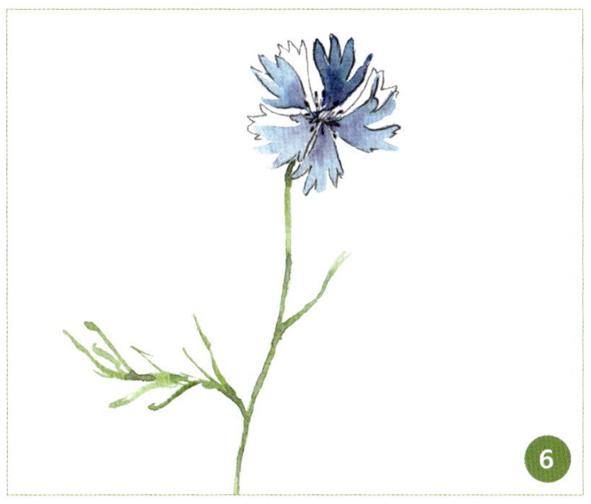

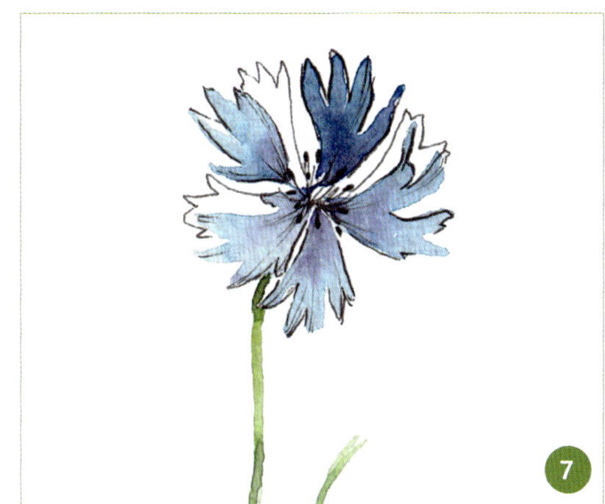

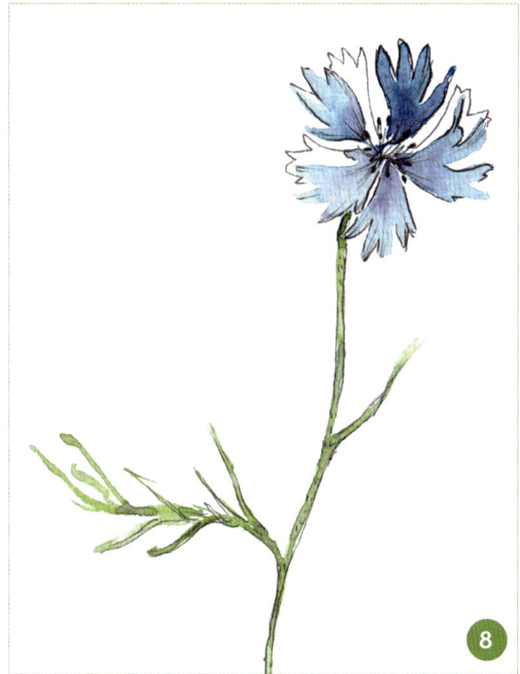

Step 6: Paint the stem with sap green, using the tip of your size 4 brush to draw a few leaves with long shapes. Drip in a bit of Prussian blue and dioxazine violet to vary the color.

Step 7: While the stem dries, draw a few direction lines on the painted petals in the flower head with the 005 fineliner.

Step 8: Finally, add a bit of detail to the stem using the same fineliner. Draw a rough outline and give the stem a few tiny hairs for texture.

Oh, I can almost feel the summer vibes and I hope you can, too. Get yourself a cold lemonade and some sunshine—you deserve it.

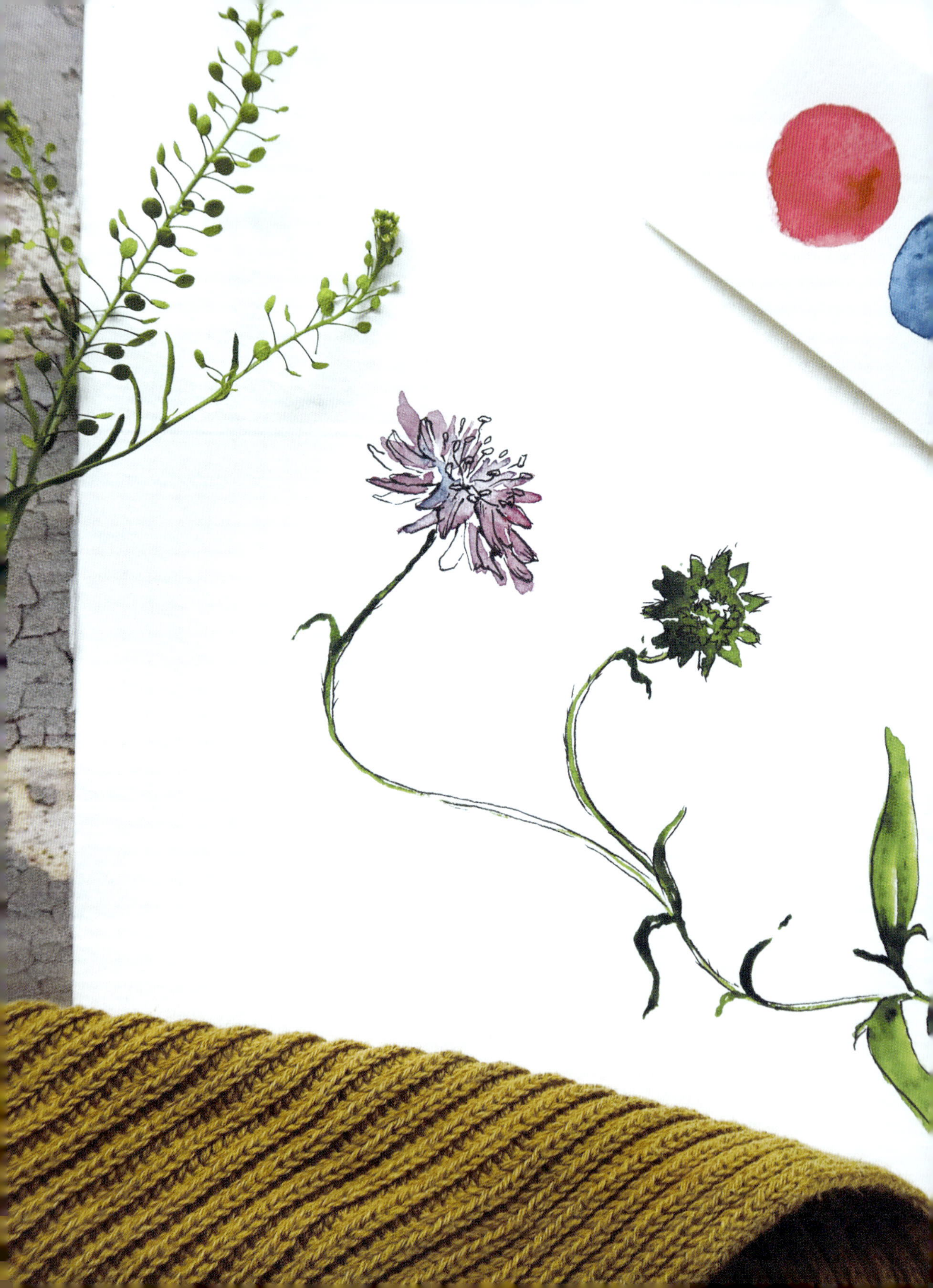

pincushion flower
a flower of peace and pins

This cutie flower looks just like a small cushion filled with pins . . . like the one your grannie always had close by so she could mend whatever needed mending. Mending broken clothes is one of the most peaceful activities I can think of. It's like giving a piece of clothing a new life in silent contemplation. But this peaceful flower is also a wild one. With its dancing stems, it's not a flower to just pick and place alone in a vase—these wildflowers need some companions to party with (see A Dreamy Summer Posy on page 145)! It's almost like grannie prefers the dance floor to a quiet night of knitting.

Materials

Paper: Canson Montval 300gsm (140lb) cold press

Watercolor brush sizes: 4 and 1

Water and cloth

Fineliner sizes: 01 and 005

Palette

Colors

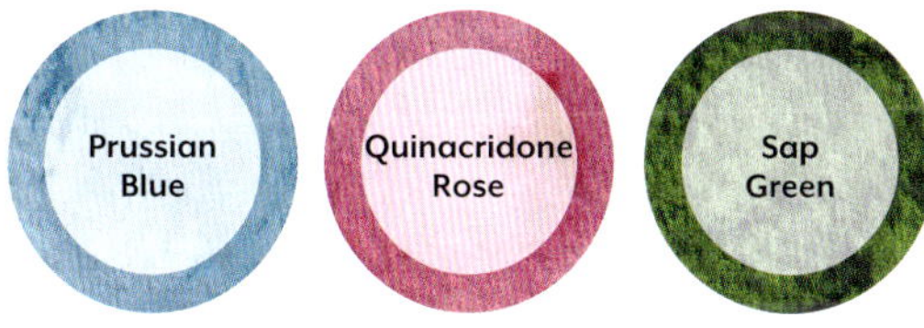

Mix

For the flower head, you will need a mix of 50% Prussian blue and 50% quinacridone rose.

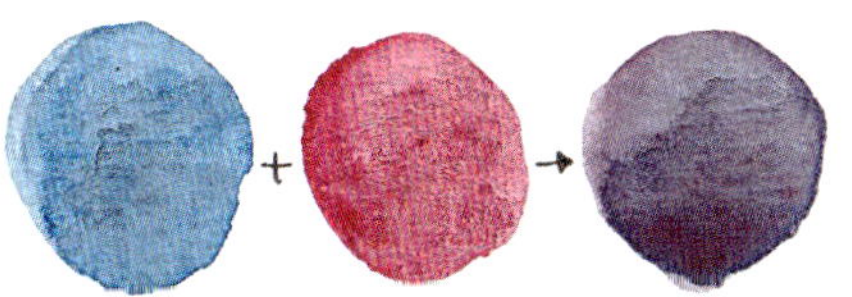

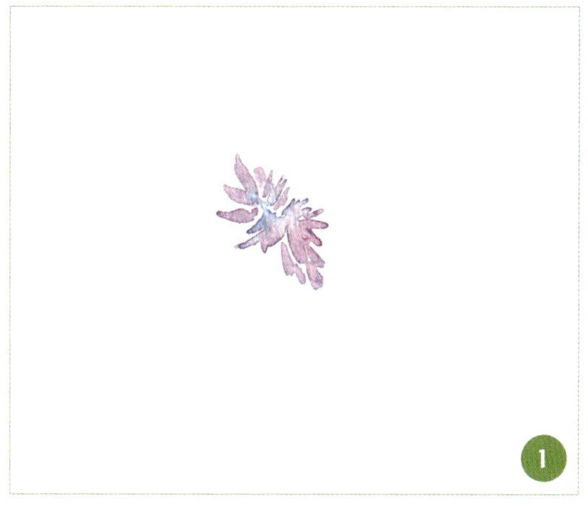

Step 1: For this power grannie flower, we start with the magical watercolor. First get a mix of Prussian blue and quinacridone rose ready and then paint the flower head with the size 4 brush. Painting wet-on-dry, start with the big petals at the bottom pointing down and to the sides. Then move to the top of the flower where you have small petals, like small spikes or pins in a cushion. Leave plenty of white space to separate the petals.

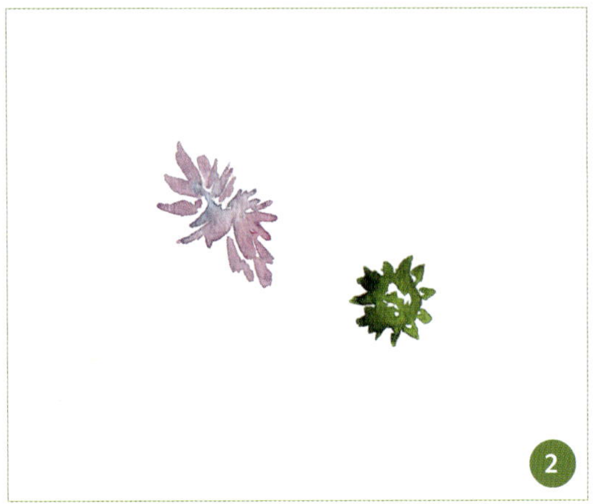

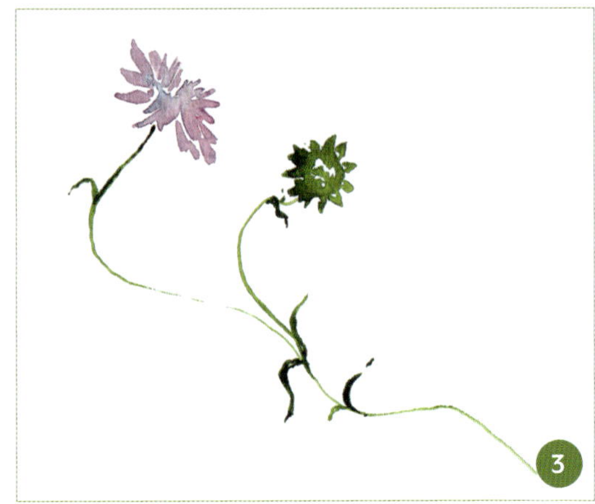

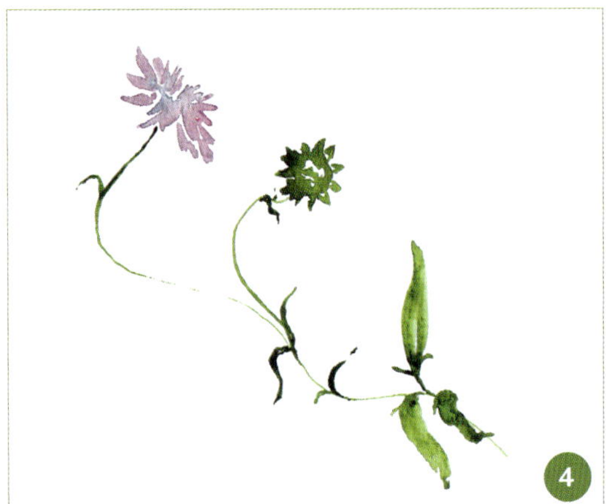

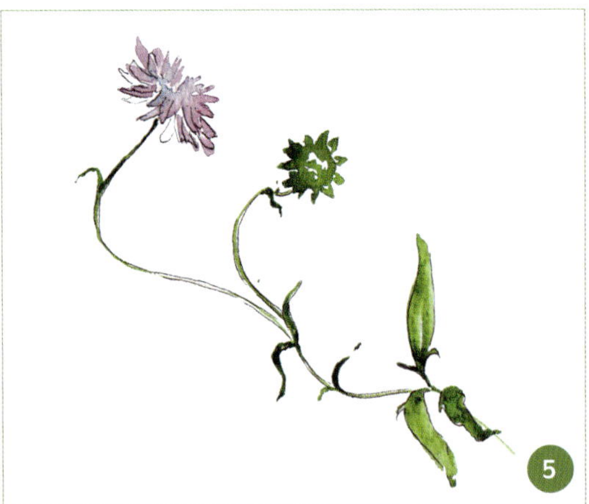

Step 2: Paint the bud with sap green. The bud is a circle shape with random spots of white space. On the outer edge, paint small triangular leaves all the way around.

Step 3: Switch to the small size 1 brush and paint the dancing stem. This will be in sap green and go all the way across the paper, dancing its way out to the right. When you have that under control, you can use the size 4 brush to paint a few narrow leaves in the same color. The leaves are very small and close to the flower head and bud. Paint a few bigger leaves where the two stems meet.

Step 4: Continue with the biggest leaves further down the stem. They are also painted in sap green, but you will drip in a bit of Prussian blue as well. These leaves have small hooks close to the stem, almost like they are going out to fish.

Step 5: When the dancing bloom is dry, draw petals on the lower part of the flower head with your 01 fineliner. You don't need to outline each painted petal . . . just add enough detail to make it easy to see the shapes. While you are drawing with the 01 fineliner, you can also outline the stem and leaves.

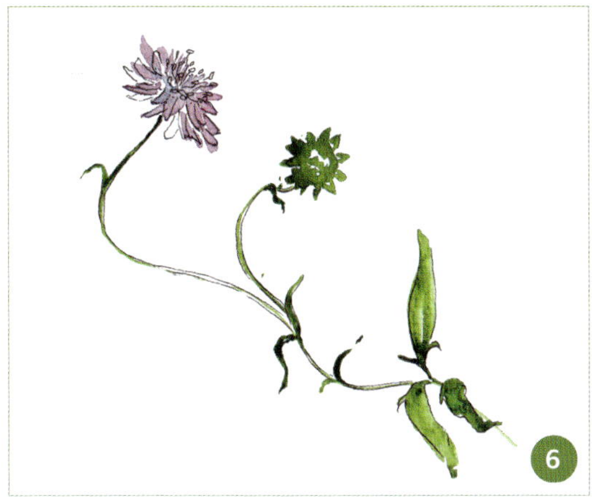

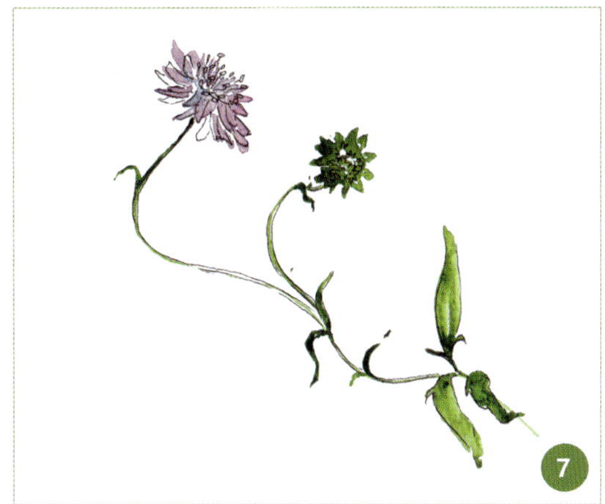

Step 6: Get your 005 fineliner and draw the pins in the center of the flower. The pins are small lines with an oval seed at the end. Have some of these seeds go further than the painted flower edge.

Step 7: Moving to the bud, draw small star shapes with the same 005 fineliner. You don't have to cover everything in small stars; just a few will create texture.

Step 8: Still using the 005 fineliner, draw an outline on the bud and give it small hairs on the triangles around the edge.

Step 9: Use your 005 fineliner and draw direction lines on the flower petals. Add a bit of shadow between some of the petals to create depth. The stem could also do with a few hairs.

I don't know about you, but this flower just reminds me of *Dirty Dancing*. Nobody puts Baby—nor grannie—in a corner. I guess wildflowers are like that, in a way.

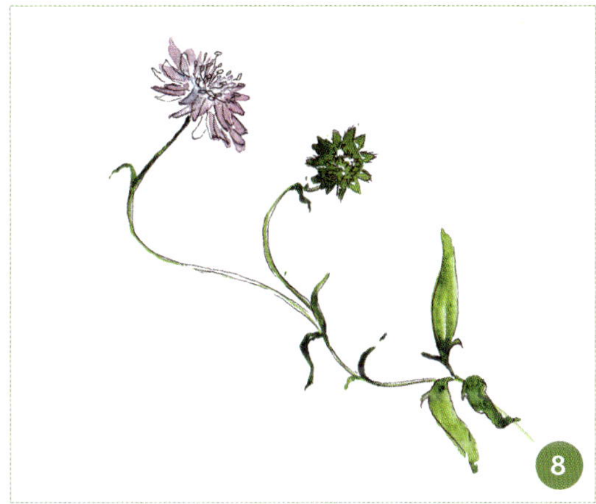

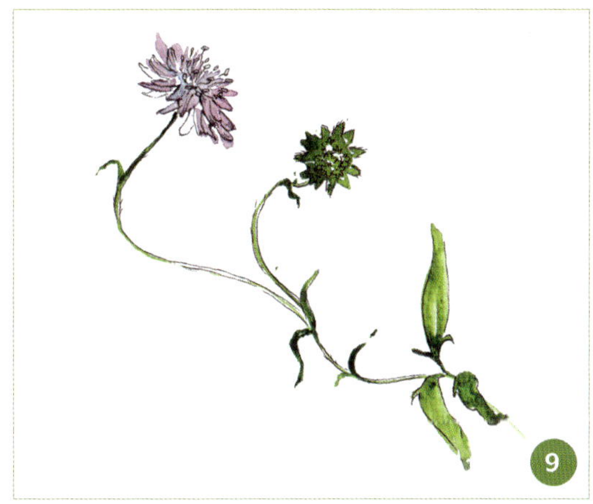

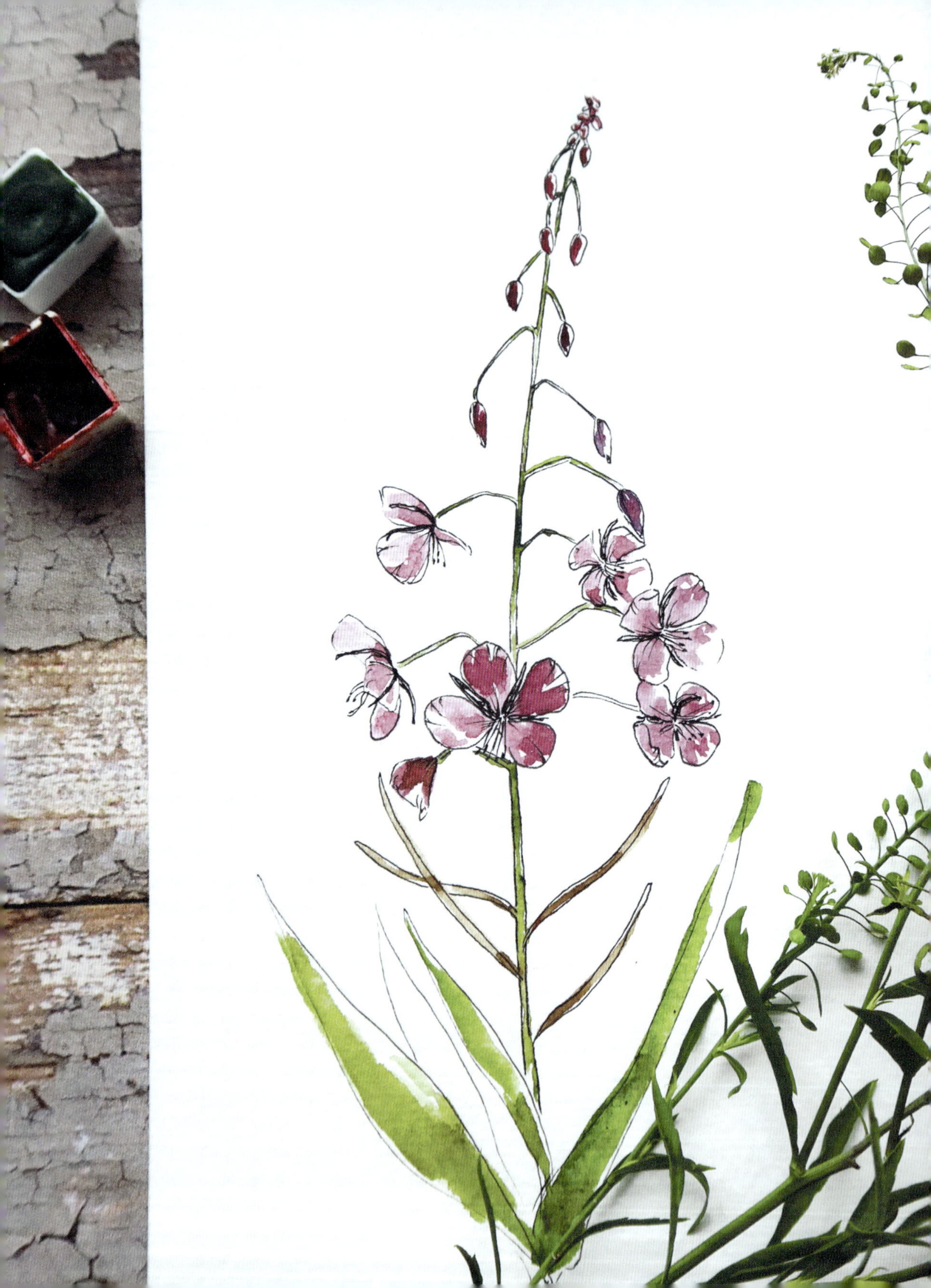

fireweed
a flower of renewed beauty and abundance

One of the most incredible things I've noticed when looking at fireweed is the way it grows in different stages. When you look closely, you will see the small young buds at the top of the stem. Then, a bit further down, you find the adults and, even further down, the elderly. They are all on the same stem, like a family living in the same house across generations, and protected by the leaves. I absolutely love that!

In this tutorial, we are going to work a bit with the change of colors across growth stages in the blooms. It's so wonderful how they change but also how they keep their colors throughout their lives.

Materials

Paper: Canson Montval 300gsm (140lb) cold press

Pencil and eraser

Fineliner sizes: 01 and 005

Watercolor brush size: 4

Water and cloth

Palette

Colors

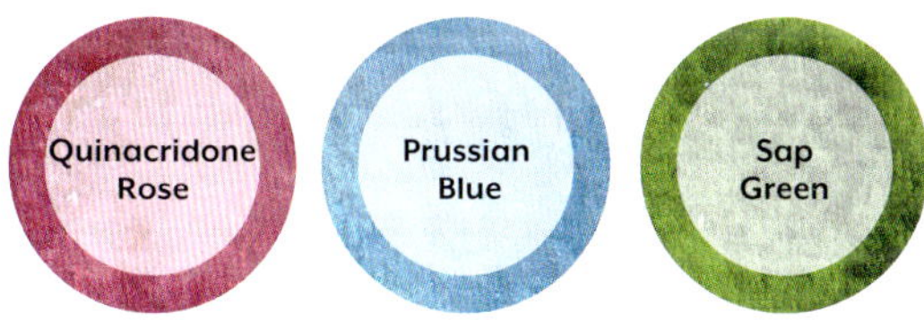

Mix

The flower mix is 50% quinacridone rose and 50% Prussian blue.

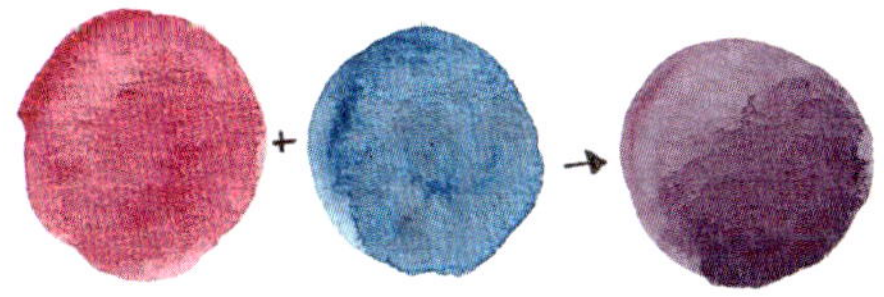

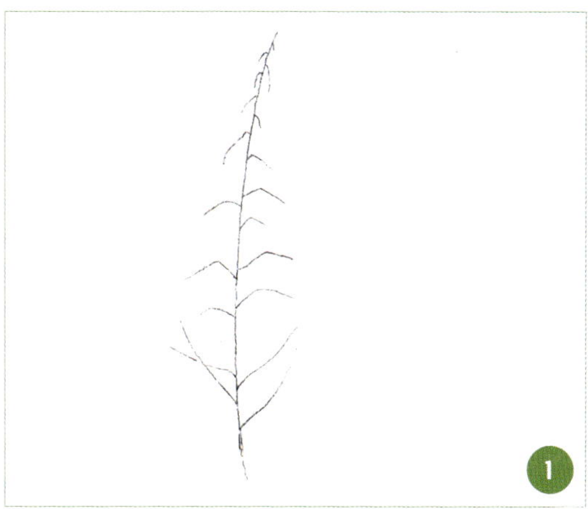

Step 1: We start by doing a nice pencil guide. So, grab your pencil and draw a slightly curved line. Add small stems on it. The ones at the top are small and bending down. When you move down the stem, they become longer, and at the bottom, the lines are long and bend upward.

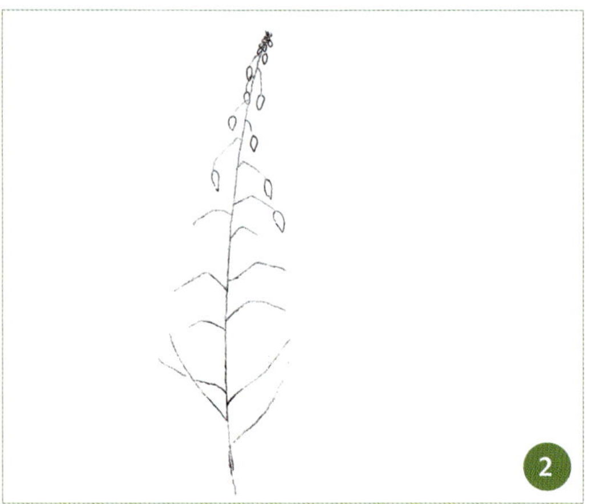

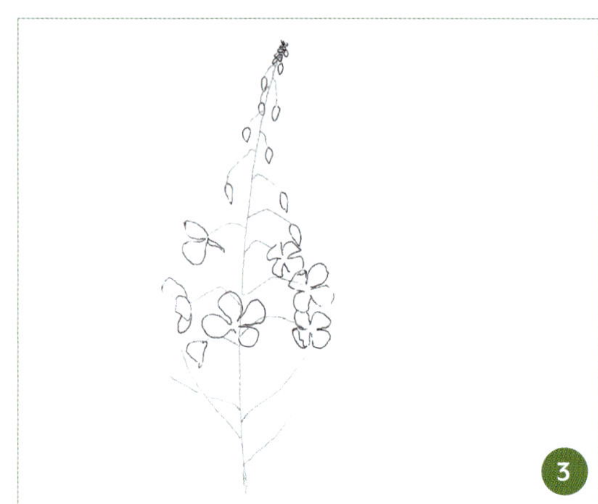

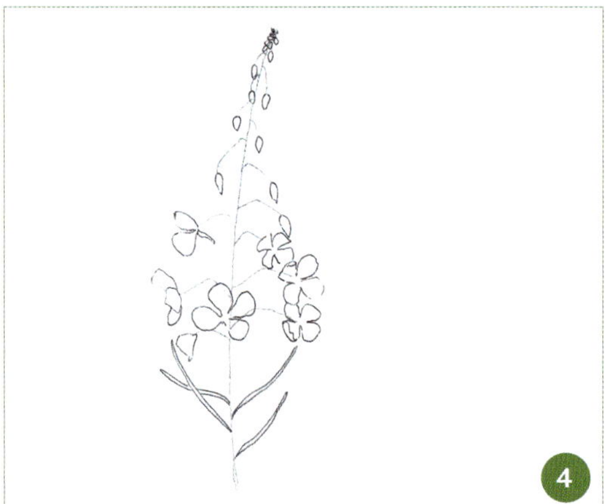

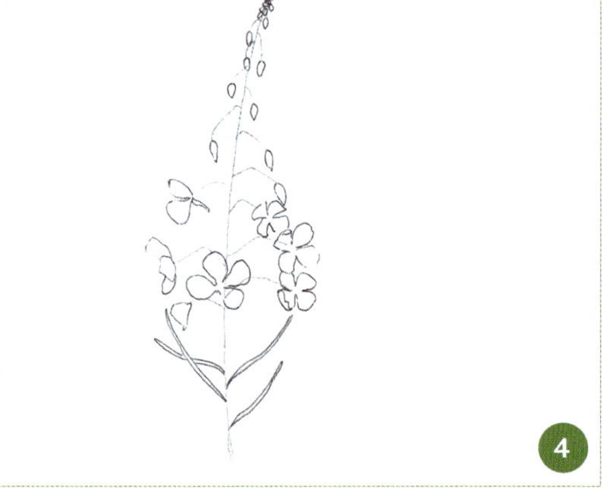

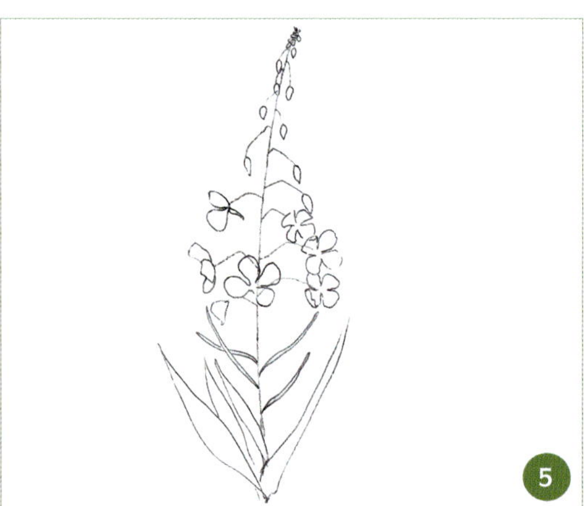

Step 2: Grab your 01 fineliner and draw the young buds at the top. They are teardrop shapes. At the very top, the buds are just small oval shapes in a cluster of cute baby buds. As you move down, they get larger with a more pronounced teardrop shape.

Step 3: Work your way down the stem to draw the flowers with the same fineliner. They have four petals, and some are seen from the side so you can only see some of the petals. Draw bends on a few of the flower petals for some life and movement.

Step 4: Draw the aging seedpods at the bottom with the same fineliner. These are shaped like a short, thicker stem without flowers.

Step 5: At the very bottom, draw loose, protecting leaves.

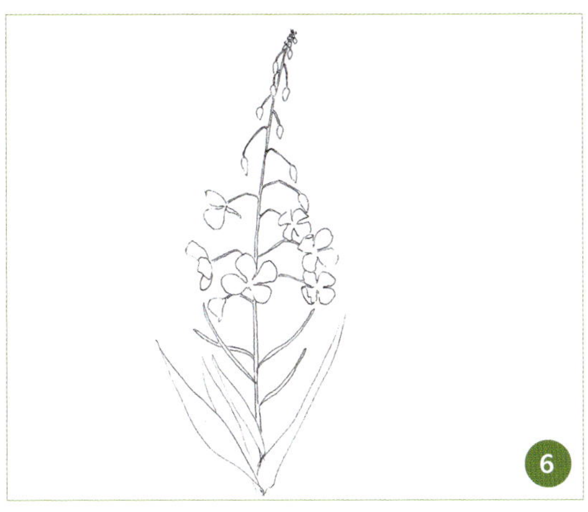

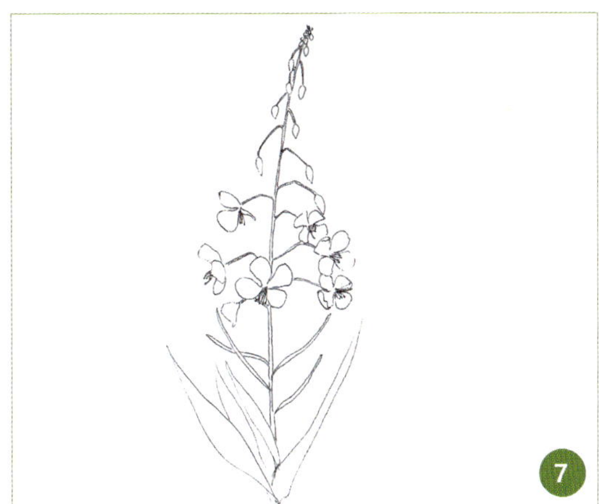

Step 6: Gather everything neatly together by drawing the stem. The fireweed has a main stem in the middle going all the way up and then additional smaller stems that attach to the blooms. A good tip is to draw the small stems first, so you keep a small gap free where it meets the main stem. What a beautiful sketch you have! Now you can erase the pencil lines because you don't need them any longer.

Step 7: Switch to the 005 fineliner and draw the stamens on the flowers in bloom. These are short, slightly curved lines with a dark spot at the end.

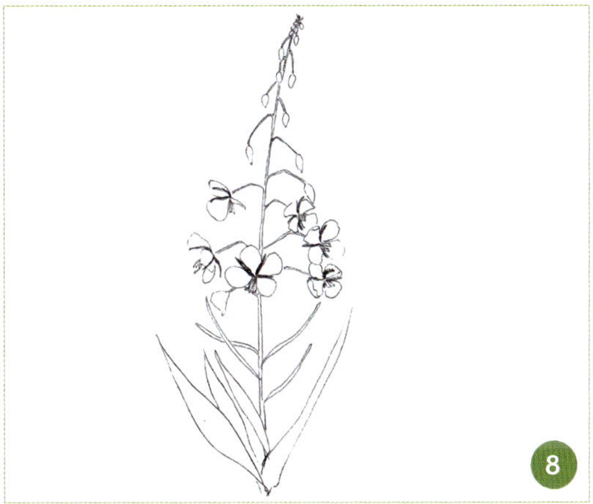

Step 8: Draw out the narrow, pointy sepals between the petals as well. Color them in with the fineliner but make sure to leave white space so they don't become too heavy.

Step 9: To finish the ink, use the fineliner to give the blooms and buds a few direction lines.

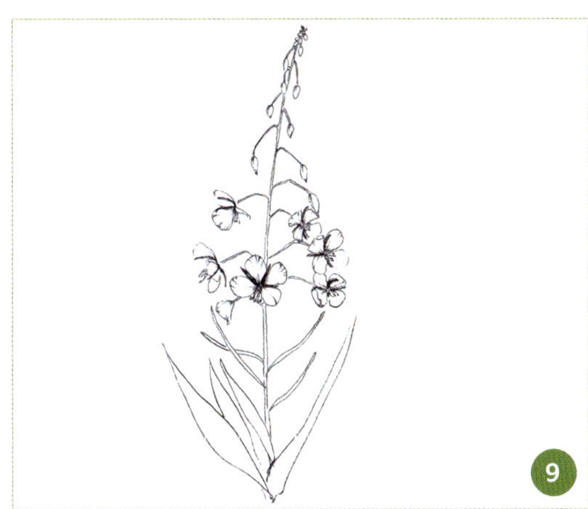

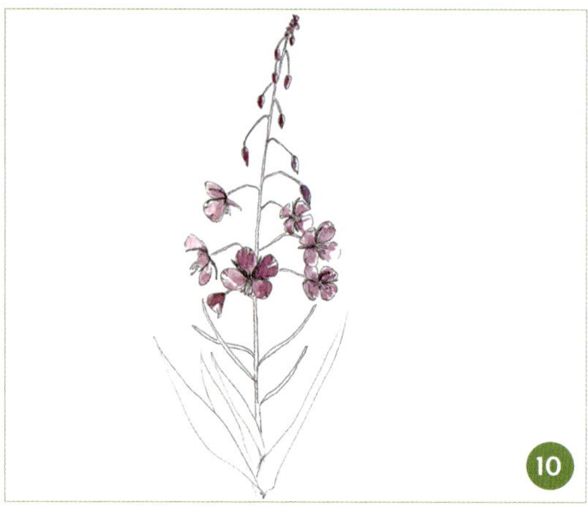

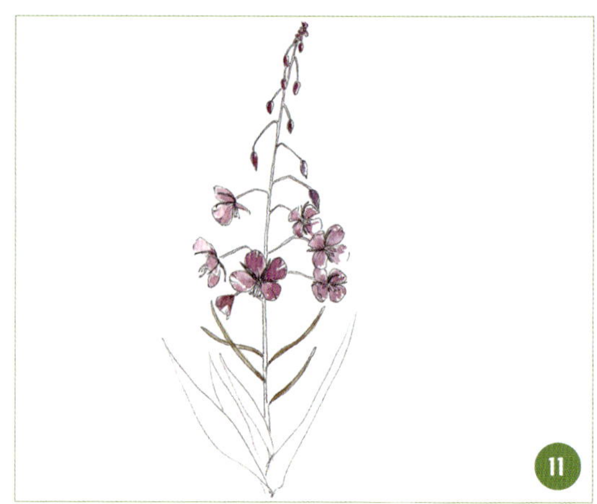

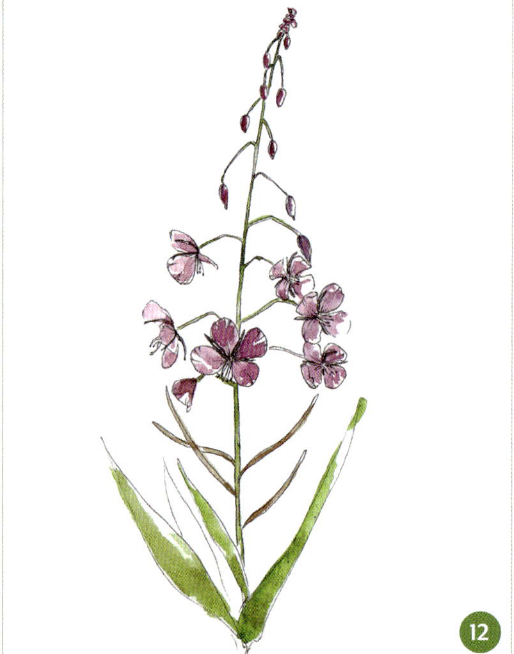

Step 10: Make a mix of quinacridone rose with Prussian blue. Paint the flowers and buds with this mix and a size 4 brush.

Step 11: Put a bit of sap green in the mix and paint the seedpods with this color. That way the seedpods still carry some of their original color, tying them together with the family while also taking them closer to the color of the stem and leaves.

Step 12: Finally, paint the stem and leaves with sap green. While it is still wet, drip in a bit of the mix from before to vary the color slightly.

Now this was great! You don't have to read that much between the lines of this flower tutorial to see how much we can learn from nature. I think that is so incredible. Well done!

wild columbine
a flower of fortitude

When we moved into our little house, there was a massive amount of ivy that we struggled hard to get rid of. We succeeded in autumn but were left with poor soil to turn into a flower bed the year after. And when May came, so did the plenitude of wild columbines. Blue, pale pink, violet, light blue and almost green. They were everywhere and they return every year now. Like magic.

The columbine can be a tricky flower because it has a lot of detail and layers. So, in this tutorial I give you a technique I use quite often: Imagine that the flower is something else.

Materials

Paper: Canson Montval 300gsm (140lb) cold press

Watercolor brush size: 4

Water and cloth

Fineliner sizes: 01 and 005

Colors

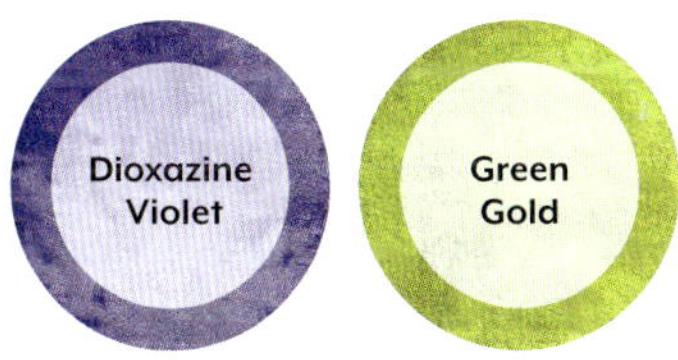

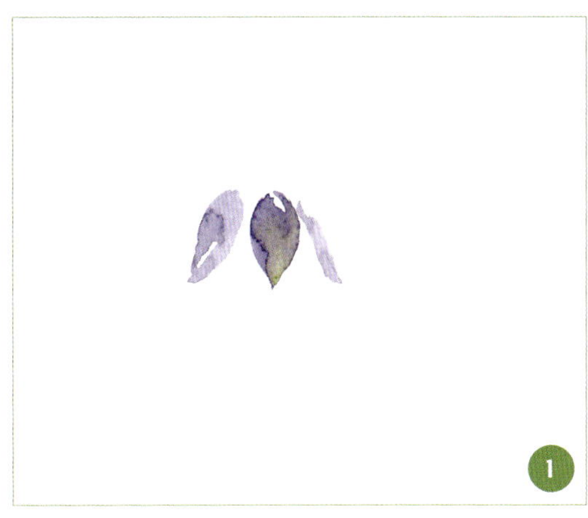

Step 1: The columbine can seem a bit scary because of all the details. So, try imagining that the flower is actually an elegant columbine fairy wearing a beautiful violet dress in two layers. Start to paint the outside part of her skirt, leaving space to also paint the inside skirt. Use your size 4 brush and the dioxazine violet. To make the colors a bit more interesting and tie them together with the rest of the drawing, drip in a bit of green gold.

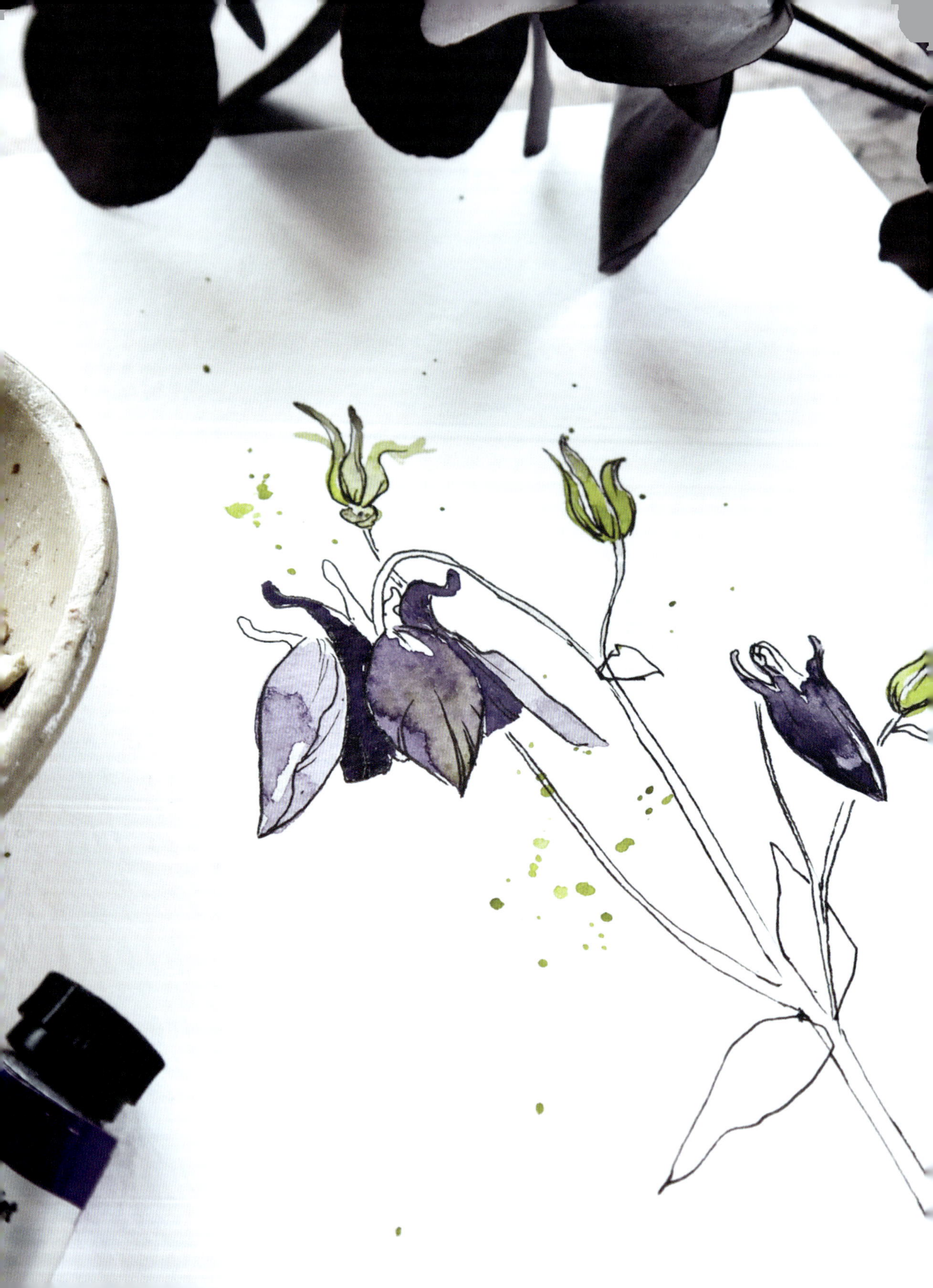

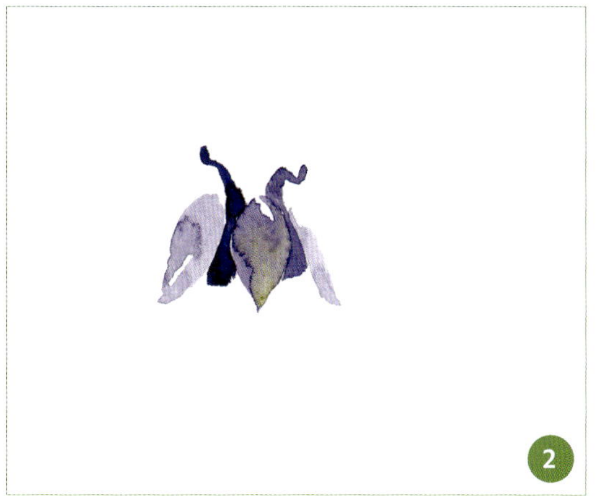

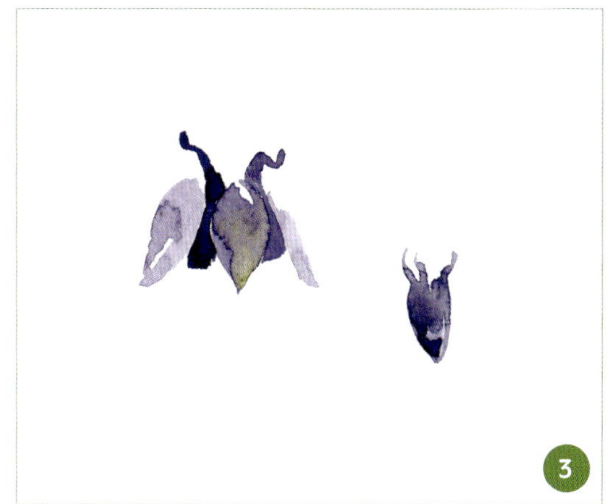

Step 2: Paint the inside skirt again using the dioxazine violet. This part of the dress is not as long as the outside skirt but has long straps to cover her shoulders. To vary the colors, paint the inside skirt with less water than the outside so it's more vibrant.

Step 3: Paint a hanging bud in violet. The bud is shaped like a drop with a pointy tip at the bottom, and this also has straps at the top. Maybe this dress is for the columbine's little sister.

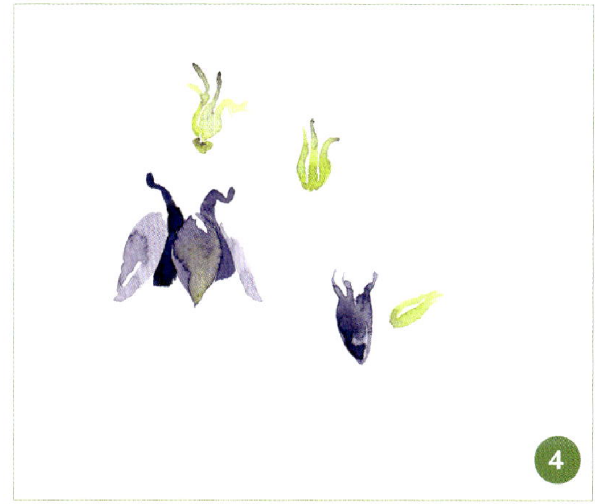

Step 4: Paint three dried seedpods around the columbines. They consist of long narrow shapes tied at the bottom. On one of them, paint a small, uneven round shape at the bottom. Paint these in green gold, and then drip in a bit of violet at the tip and the bottom to tie the colors together.

Step 5: Once dry, it's time to get your 01 fineliner and draw a stem. Draw one main stem and make the bud, wilted seedpods and blooms meet in different spots on that stem.

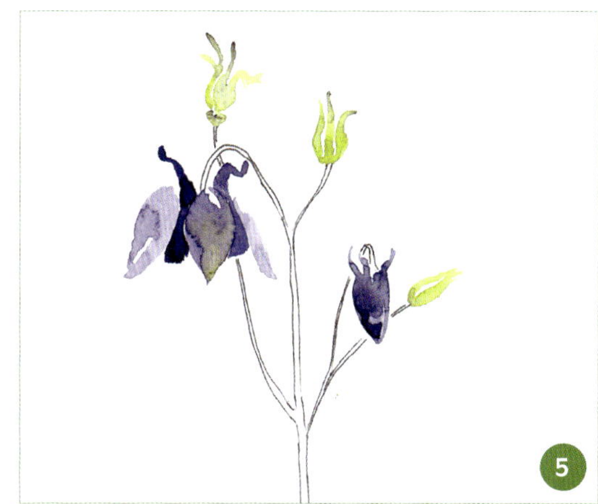

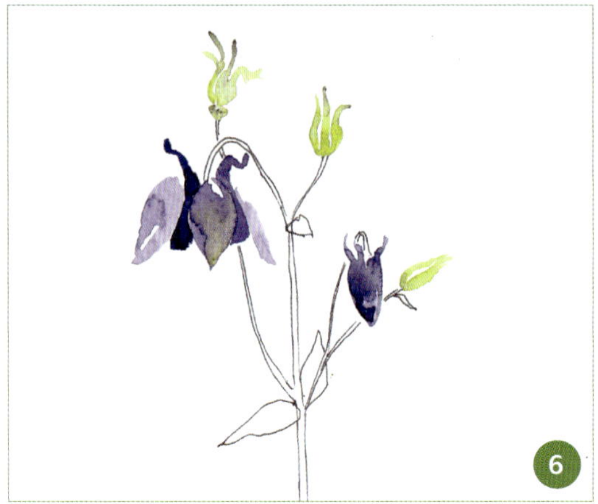

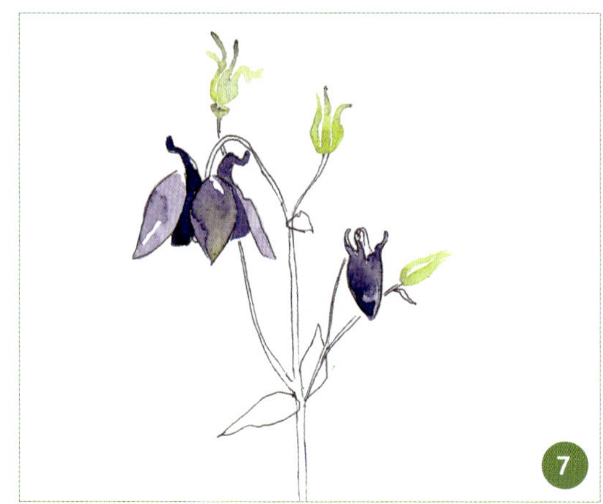

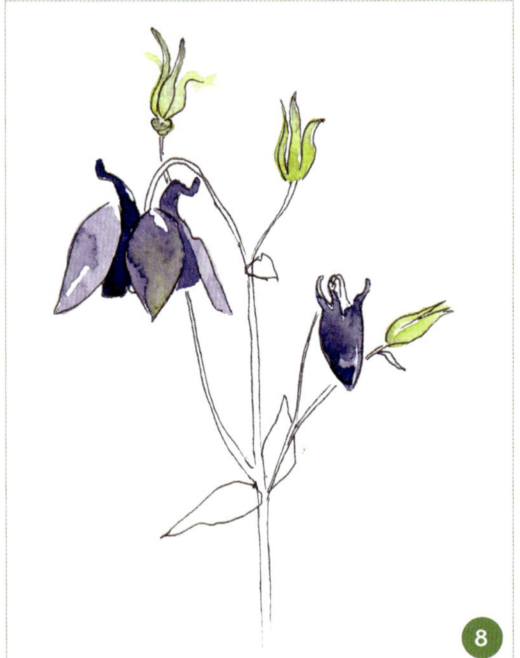

Step 6: Where the stems meet draw a few teardrop-shaped leaves with the same fineliner.

Step 7: Still holding your 01 fineliner, draw an outline on the bud and bloom.

Step 8: Draw an outline with the 005 fineliner on the wilted seedpods.

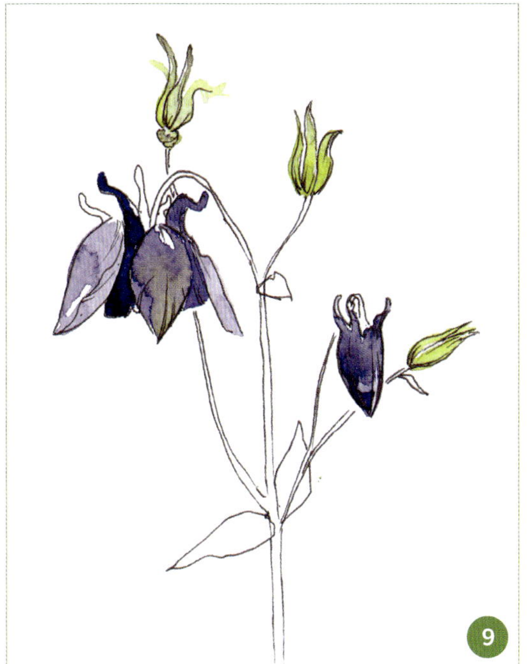

Step 9: The columbine wants a few more straps for her dress, so draw them hiding behind the full bloom with the 005 fineliner. Draw direction lines on the petals of the flower as well as the bud and seedpods.

Step 10: Finally, let's celebrate this beautiful columbine with a splatter in green gold . . . like confetti after a beautiful dance.

Yes, you did it! The columbine can be tricky, but I often find it helpful to imagine something other than the flower to help me. Like in this case, I thought of a dress in layers. Maybe you can use this technique on a different flower?

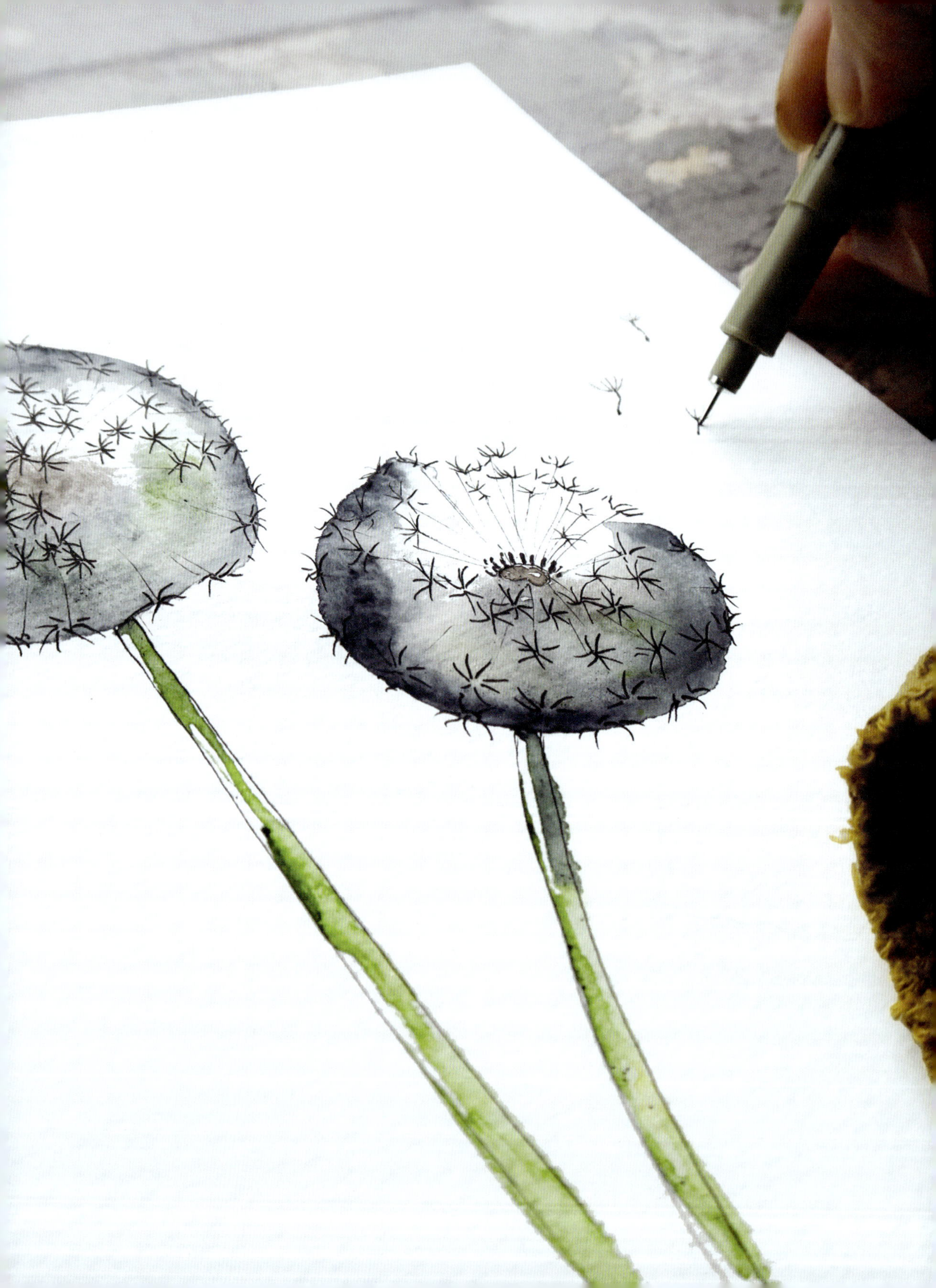

dandelion
a flower of healing and resilience

There are so many opinions on dandelions these days. Some see them as annoying weeds in their lawn, and some enjoy the bright pops of color and the whimsical spheres when the flower ages. I must admit that I lean toward the latter team. I mean, a flower that is colorful, abundant, can be turned into floral wreaths by my kids and is even named after a lion is just pretty incredible.

In this tutorial, you'll learn how to create a mature beauty, showcasing how to combine watercolor and fineliner to create the feeling of a transparent sphere of seeds.

Materials

Paper: Canson Montval 300gsm (140lb) cold press

Watercolor brush size: 4

Water and cloth

Fineliner sizes: 01 and 005

Colors

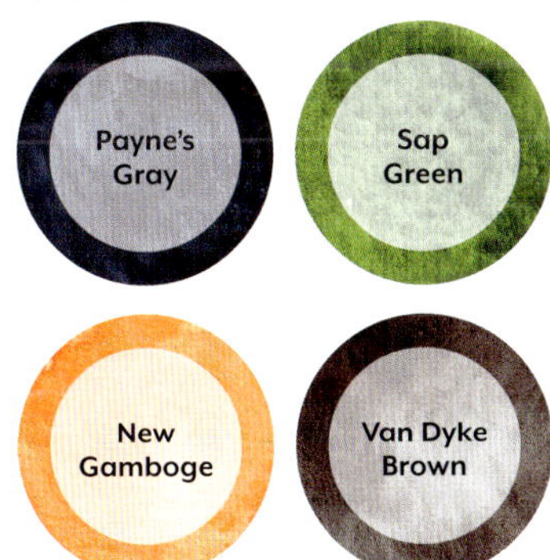

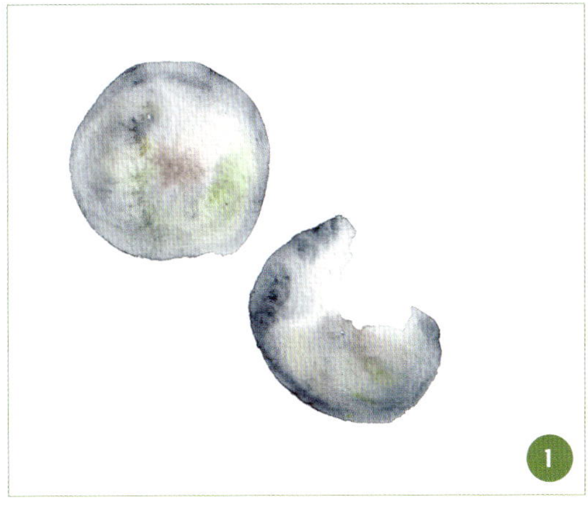

Step 1: Using your size 4 brush, paint one full circle with water and three-fourths of a circle, a little lower, also in clean water. Carefully drip a watery Payne's gray into the clear water wash you just painted. Do the same with a bit of sap green and a small droplet of new gamboge. The green will tie the flower head together with the stem, and the yellow is a memory of the flower it's been.

Count to 20 and in the center of both circles, drip a bit of Van Dyke brown. Let the colors mix gently and wait for them to dry completely. While you wait, you can enjoy watching the blooms you just created turn into a beautiful texture.

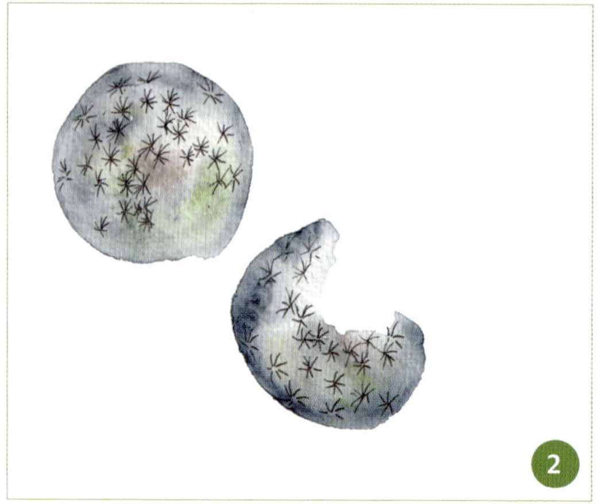

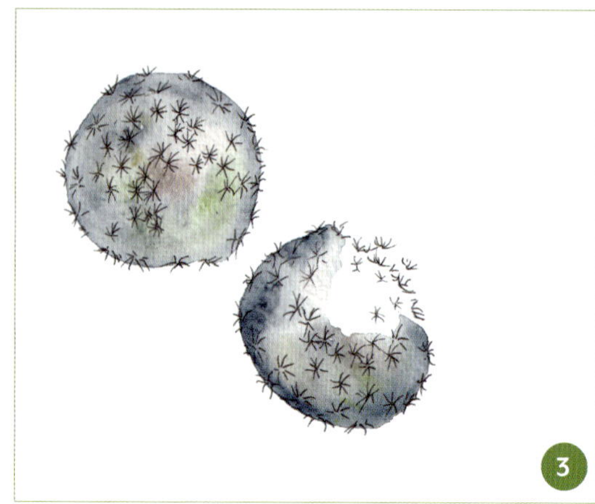

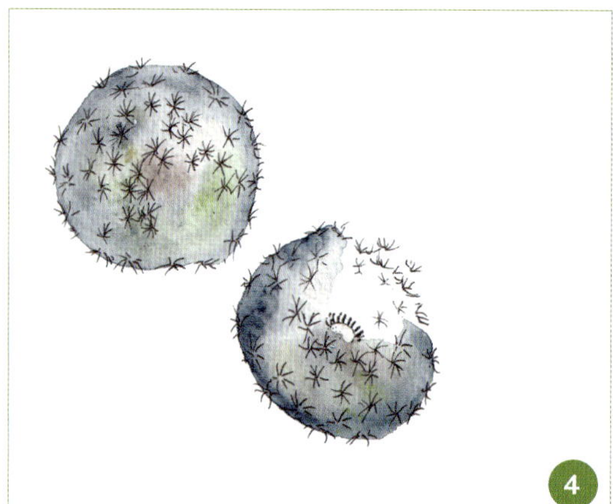

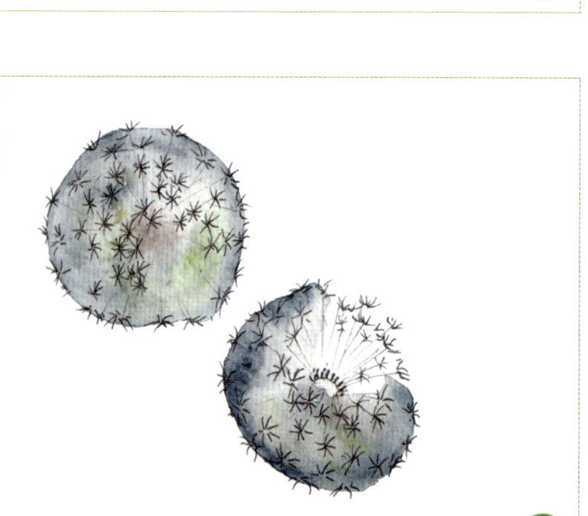

Step 2: Using your 01 fineliner, draw small starbursts across the two spheres. Each starburst is simply six to eight lines meeting in a point. Draw as many as you like. Let some overlap and make sure to leave space without any starbursts to let the watercolor and texture shine. When you get closer to the edge you can let the stars become a bit flatter. To do this, the lines at the sides of the stars will be longer than the top and bottom to show that they are being seen from the side.

Step 3: Now we are going to work on the edges of the dandelions. Still using your 01 fineliner, draw half starbursts that go outside the edge of the watercolor. This will bring more life and movement to the bloom. On the open dandelion, you can also draw these half starbursts at the edge and fill in the gap with a few seen from the side as well.

Step 4: Draw the oval center of the open dandelion now. Draw the part of the center that is visible and let the rest hide behind the watercolor. Give it a few dots for texture and then draw small dark ovals attaching to the center. These are the bottom parts of the seeds that will soon fly away.

Step 5: Changing to a 005 fineliner, you can now draw the lines going from the starbursts toward the center of the dandelion. Let some of the lines go all the way to the center and let some be just barely visible in places. The open area on the right dandelion will have the most visible lines.

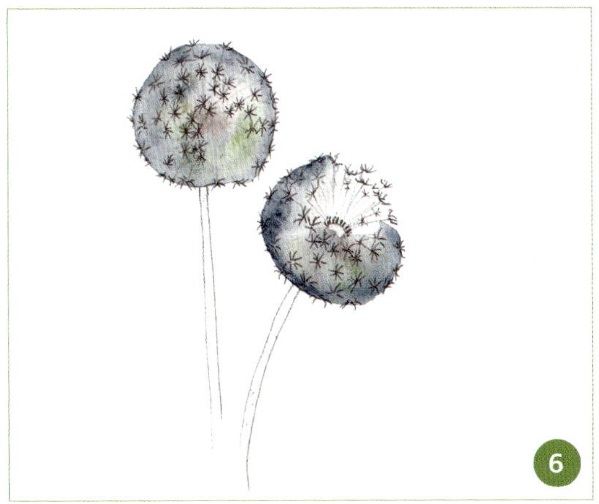

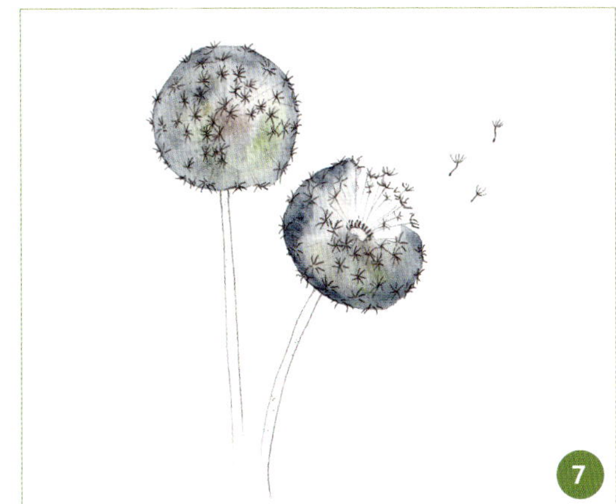

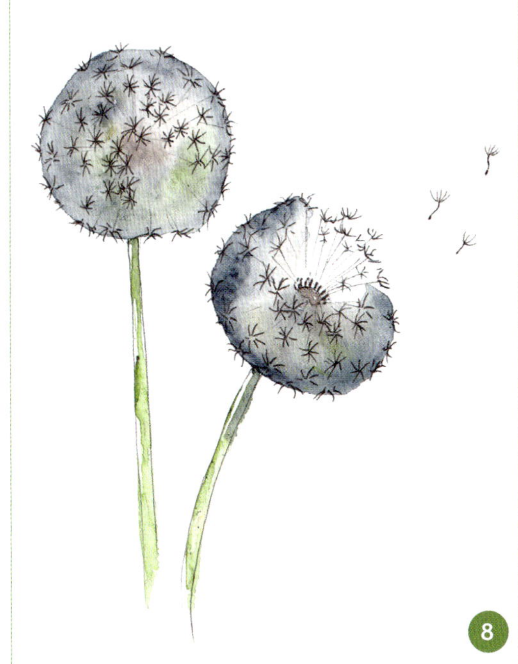

Step 6: With your 01 fineliner, draw the stems. These are two straight lines next to each other. Keep the left one tall and the right one slightly bent. For a bit of texture, take your 005 fineliner and draw small dots in a few places on each stem.

Step 7: To add a bit of movement to these blooms, take the 01 fineliner and draw three flying seeds on their way to see the world. These flying seeds are created with half of a starburst, a small stem and a small oval at the bottom. Let them bend in the wind so they all look unique.

Step 8: For the final touch, add a bit of color on the stem. Grab your size 4 brush and load it with sap green. Paint the stem wet-on-dry, leaving white space along the edges of the stem. Drip in a bit of Payne's gray at the top for a bit of shadow, just below the flower head. Add a bit of new gamboge in the center of the seed heads, tying the colors together with the colorful bloom it was a short while ago.

And well done! You have just created one of the most whimsical and iconic shapes in the spring floral field! Imagine an entire drawing just with these spheres—that would be so magical!

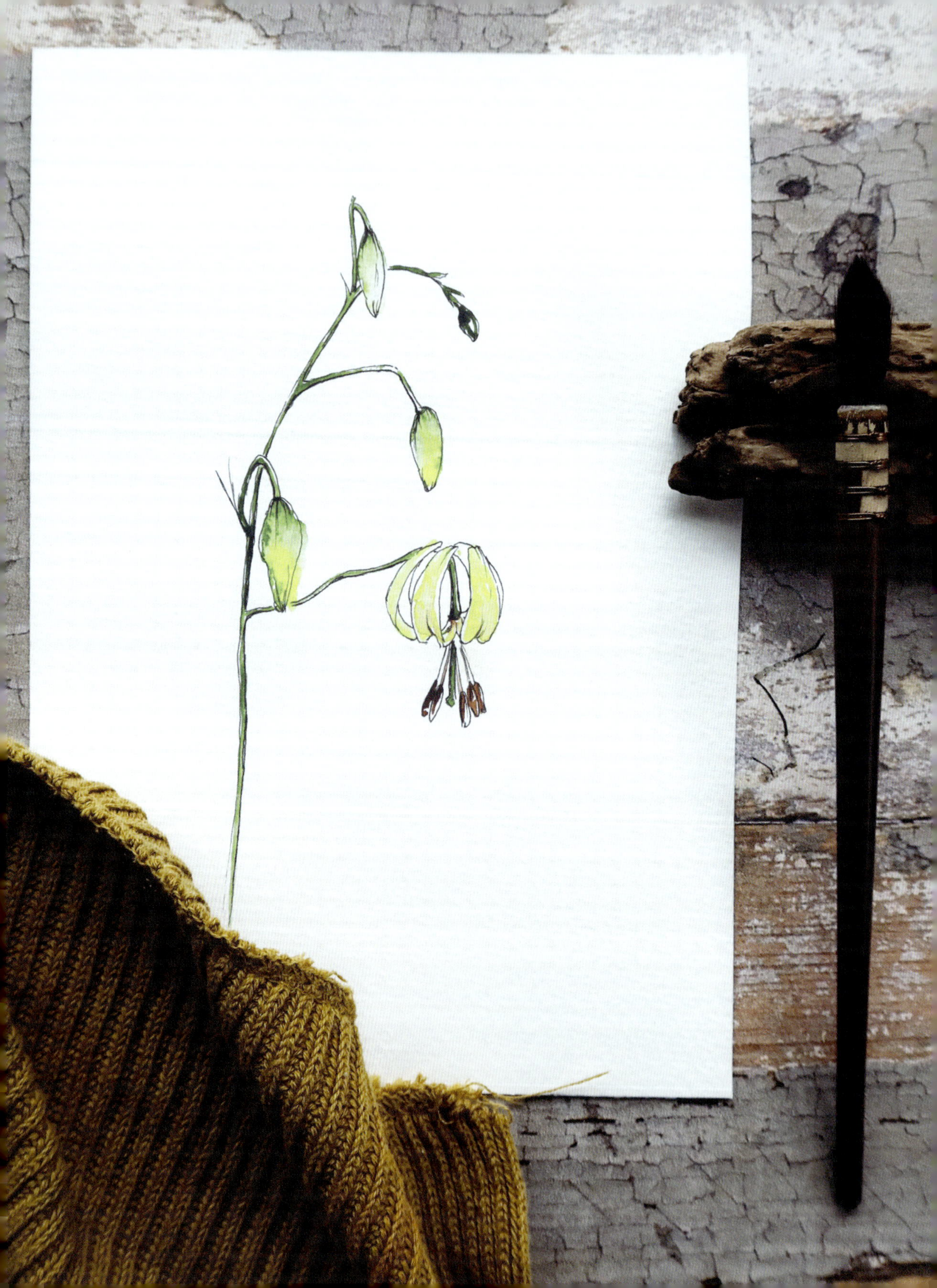

dogtooth violet
a flower of healing and early spring

The dogtooth violet that blooms in the early spring is a flower that reminds us of the constant circle of life. It has a deep meaning of hope, resilience and healing, which is what we all crave after a long winter. The dogtooth violet actually comes in different colors other than violet. So to shake it up, I thought we should try a yellow flower this time.

Materials

Paper: Canson Montval 300gsm (140lb) cold press

Pencil and eraser

Fineliner sizes: 005 and 01

Watercolor brush size: 4

Water and cloth

Colors

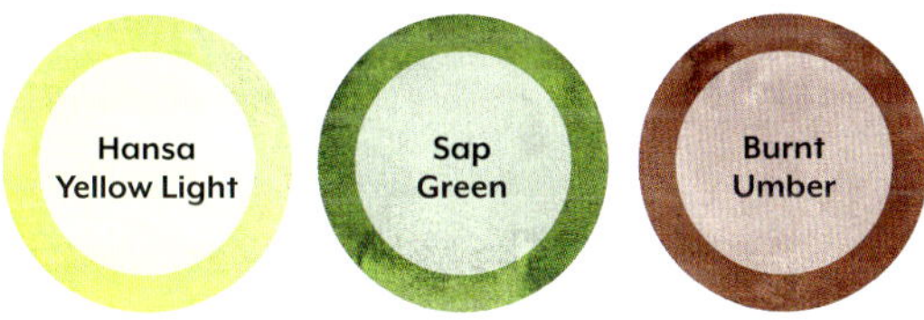

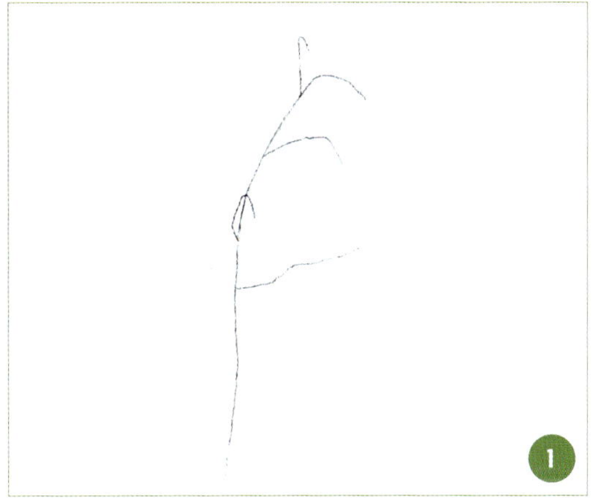

Step 1: Start by drawing a guide for a stem that bends to the right. Add four extra flower stems. Two of them are on the right side of the stem pointing to the right and the other two are on the left side pointing up and bending down to the right.

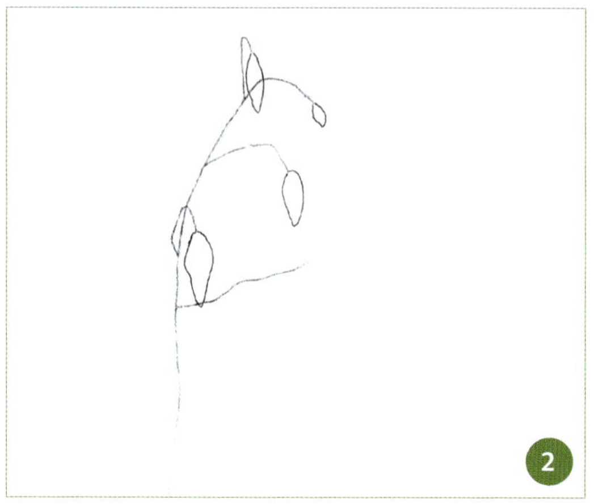

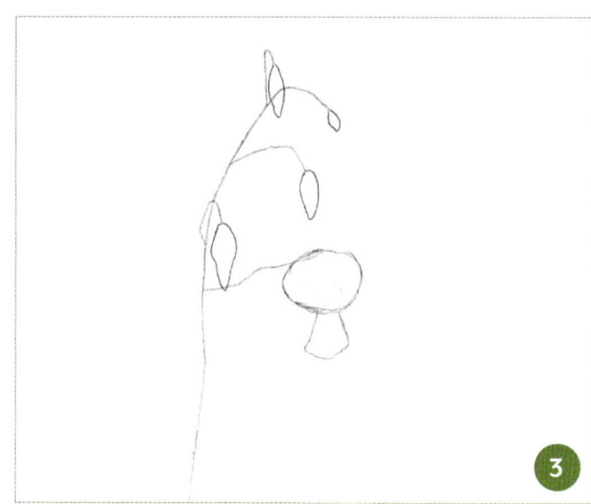

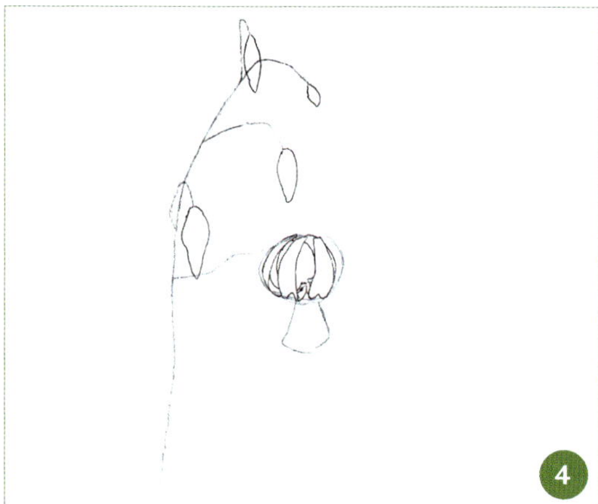

Step 2: Draw teardrop-shaped buds on the four top stems with the 005 fineliner. The top bud here is the youngest baby bud, so make sure that it is smaller than the rest.

Step 3: On the lowest stem, draw an extra guide for the flower with the pencil. This guide is a fat oval with a thimble shape below.

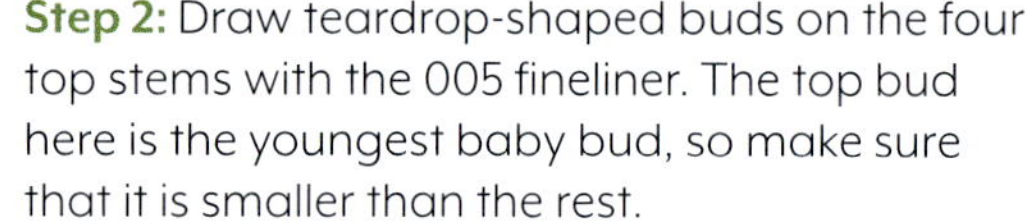

Step 4: Draw the petals on the flower with the 005 fineliner. The flower is facing down but the petals quickly bend backward and up . . . like a very hard yoga pose. Get tips on drawing bent petals on page 20 and then make these petals bend even more.

Step 5: Use the 005 fineliner and draw stamens with oval seeds below the flower petals.

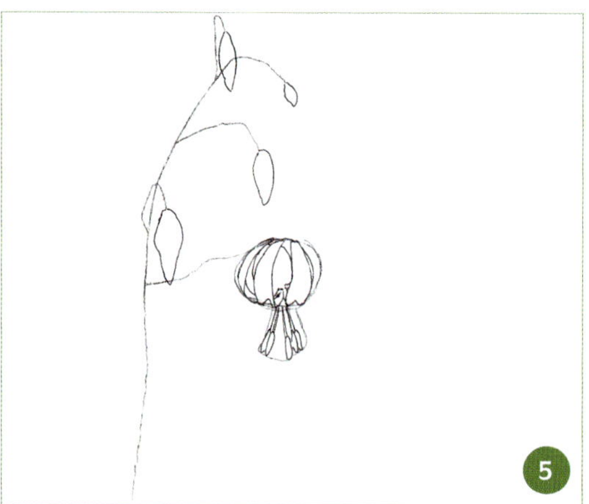

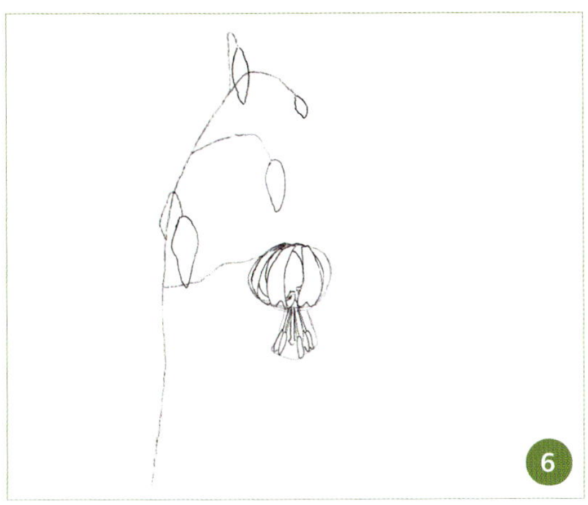

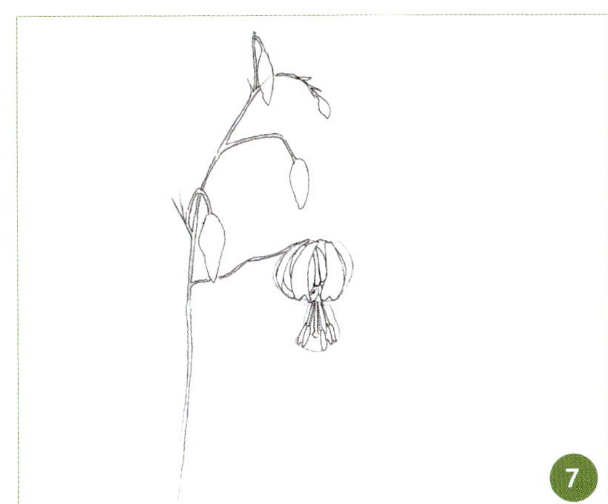

Step 6: To finish the flower, draw the long stigma inside the bloom with the 005 fineliner. Make sure it's hiding a bit behind the seeds.

Step 7: Draw the stem from inside the yoga petals all the way to the main stem. Still using the 005 fineliner, draw the rest of the stems. Give the stem a few thin leaves where it bends, close to the small bud at the top.

Step 8: Draw direction lines on the buds, showing the smooth texture of a young bud with long lines.

Step 9: Then return to the beautiful yoga flower. Show the bend with a shaping line in the middle of the petal bend. When you are happy with your sketch, erase the pencil lines.

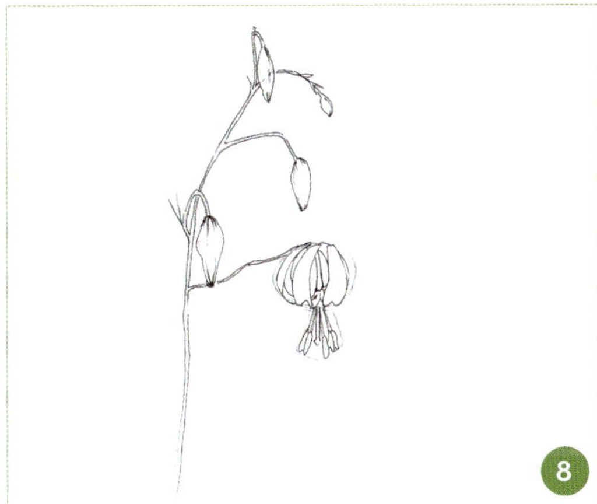

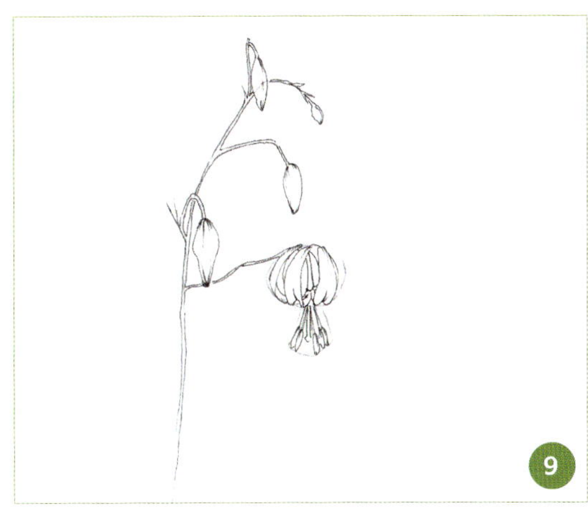

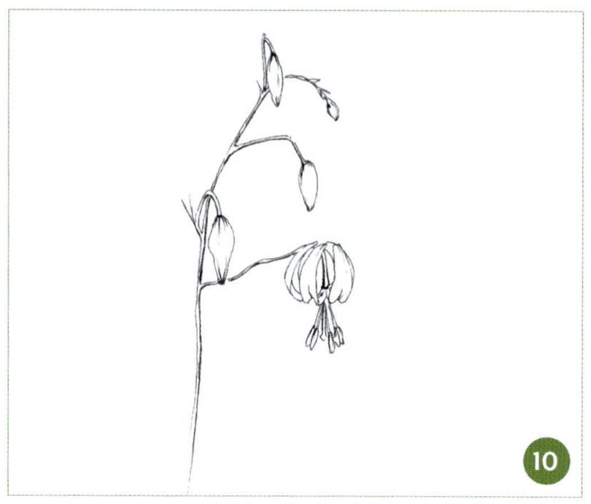

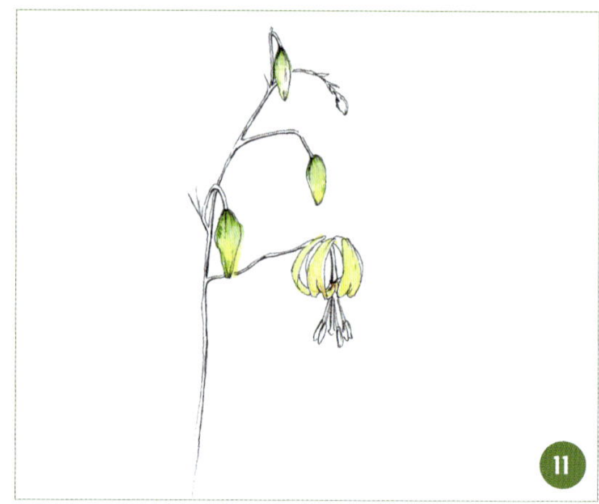

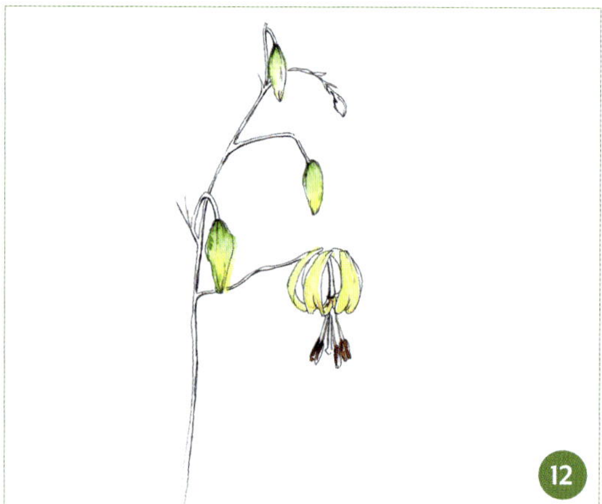

Step 10: Add a bit of shadow. Take your 01 fine-liner and draw a line on the right inside of the stems.

Step 11: Add some color. Get your size 4 brush and add clean water to the buds. Paint the tip of the buds with hansa yellow light and the top with sap green. Paint the flower petals with hansa yellow light as well. Drip in a bit of burnt umber in the petals. This will create a warmer look than the buds, which are in the cooler color.

Step 12: Paint the seeds in the flower head with the burnt umber. Make sure to leave white space here to avoid them getting too heavy.

Step 13: Finally, once everything is dry, paint the stem and the stigma inside the flower with sap green. Drip in hansa yellow light in a few places to tie the colors together.

You are done and it looks incredible! If you feel inspired, you can go and get out your yoga mat and try to see if you can bend like the flower (or you can skip the exercise and just go to the next flower—it's all up to you).

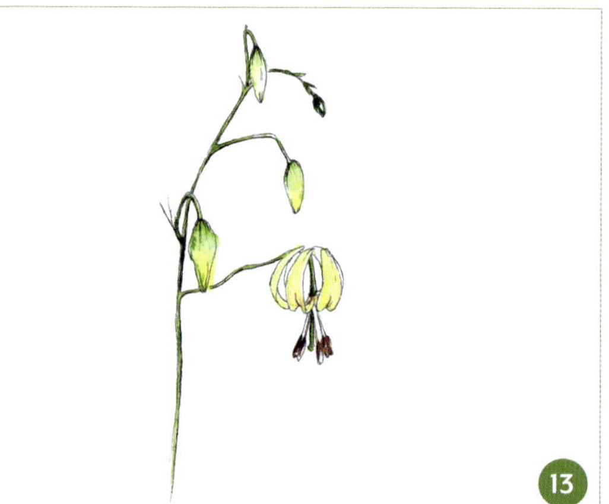

thistle
a flower of power and strength

One flower that is highly underrated is the thistle. It's like that kid in school no one wants to play with. She may look different than the rest, but she is by far the most powerful. She grows and blooms for the entire season. Even though she has thorns to protect herself, she also has the softest heart that, when she grows older, reveals itself as furry cotton wool.

In this tutorial, we explore the difference in texture between the prickly flowers and soft cotton heads.

Materials

Paper: Canson Montval 300gsm (140lb) cold press

Watercolor brush sizes: 4 and 1

Water and cloth

Fineliner size: 005

Palette

Colors

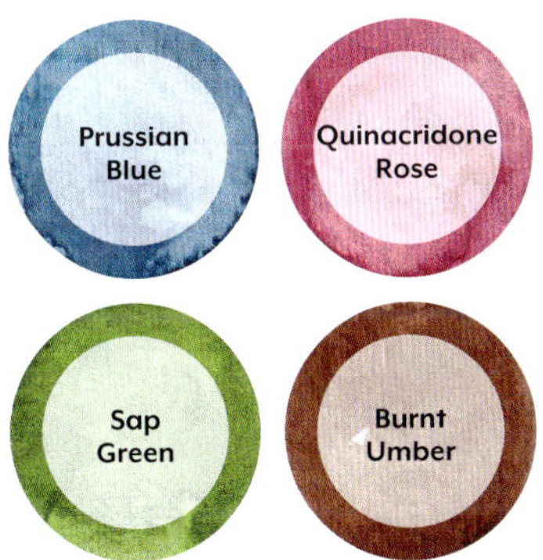

Prussian Blue

Quinacridone Rose

Sap Green

Burnt Umber

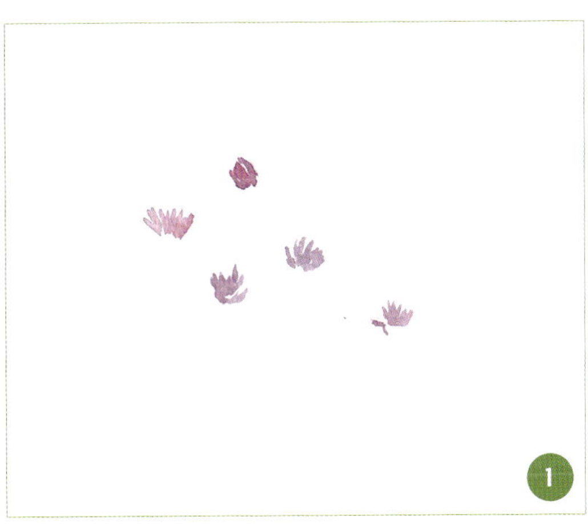

Step 1: Paint five thistle head tops with a size 4 brush and a mix of Prussian blue and quinacridone rose. Let the colors vary when you paint these bristly hairs. Let the thistle heads dry.

Mix

To get the color of the flower heads, mix 50% Prussian blue and 50% quinacridone rose. When you mix it on your palette, don't just mix to one color but keep lots of color variations, so you have lots of shades to choose from. Some will be more blue and some more pink.

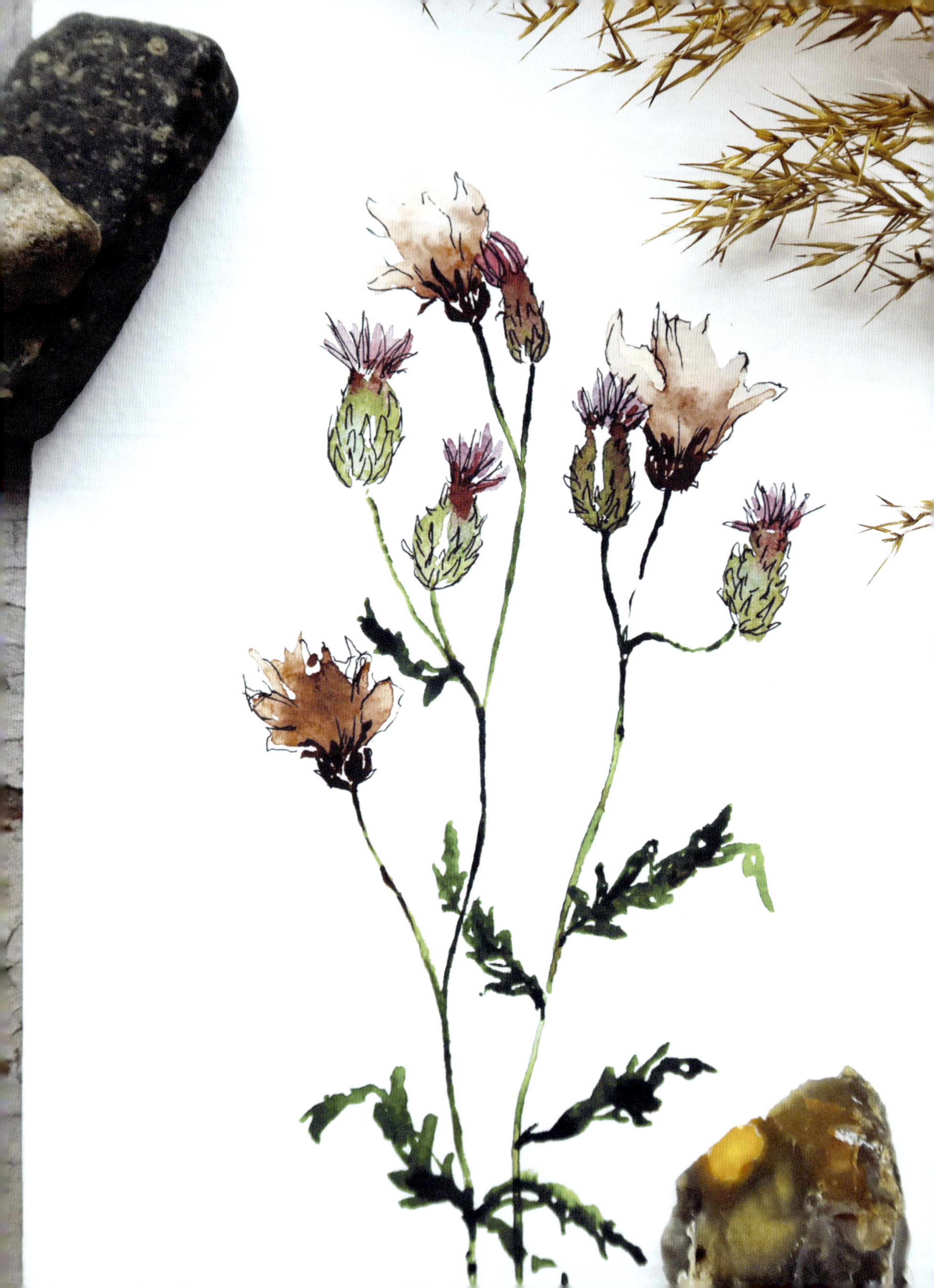

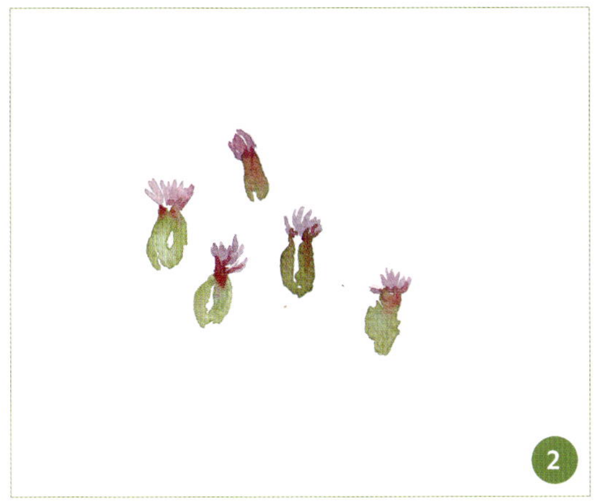

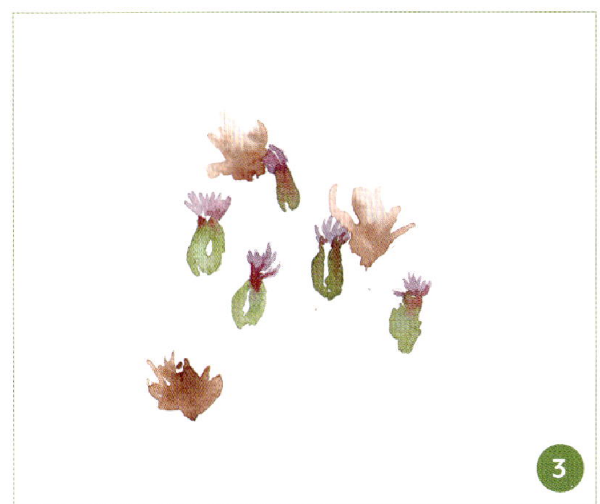

Step 2: Put a bit of sap green into the blue/rose mix and paint the bottoms of the flower heads. Keep white space in the shapes to make them light. Drip in quinacridone rose at the top where the shapes meet the hairs. Use the tip of the brush to drag the wet paint on to the dry tops of the flowers as a second layer.

Step 3: Paint the old soft cotton wet-on-wet. Start by wetting three shapes with clean water and drip in burnt umber at the bottom of the wet patches. Let it spread and then drip in a very small amount of quinacridone rose to make the colors look cohesive.

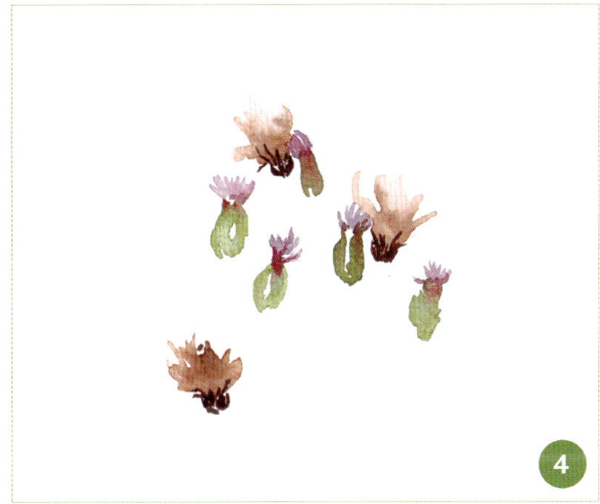

Step 4: When the soft patches have dried, paint the bottom parts of the wilted blooms with burnt umber. This shape should look a bit like a hand with fingers, holding and protecting the wilted flower.

Step 5: Paint two main stems branching out to meet the flower parts using a small size 1 brush and sap green. Drip in burnt umber close to the wilted heads and a bit of quinacridone rose in the greens.

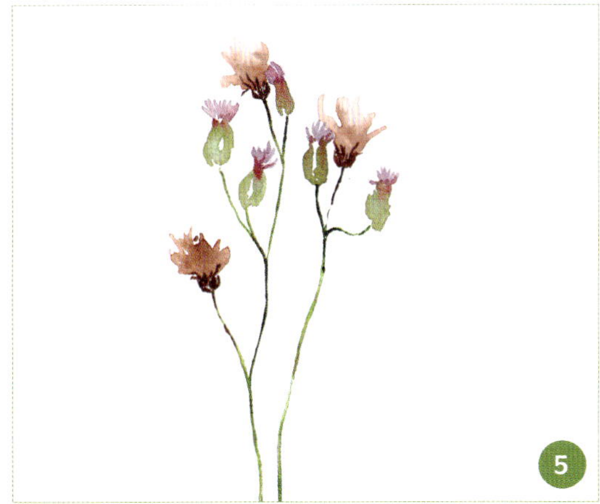

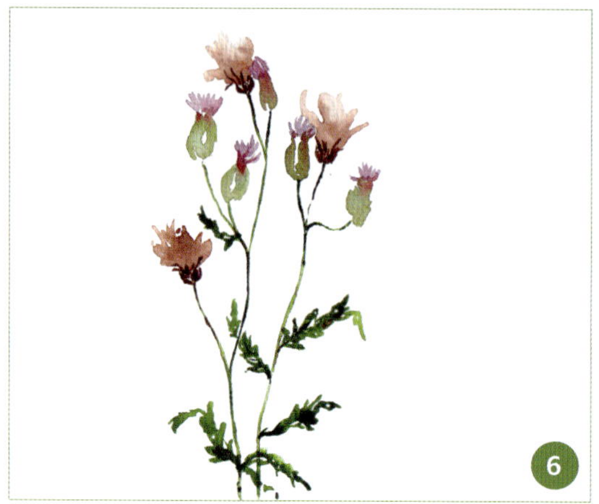

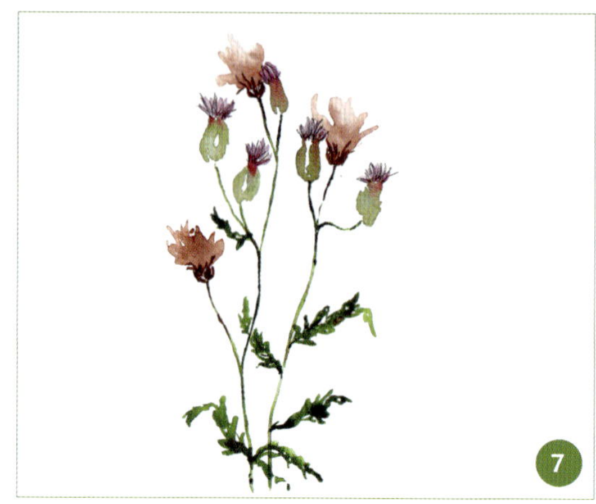

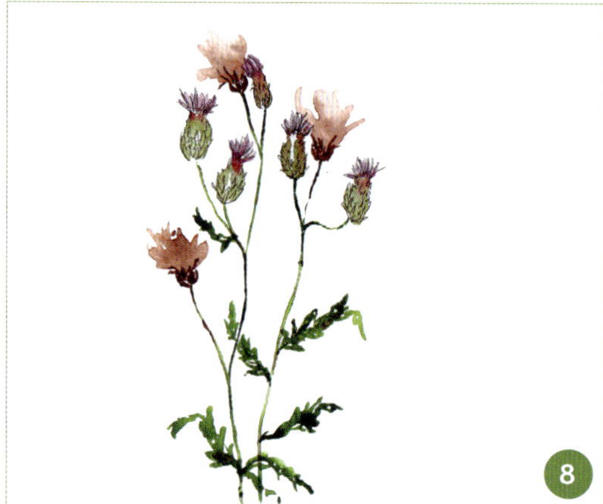

Step 6: Paint the pointy leaves in sap green using your size 4 brush. Keep these leaves super loose and with plenty of white space.

Step 7: Draw the bristly hairs on top of the thistle flowers with a 005 fineliner.

Step 8: The thistle has armor to protect itself that looks a lot like scales on a pinecone. Draw this with the 005 fineliner. Start at the bottom and work your way up, having the shapes hide behind each other.

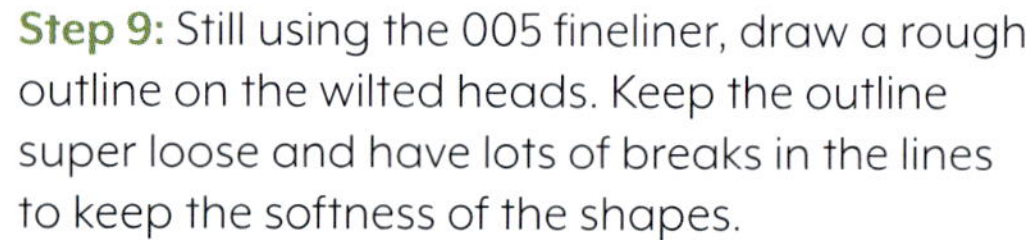

Step 9: Still using the 005 fineliner, draw a rough outline on the wilted heads. Keep the outline super loose and have lots of breaks in the lines to keep the softness of the shapes.

Next time you meet a thistle with your sketchbook, give it some attention. Observe its harsh outside and remember its soft inside. Sometimes we just need to get to know each other to understand. And yes, that goes for people as well as flowers.

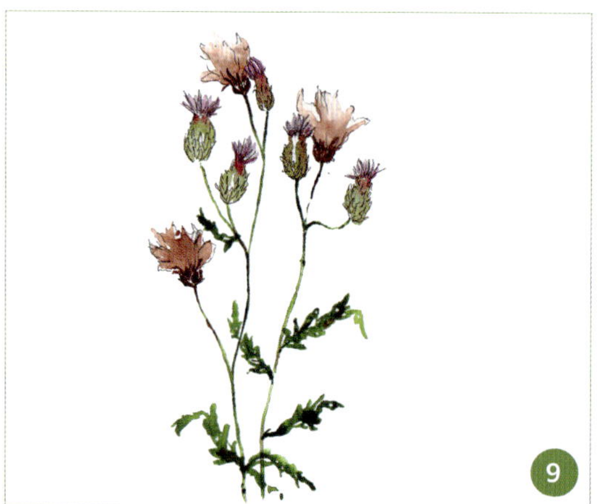

lupin
a flower of imagination

Did you know that *lupin* is Latin for wolf? Pretty cool and to be honest I went down a rabbit hole to research the lupin before writing this. But spoiler alert: This flower does not go out hunting at night, turn into a howling were-flower or raise Mowgli as its own. But in ancient times they thought that lupins drained the soil, like a pack of wolves. Compared to all of that, the lupin is a bit boring to be honest. But it's the flower of imagination. So why not just let our imagination run free? Imagine a beautiful pack of pink and violet lupins howling to the moon.

The lupin is extra special because its wilted look is just as stunning as the full bloom, and maybe even more extravagant.
We are going to explore that in this tutorial.

Materials

Paper: Canson Montval 300gsm (140lb) cold press
Pencil and eraser
Fineliner sizes: 01 and 005
Watercolor brush size: 4
Water and cloth

Colors

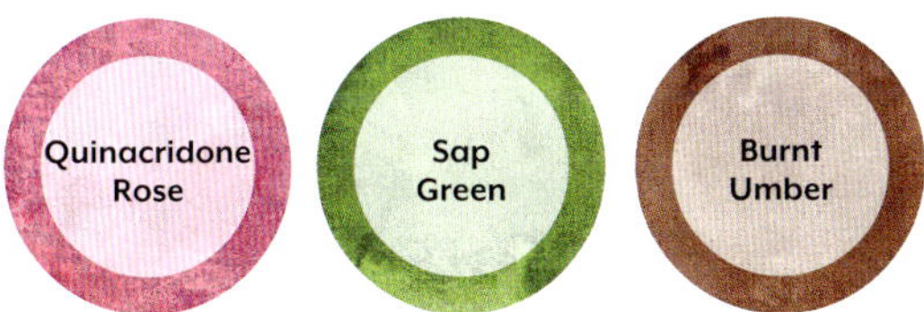

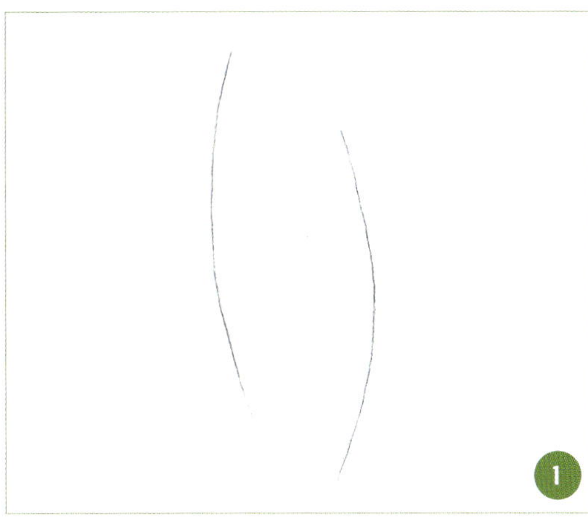

Step 1: Use your pencil to draw two lines, curving like they are greeting each other with a bow.

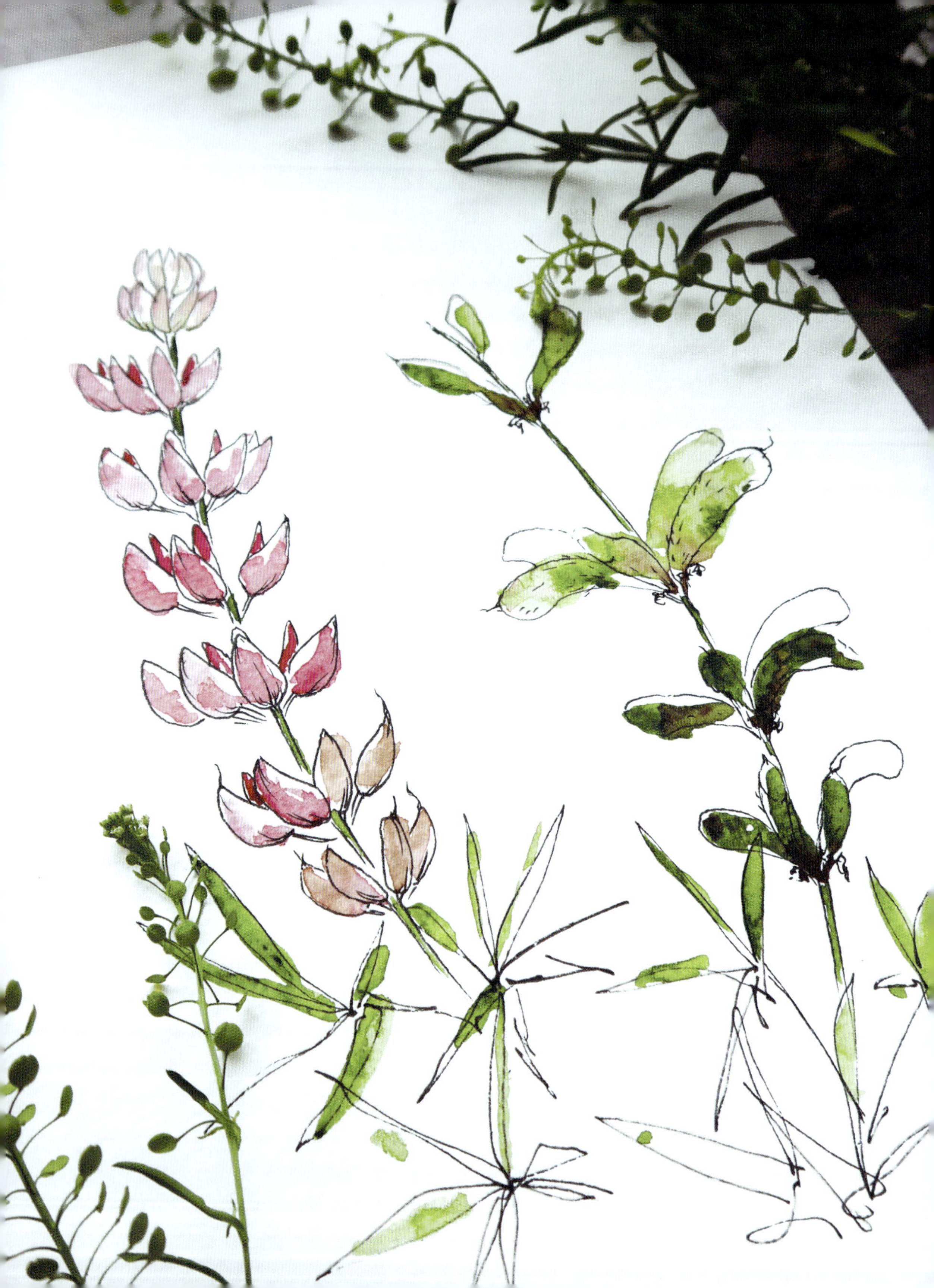

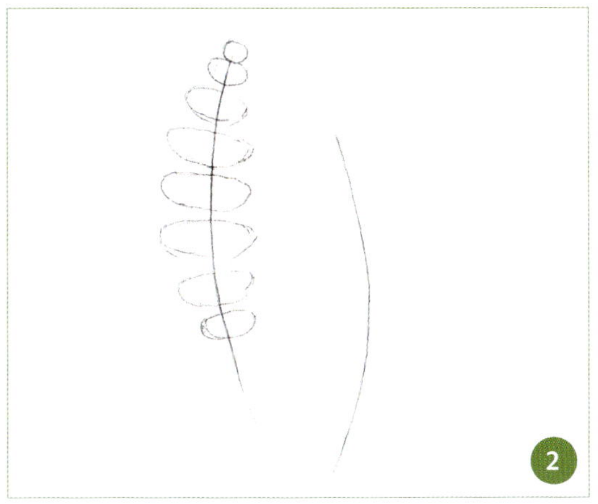

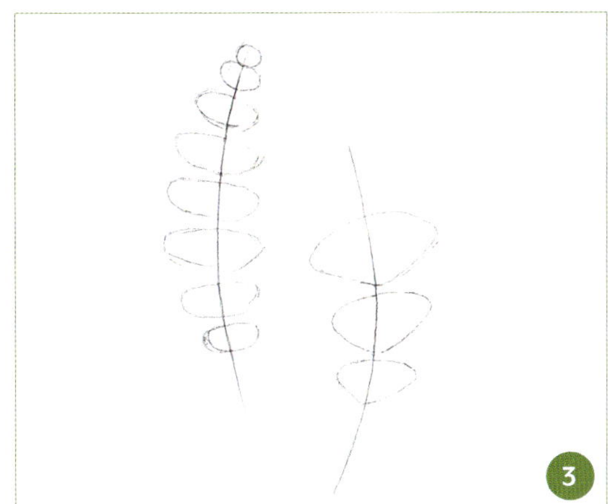

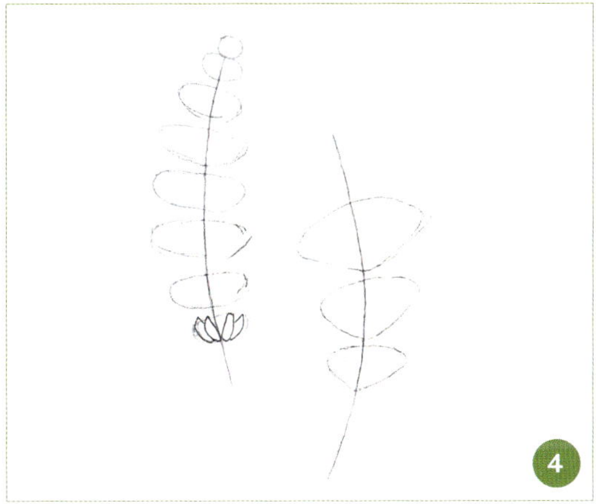

Step 2: Starting with the left line, draw fat ovals all the way up the stem. Let the top and bottom shapes be smaller, with the top one shaped almost like a circle with no space between it and the one below.

Step 3: Draw three ovals on the right line, with tips pointing down like upside-down umbrellas.

Step 4: Take your 01 fineliner and draw four small bean shapes at the bottom of the left lupin.

Step 5: Draw the middle part of the flower with the same fineliner. This part is made of clusters of shapes that look a bit like an angry cat eye, but don't let them scare you. Some are seen from the side and some from the front. Keep each oval different and let some of the shapes overlap.

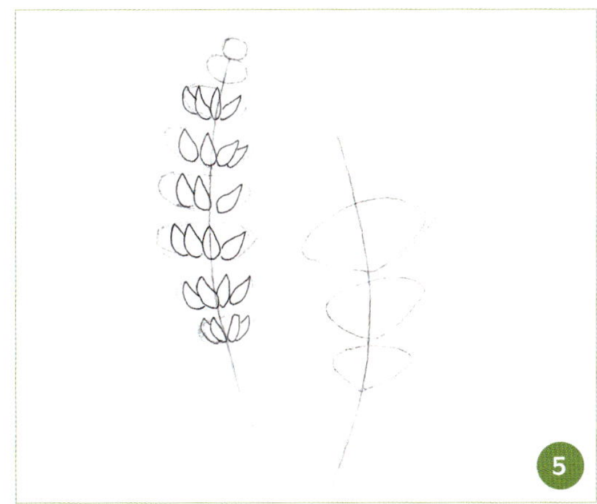

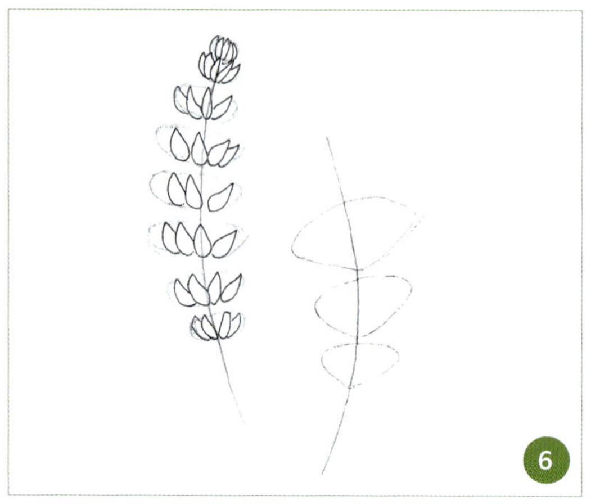

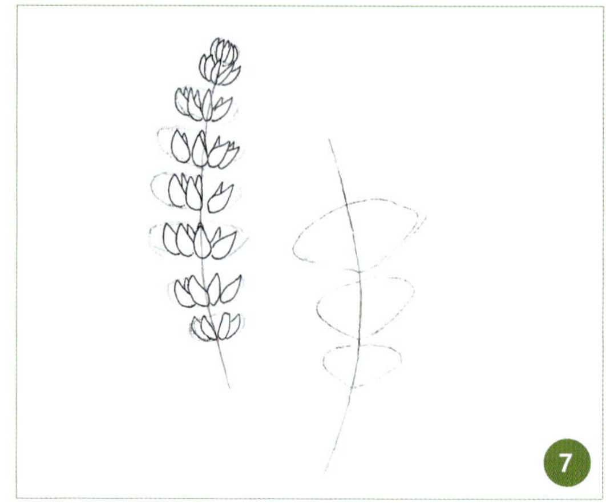

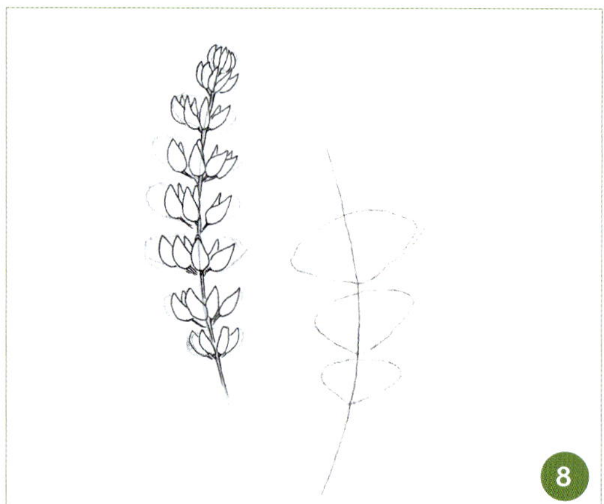

Step 6: Add the top blossoms, still using the 01 fineliner. They almost look like banana clusters. Let the bottom oval overlap the top a bit for some nice depth.

Step 7: With the 005 fineliner, draw a small triangle inside the biggest petals. This is the inside of the flowers. You can only see them on the flowers in full bloom, so there is no need to put them on the top or bottom ovals.

Step 8: Draw the stem with the 01 fineliner and draw small stems from the single blooms to the main stem with the 005 fineliner.

Step 9: Now we will shift to the wilted lupin to the right, and this one has some super quirky shapes. Draw oval, uneven shapes close to the stem. These are the seedpods seen from the front. Let them point upward and have a shape like a crazy bean.

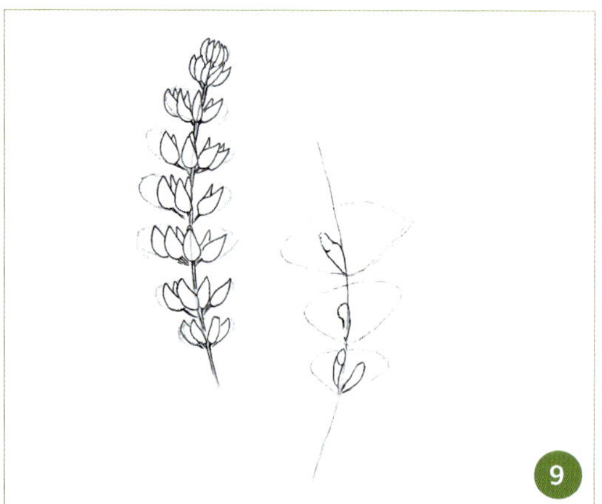

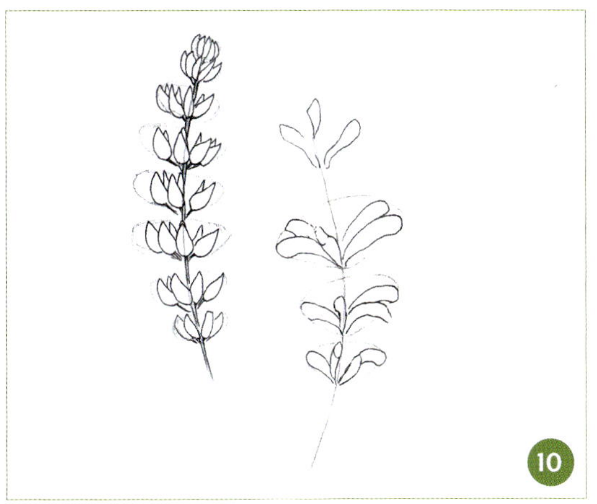

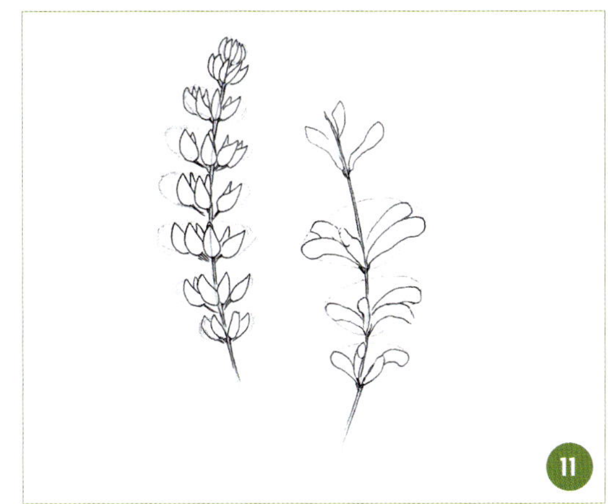

Step 10: Draw the big seedpods, shaped like beans. Let each ring of seedpods meet in the same place on the stem. You can always sketch further than your pencil guides as you go along. I decided to add three smaller beans at the top.

Step 11: Draw the stem like before with the 01 fineliner and then use the 005 fineliner to create small stems from the single beans to the main stem.

Step 12: Go crazy with your 01 fineliner and draw some quick leaves, long and shaped like stars. To make them, just move your hand as quickly as you dare. Finally, erase the pencil.

Step 13: Add details to the left lupin with the 005 fineliner, shaping lines and small hairs at the tips of the bottom blooms.

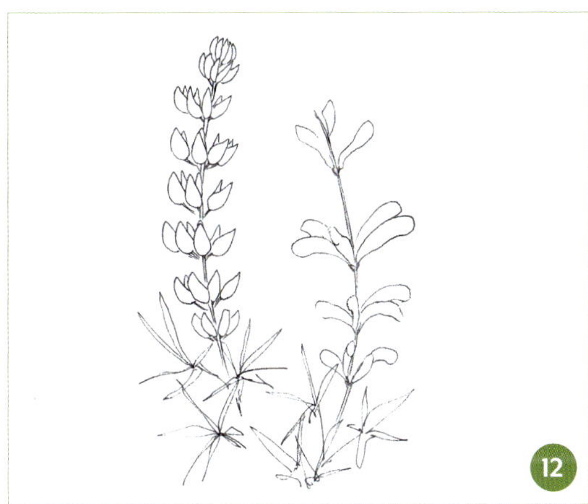

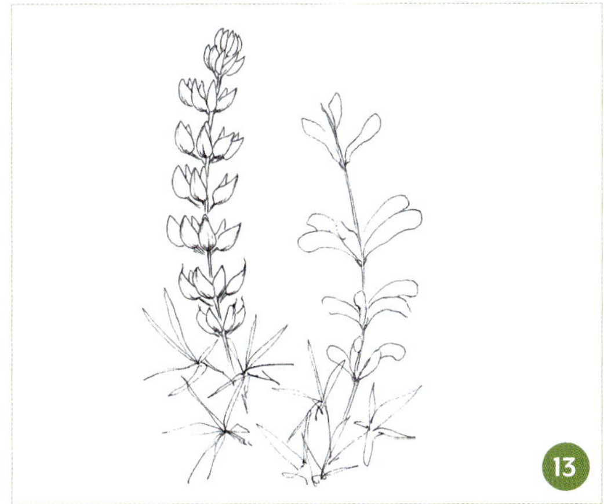

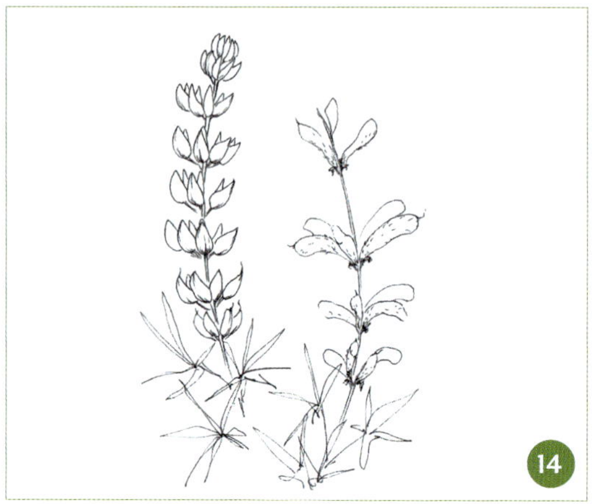

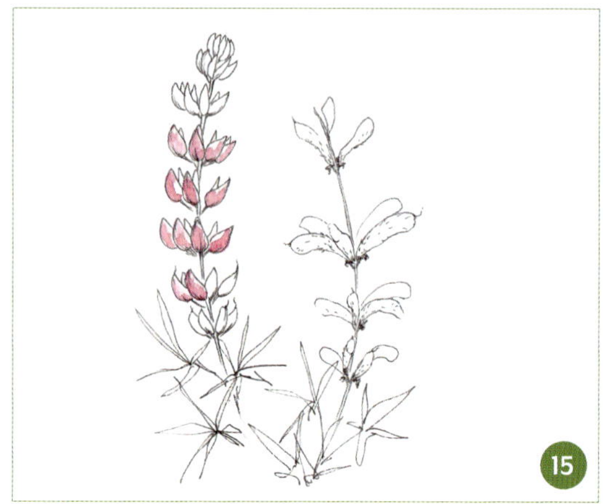

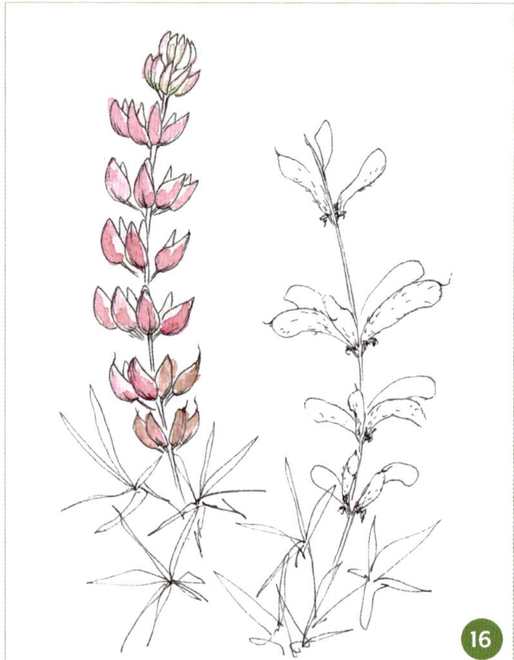

Step 14: Use the same fineliner to add details to the right lupin. Give the beans hair and a small stray hair at the tip of each bean, almost as if it had a tiny mustache. Finally, draw a small doodle where the beans meet the stems. This is what is left of the wilted bloom after losing its petals.

Step 15: Paint the middle section of the blooms on the left lupin with a watery quinacridone rose and a size 4 brush.

Step 16: Paint the top blooms with the quinacridone rose, but drip in a bit of sap green to show that they are younger blooms. On the bottom blooms, do the same but with burnt umber to reveal their age. Let it dry.

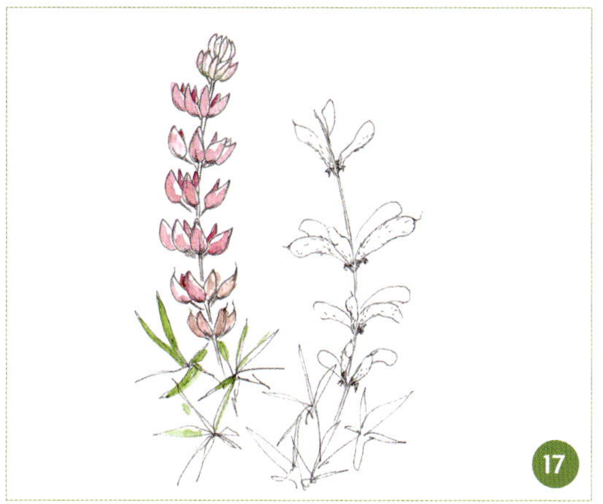

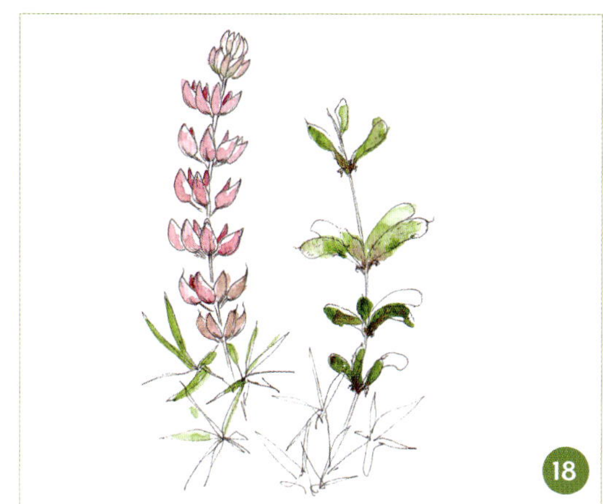

Step 17: Paint the triangular shapes in the center of the flowers with a bright quinacridone rose and the leaves with sap green.

Step 18: Paint the beans of the lupin on the right with sap green. While they are still wet, drip in a bit of burnt umber where the beans meet the stem. You can also drip in a bit of quinacridone rose in a few places.

Step 19: Finally, paint the leaves on the right lupin as well as the stems on both.

And you have now created two blooms in one tutorial! Yay you! You deserve to take a walk, stretch your legs and just imagine what would happen if lupins were actually wolves.

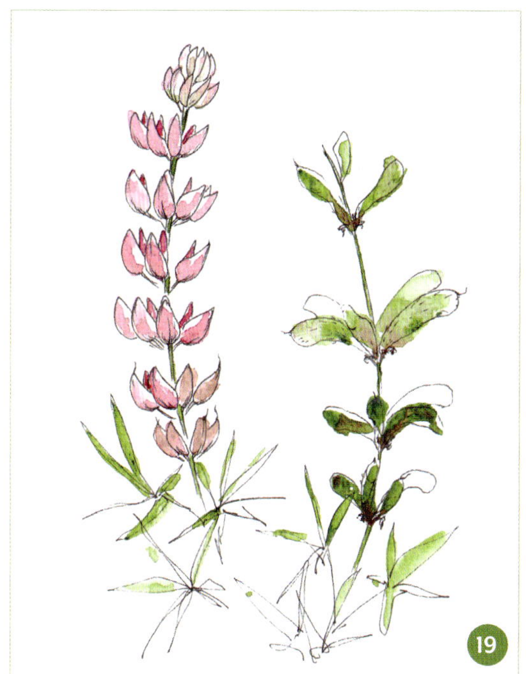

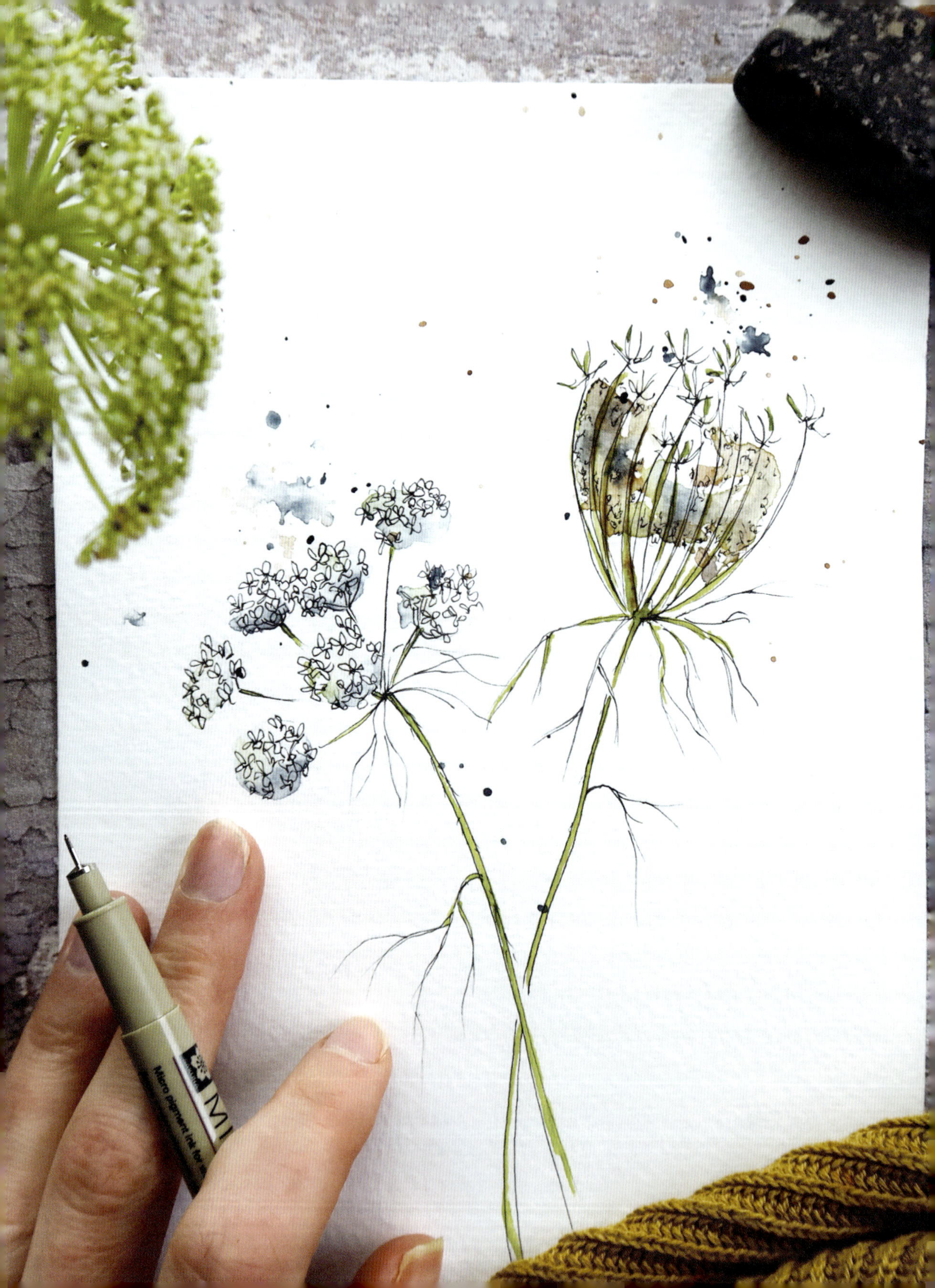

queen anne's lace
a flower of sanctuary and safety

Did you know that Queen Anne's lace is also called a bird's nest flower? And the reason for that is when the flower wilts, it creates a nest-like shape that reminds you of a bird's warm, safe home. That is super poetic in my mind. And I actually feel like planting even more of these delicate wildflowers around my home to spread some of that homey feeling. In this tutorial, we are of course doing the bird nest-shaped, wilted bloom as well as one in full bloom.

Materials

Paper: Canson Montval 300gsm (140lb) cold press
Pencil and eraser
Fineliner sizes: 005 and 01
Watercolor brush size: 4
Water and cloth

Colors

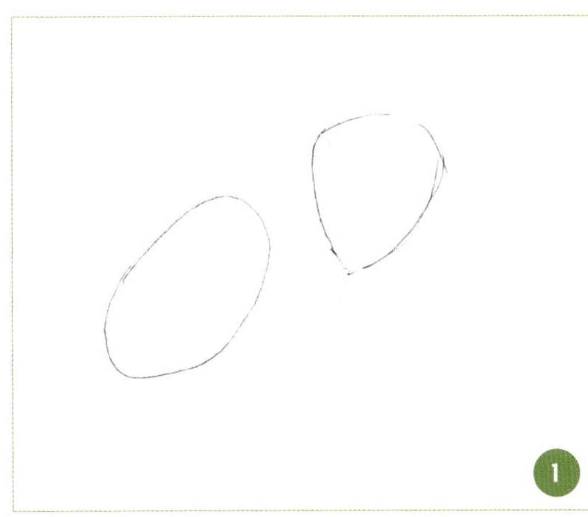

Step 1: Draw two guides in pencil. One guide is an oval on the left that will become the full bloom. The other has the shape of an egg, but with a point at the bottom that will turn into a wilted flower.

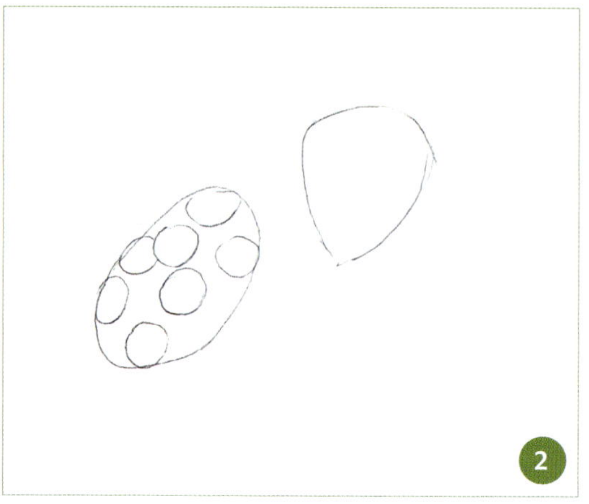

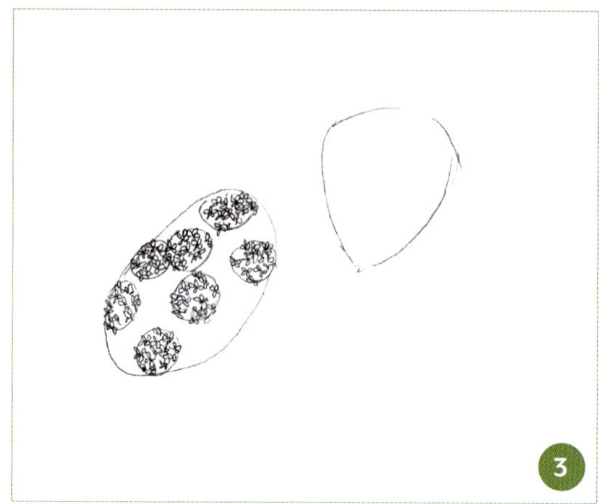

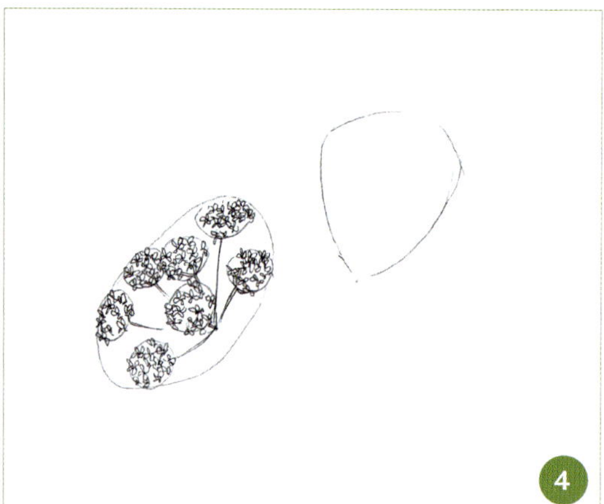

Step 2: Draw small circles inside the oval still using pencil.

Step 3: Fill the small circles with tiny, loose and doodly four-petaled blooms using the 005 fineliner. These are the small flower clusters in the Queen Anne's lace.

Step 4: Decide on a point in the middle of the oval and grab your 01 fineliner. Now draw small stems to each of the smaller clusters from a point you choose. A few of the clusters can get additional smaller stems to hold the blooms.

Step 5: For the wilted Queen Anne's lace, draw a bunch of long, flat C-shaped lines using the 01 fineliner . . . some short and some long. On the left side of the flower, the lines bend to the right, and on the right side, they bend left. This will emphasize the shape.

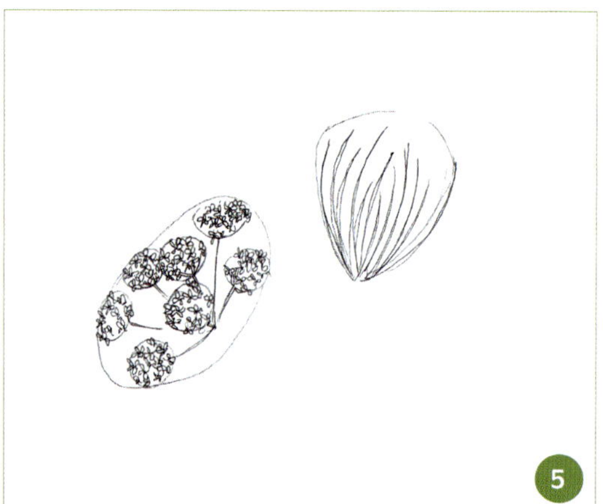

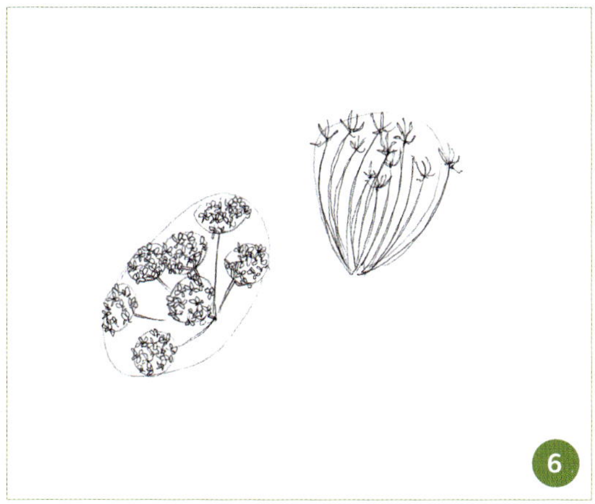

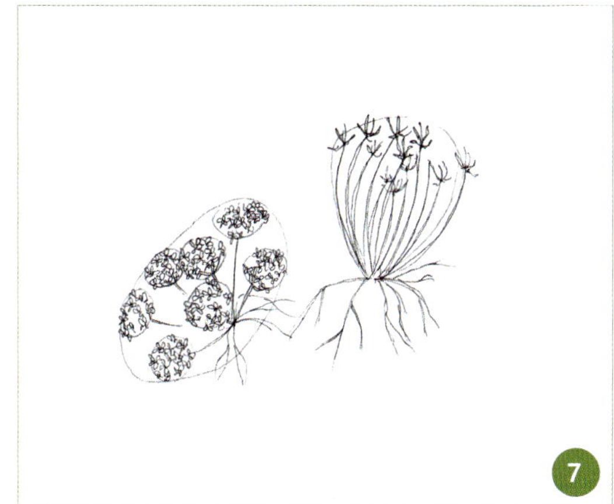

Step 6: Draw small, loose stars from the top of each of the C-shaped lines with a 005 fineliner.

Step 7: Draw the leaves just below the two blooms with the same fineliner. They are long and thin with a few extra lines on them. I always think they look a bit like skeleton hands, but that might just be my imagination.

Step 8: Draw the stems with your 01 fineliner. Let them cross each other for some depth and movement.

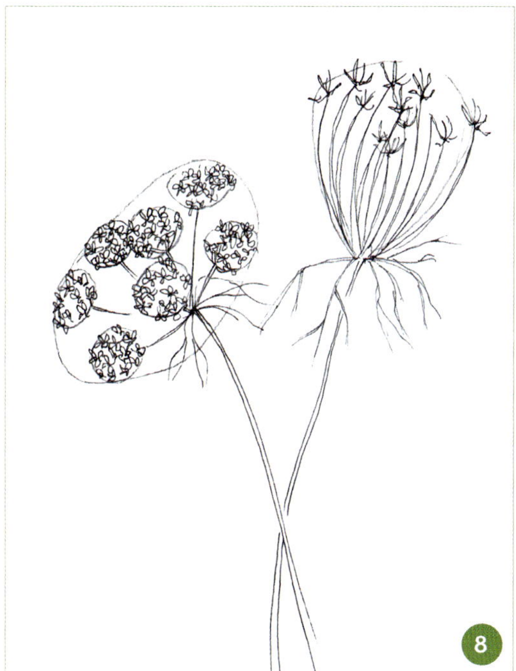

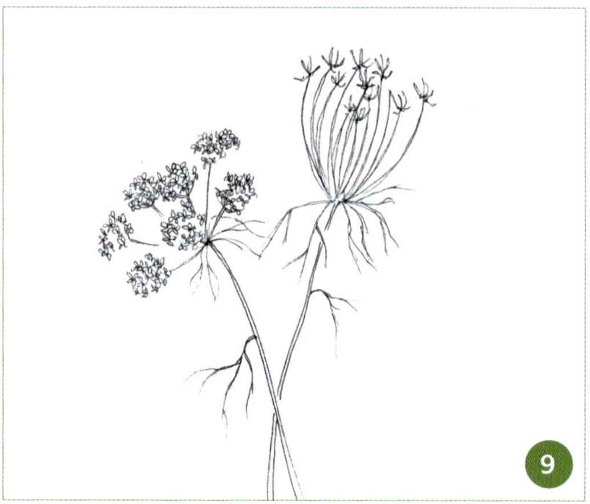

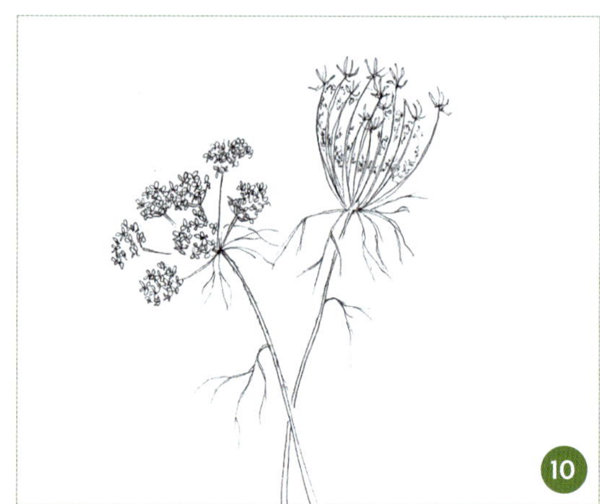

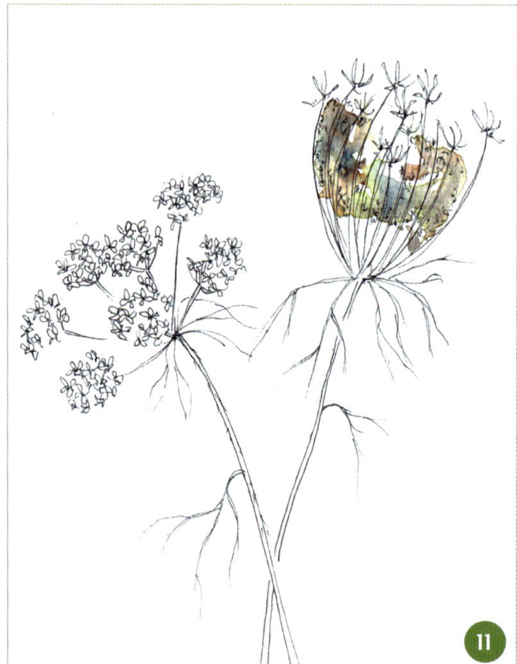

Step 9: Grab your 005 fineliner again and draw a few leaves on the stems as well in the same way you did before. Ah, beautiful! Now you can erase the pencil lines.

Step 10: With your 005 fineliner, add the final details. A few doodles inside the wilted flower will create some texture. Only add texture to the top two-thirds of the flower. The bottom part is left free. Finally, draw a few hairs on the stems.

Step 11: Wet the area inside the wilted bloom, and with your size 4 brush, drip green gold, burnt umber and Payne's gray into the water. Don't force the mix . . . just let it mingle and spread by itself. Leave some white space so it doesn't feel too heavy.

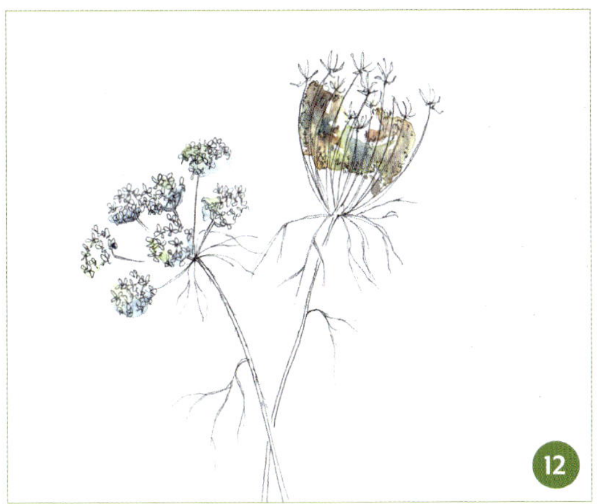

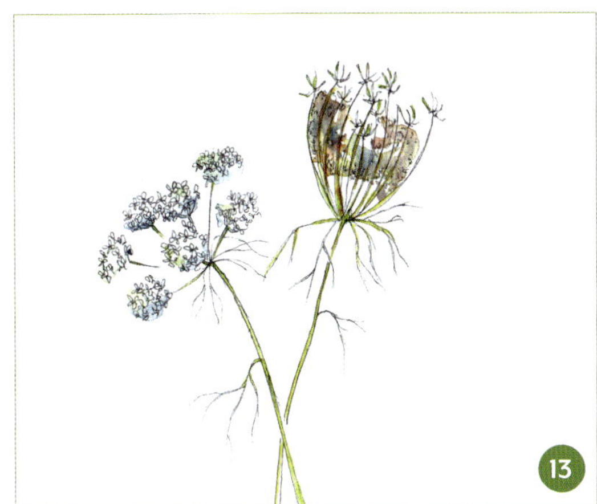

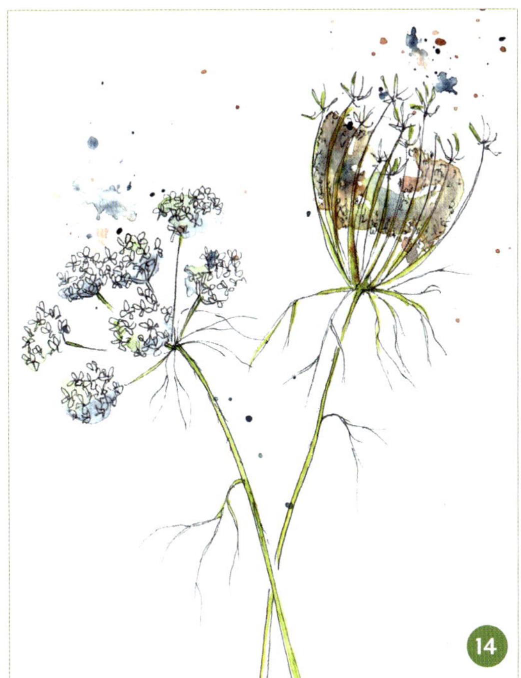

Step 12: Wet all the small clusters in the full bloom and then drip in a very watery Payne's gray at the bottom of the clusters. After that, drip in a bit of green gold at the top and let it dry.

Step 13: Finally, add a bit of color to the stem using the same size 4 brush. On the full bloom, paint the entire stem with green gold. Drip in a bit of Payne's gray just below the flower head to add shadow beneath the clusters. Paint the stem of the wilted bird's nest with green gold as well, but drip in a bit of burnt umber.

Step 14: Finish it off with a few artsy splatters of burnt umber and Payne's gray. Load your brush with each color separately and gently tap on the handle with your finger or another brush to send the color flying! The closer you are to your paper (and the more paint on your brush), the larger the droplets; the further away, the smaller the droplets.

You are done! There's so much beauty in this painting, and you did that! I just know the birdies outside are cheering you on Cinderella style.

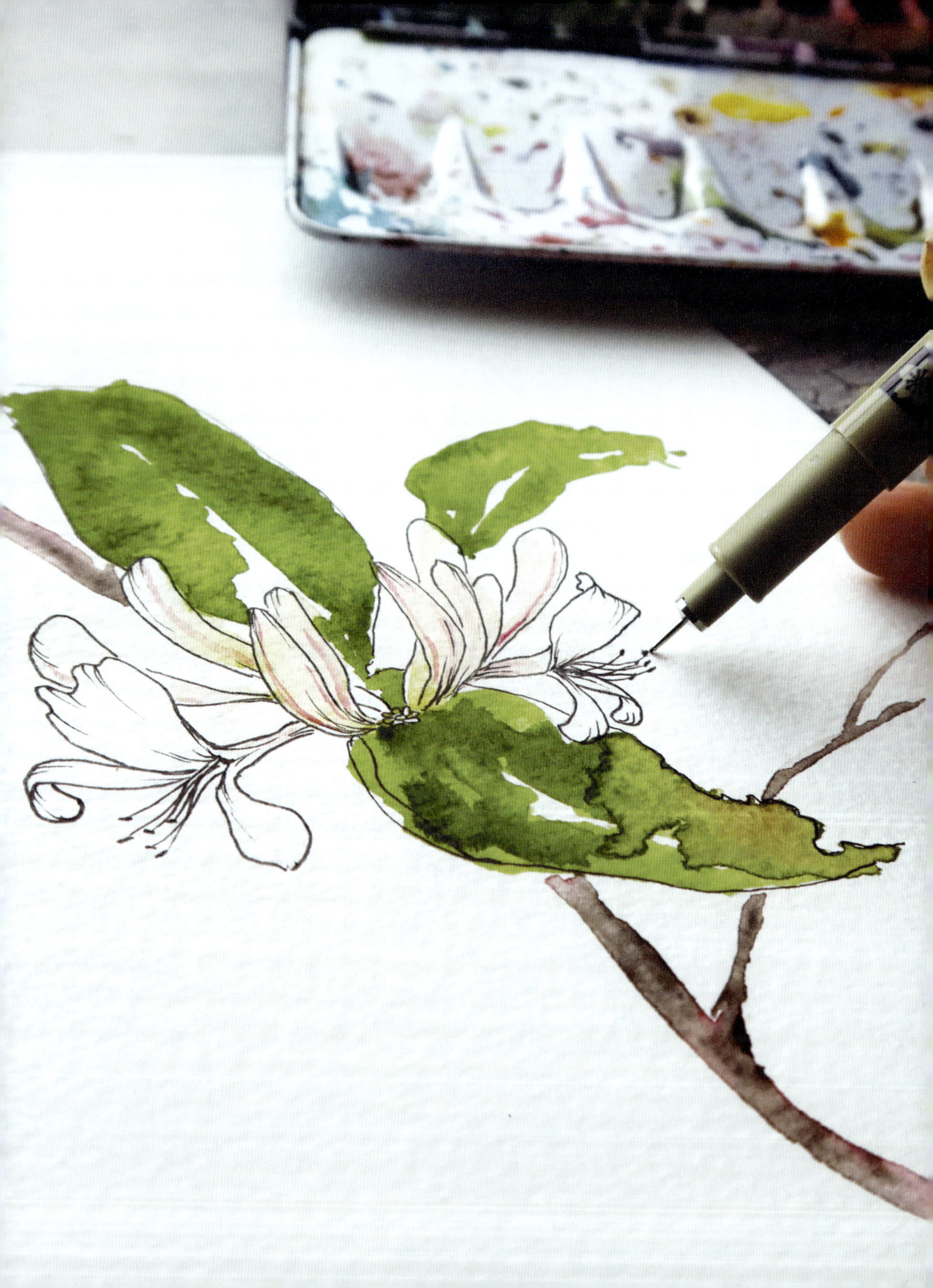

honeysuckle
a flower of first love
and old flames

This is such a romantic flower. Like, blockbuster romantic. In Greek mythology, it was said that two lovers, Daphnis and Chloe, could only be together when the honeysuckle bloomed . . . which was not a long period of time. So, they turned to the goddess of love, Aphrodite, for help. She expanded the time of the growth for the honeysuckle, which may be why it blooms all season long. In this tutorial, we are going to sketch this romantic flower while sending a loving thought to Daphnis and Chloe. Maybe by immortalizing it on paper, we can help them be together all year long.

Materials

Paper: Canson Montval 300gsm (140lb) cold press

Pencil and eraser

Fineliner sizes: 01 and 005

Watercolor brush sizes: 8, 4 and 1

Water and cloth

Colors

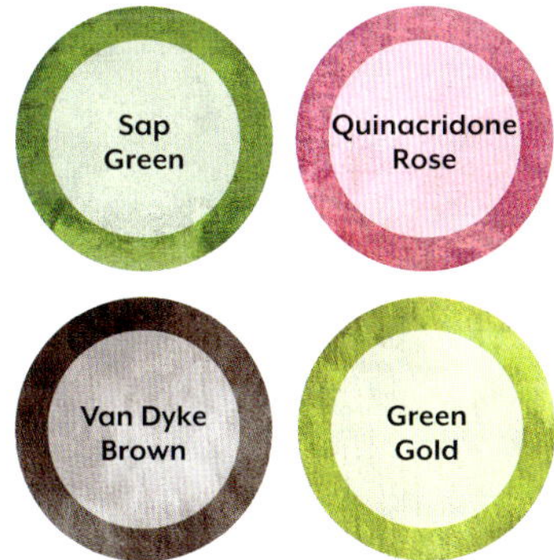

Mix

For the stem, create a mix of 50% Van Dyke brown and 50% quinacridone rose.

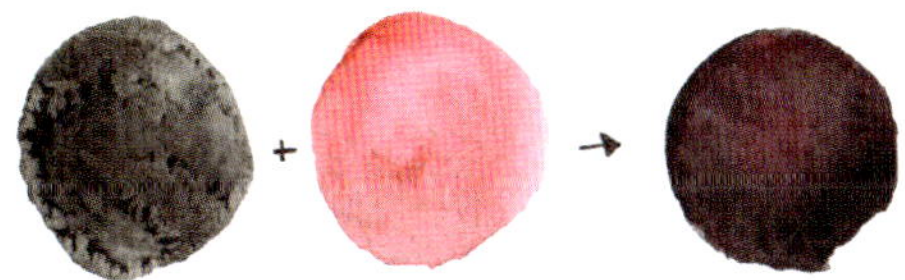

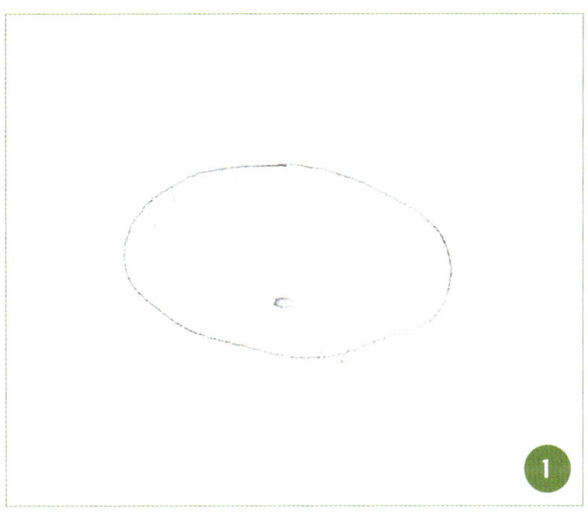

Step 1: The honeysuckle is a bit complex, so we are going to work a bit on our pencil guides first. Start by drawing an oval guide with a small oval on the lower part of the center inside.

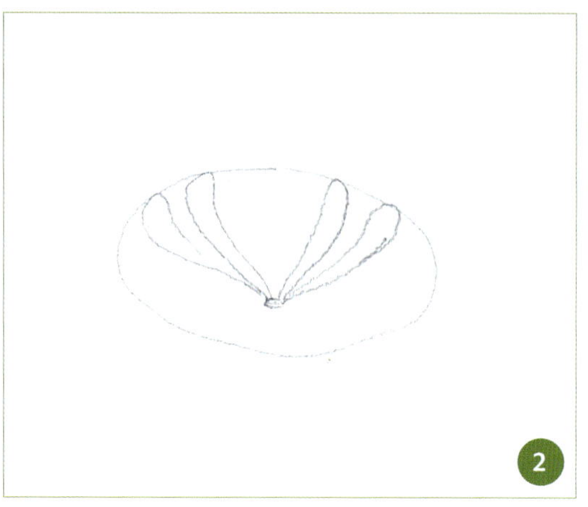

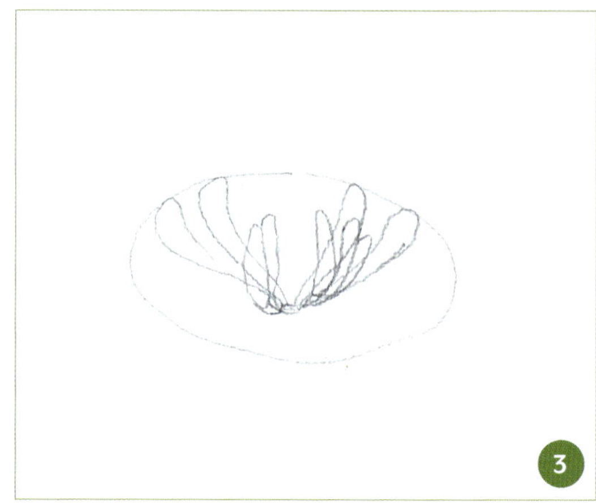

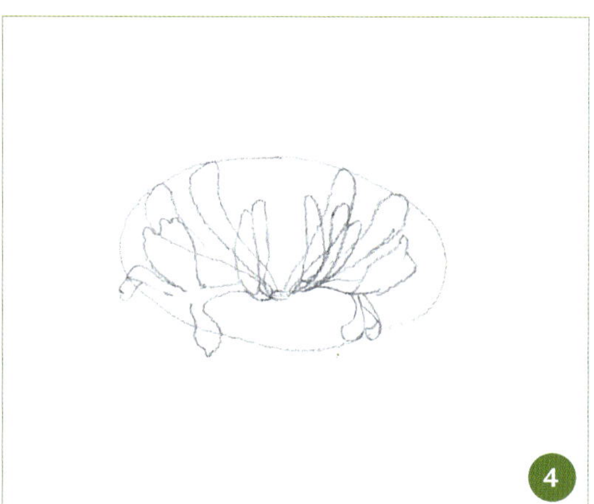

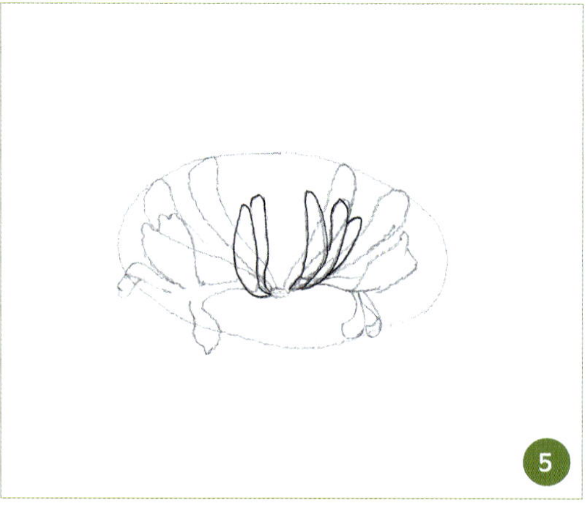

Step 2: Draw the four inner petals of the honey-suckle, called umbels. They look like a long bean that is narrow closest to the center, attaching at the small oval.

Step 3: Draw the front umbels, too. Let them overlap the back ones and be shaped more upward. Don't worry about having pencil lines crossing each other; everything will be erased soon and it's great to guide our fineliner sketch.

Step 4: Draw two flowers seen from the side. They have one big petal on the top and two thin ones at the bottom. The right one has two thin petals curling downward and a big one curling up. The left flower also has a big petal curling up, but its two thin petals at the bottom both curl down and up for some variation in the shape.

Step 5: Now it's time to make good use of the pencil guides. Grab your 01 fineliner and outline the five umbels in the front.

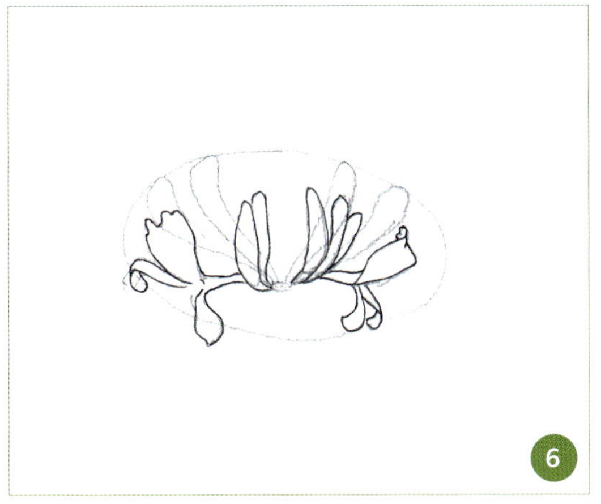

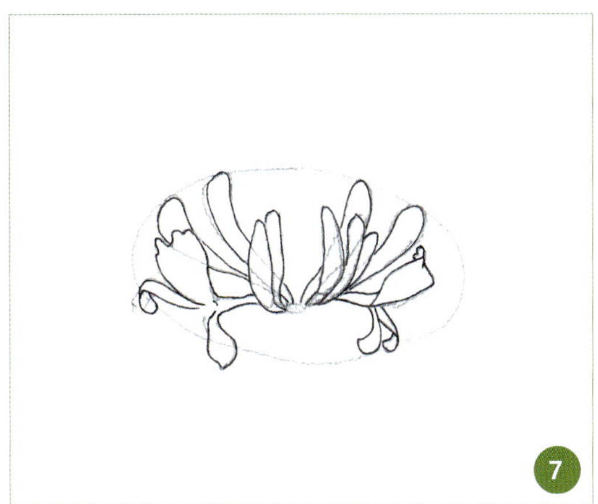

Step 6: Outline the flowers on the sides with the same fineliner. If you are unsure how to get the right curl, you can go to page 20 for some tips.

Step 7: Finally, outline the rest of the flower. Be careful to draw the umbels hiding behind the front ones to get the right depth in your flower.

Step 8: Get out your 005 fineliner and start drawing the stamens in the center of the flowers. When they are done, you can draw a tiny seven petaled flower in the small oval. When you have done that, you can erase the pencil guides and admire your sketch before adding the watercolor.

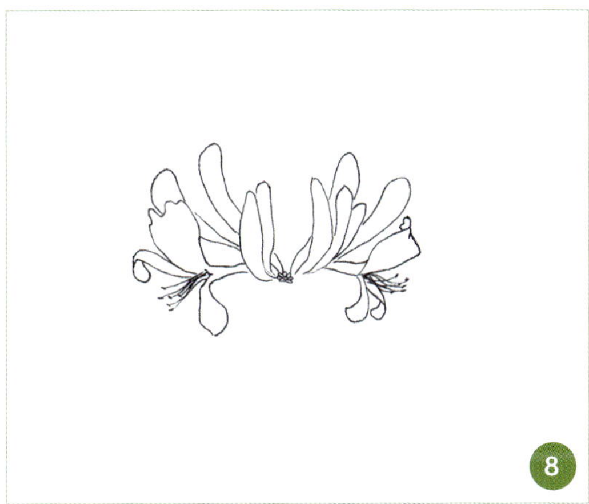

Step 9: Get out your big size 8 brush and load it with sap green. Paint three leaves behind the flower, leaving white space where the leaves would have their middle veins. Add a bit of quin- acridone rose at the right edge of the bottom leaf. This will make the leaves unique and will tie the colors together.

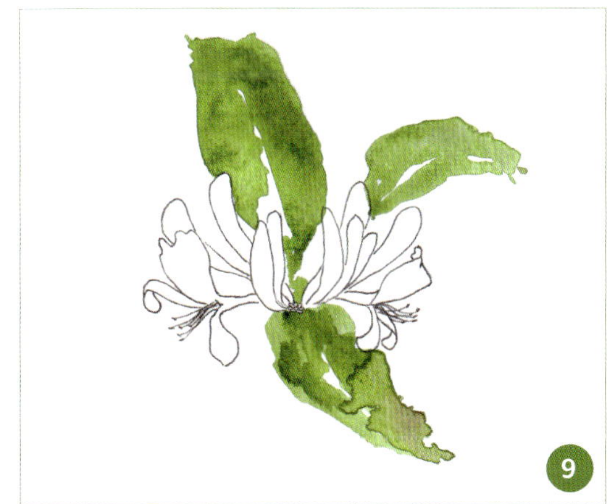

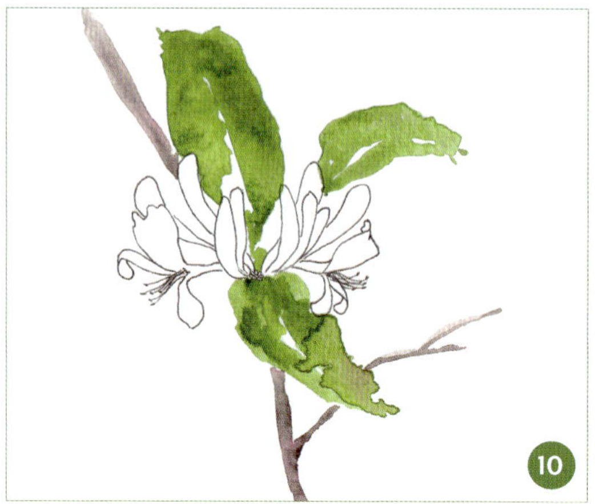

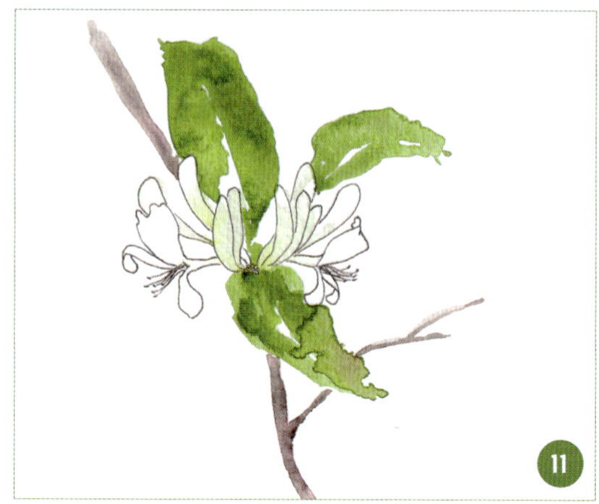

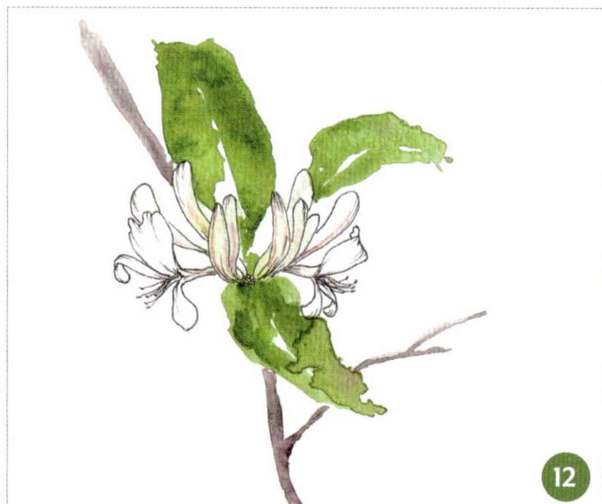

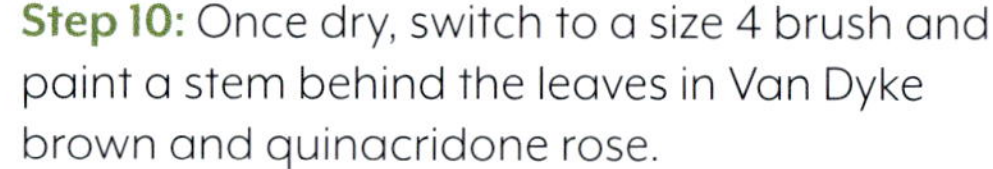

Step 10: Once dry, switch to a size 4 brush and paint a stem behind the leaves in Van Dyke brown and quinacridone rose.

Step 11: Load the brush with a watery green gold and paint the umbels in a very light wash.

Step 12: When the green is dry, dip a small size 1 brush in quinacridone rose and carefully paint direction lines on the umbels.

Step 13: Once dry, outline the two leaves closest to the flower with your 005 fineliner. Give the bottom leaf a bend and make the edge a bit uneven where you dripped in the rose earlier. This will add to the uniqueness of the leaf and show that an insect may have had its lunch there at some point.

You did it! I am sure that Daphnis and Chloe will be thrilled to learn that they can now be together for good. Wonderful job! And maybe if you have someone special you want to be with, you could create a card or something with a honeysuckle on it. Just saying.

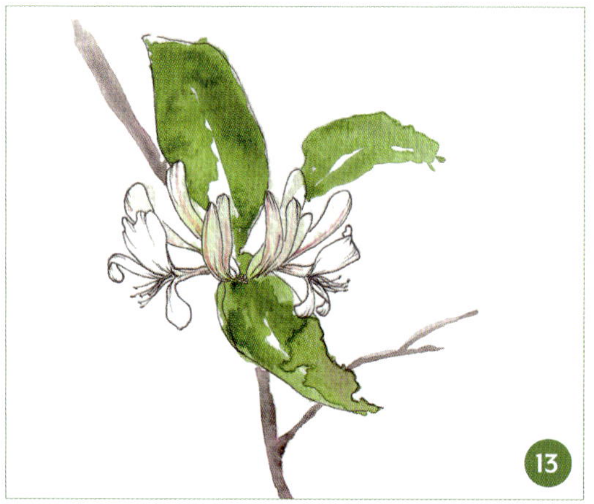

wild rose
a flower of immortal love

The beautiful wild beach rose is a personal favorite of mine. It grows wild in a lot of places here in Denmark. It is not high maintenance like a lot of the other roses, but just blooms wild and free wherever it likes. Native to East Asia, specifically China, Korea and Japan, these hardy roses have naturalized in parts of North America and Europe. In fact, beach roses are actually on the list of invasive plants here in Denmark; that is how much this fragrant beauty believes in itself! One of the wonderful things about the wild rose is how long we get to enjoy it. From the first buds, to the bloom and all the way to the colorful seedpods (called rosehips), it truly is immortal love. In this step-by-step tutorial, we dive into the early days of the autumn season when the flower begins to create its rosehips that are not vibrant red just yet.

Materials

Paper: Canson Montval 300gsm (140lb) cold press
Pencil and eraser
Fineliner sizes: 005 and 01
Watercolor brush sizes: 4 and 8
Water and cloth
Palette

Colors

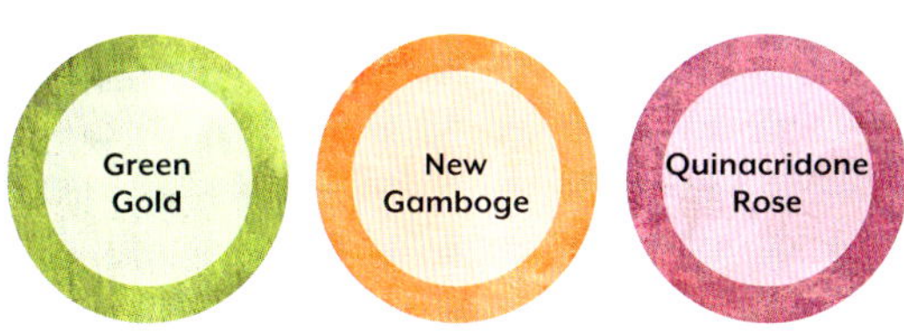

Mixes

For the seeds in the rose, create a mix of 50% green gold and 50% new gamboge.

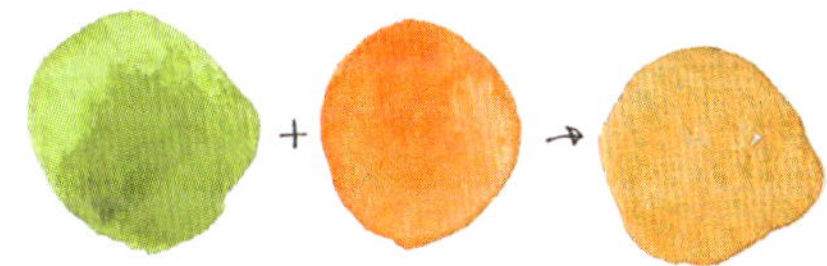

For the color variation in the rose, use 50% green gold and 50% quinacridone rose.

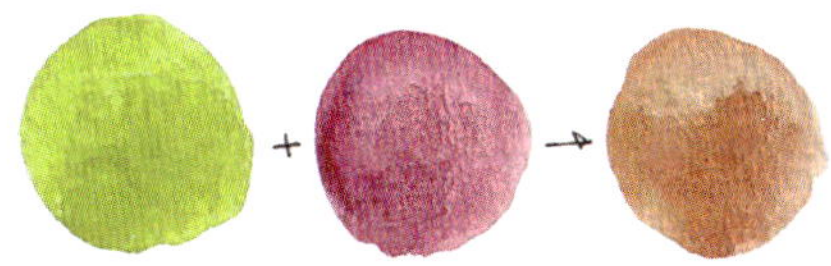

To get the color variation in the rosehips, mix 50% quinacridone rose and 50% new gamboge.

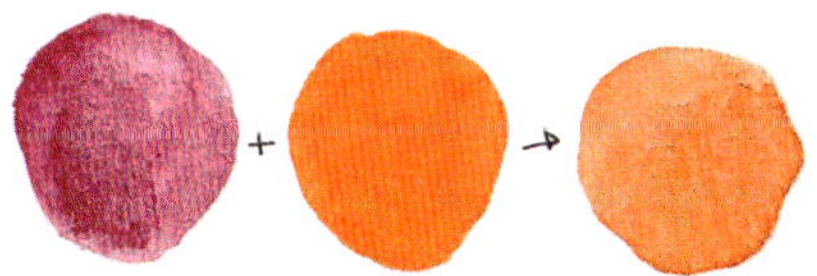

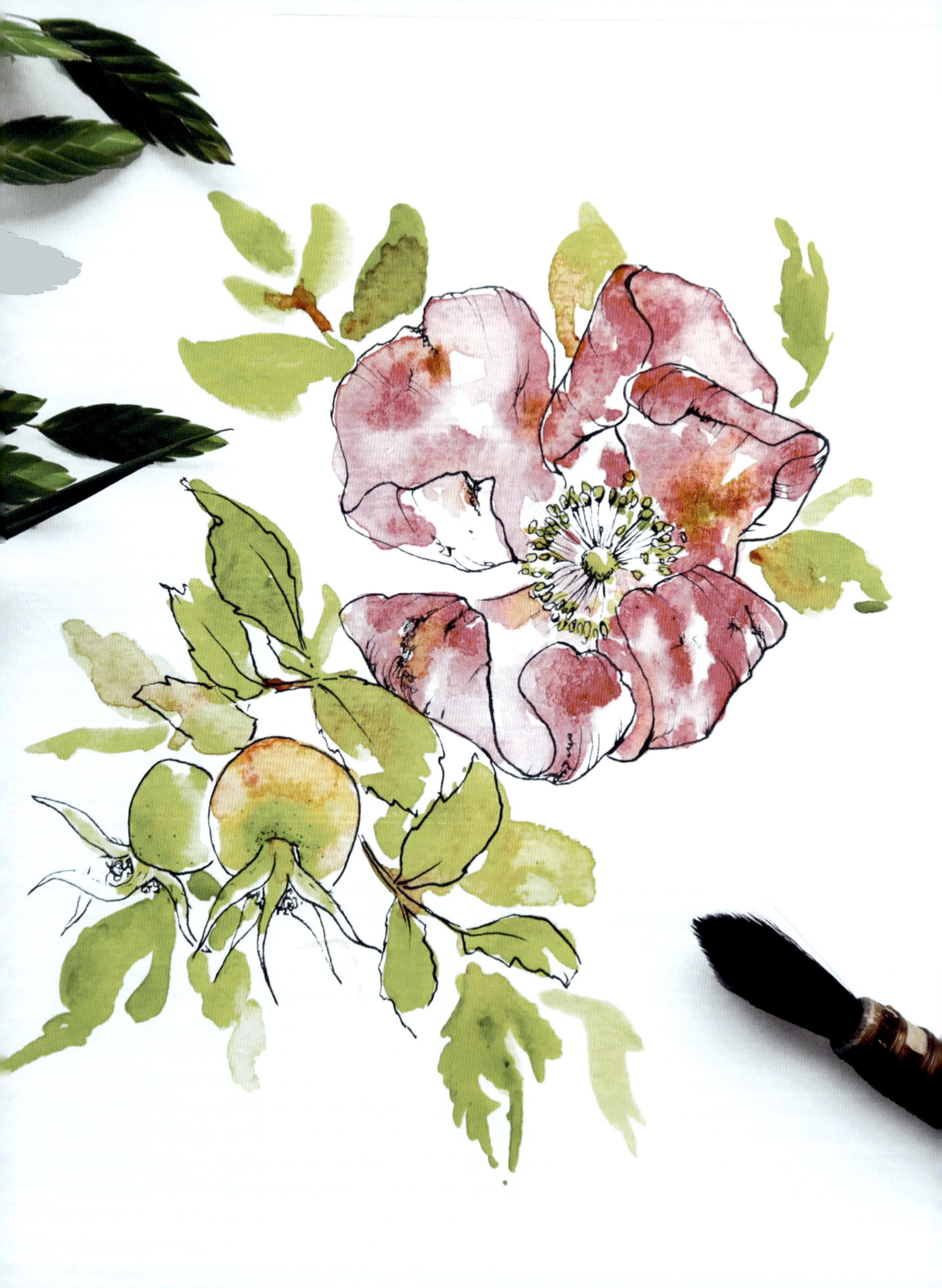

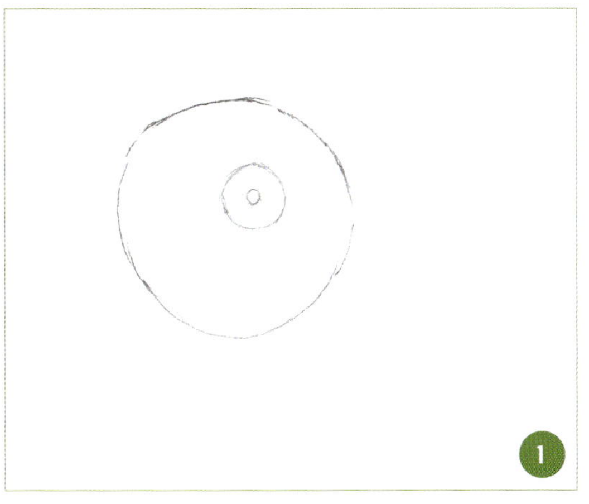

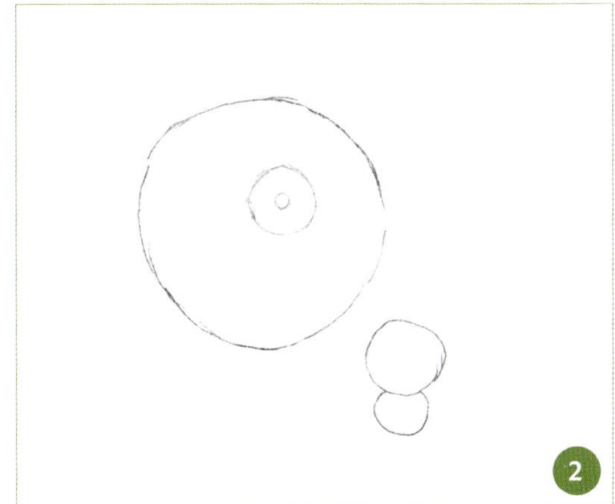

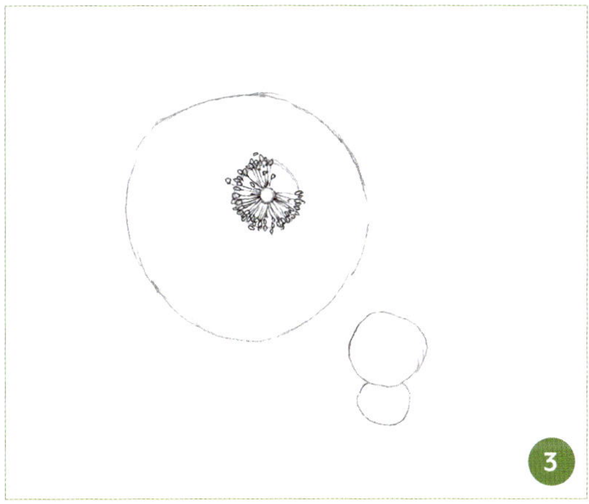

Step 1: First draw three circle guides in pencil inside each other. This will become your main flower soon.

Step 2: Draw two more circles a bit below the rose to the right. Let the biggest one be in front and the small one hiding behind. These will become two cute, little rosehips.

Step 3: Take the 005 fineliner and draw small seeds around the edge of the middle circle on the rose. Let some break the pattern and leave an area entirely free from seeds. When you finish the seeds, draw lines from the seeds to the inner circle.

Step 4: The wild rose is intricate with a lot of bending petals, so we will draw them one at a time and in pencil first. Start with a deep breath and then confidently begin with the first petal. Draw the outline first and then the bend afterward as discussed on page 20. Leave a bit of white space where the line should have otherwise met the center.

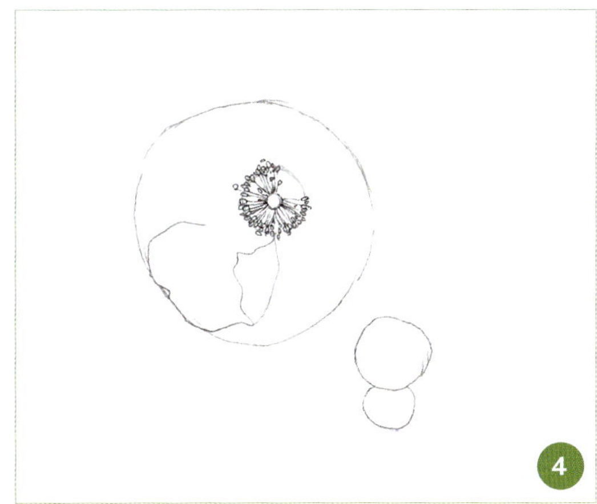

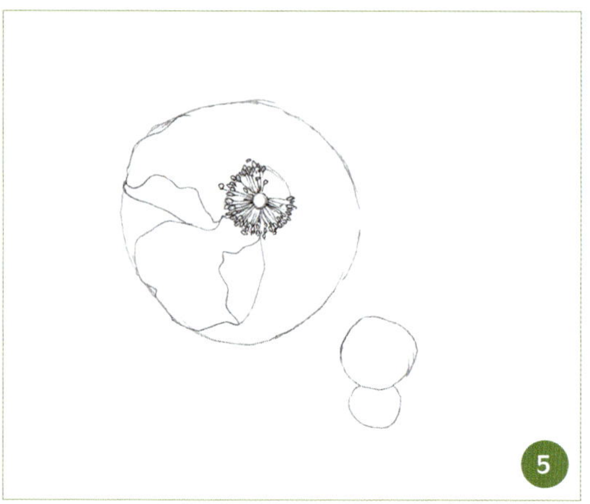

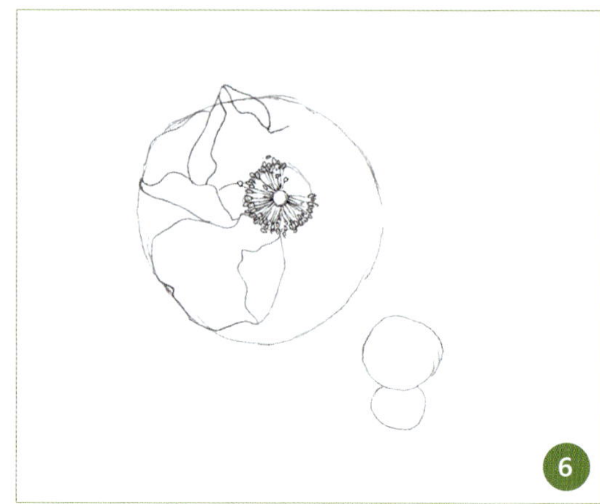

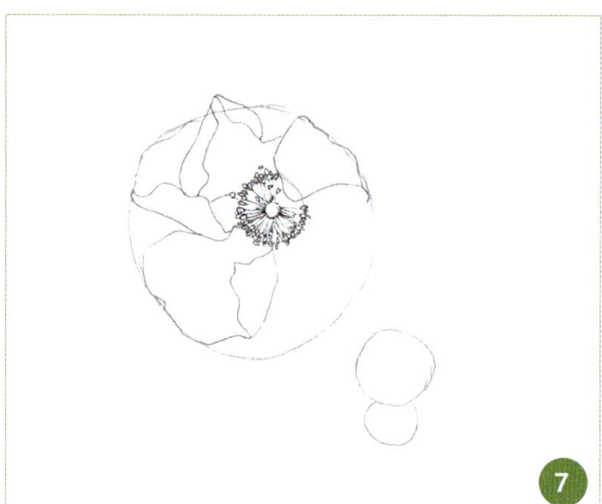

Step 5: You've got this! Draw the second petal. This one will overlap the first, which is why we created the white space before. With this petal do the same as before, leaving white space for an overlapping petal.

Step 6: To shake things up, draw a petal that both overlaps and tucks behind. Start with the outline and let the outline break where you meet the left petal. Draw two bends on the petal. This will give us some variation in the flower.

Step 7: The next petal is seen from the front and bends in front of the center. That is why we left space in the seeds. You are almost there now.

Step 8: The last petal is also curved in two places and here you can see the inside of the petal where it meets the center.

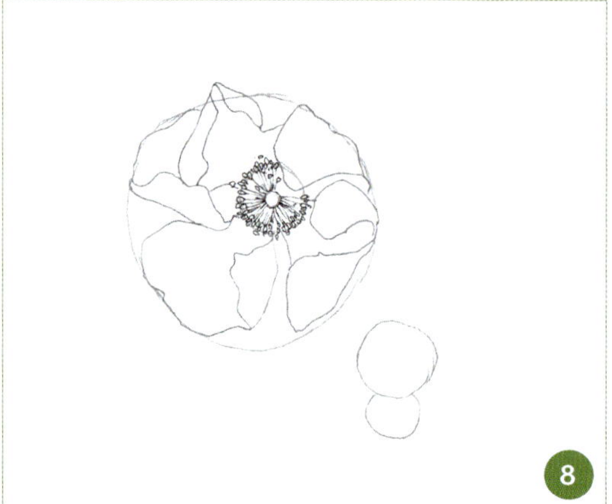

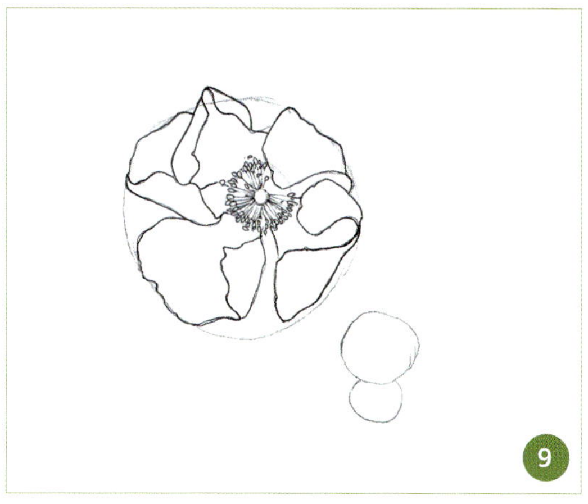

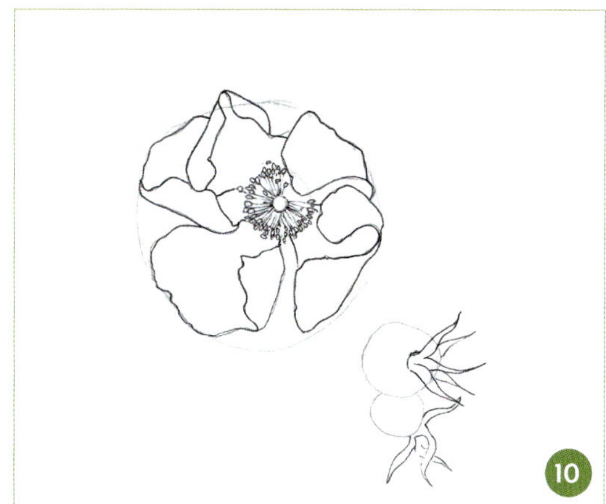

Step 9: Your pencil guide is done, and you can pat yourself on the back. A rose like this can be tricky but a good pencil guide is gold. Now you can get your fineliner size 01 and draw the outline for the petals without fear.

Step 10: Now we switch our focus to the rosehips. Start with the sepals, drawing with the 01 fineliner. Sepals are long and pointy and almost look like arms on a jellyfish.

Step 11: Outline the rest of each rosehip in 01 fineliner.

Step 12: Get out your 005 fineliner and draw direction lines and texture on the rose. Give the rose small wrinkles and doodle in places where you want texture, especially in the areas of the edge where there are bends and on the big petals with a clean surface that you will want to break up a bit.

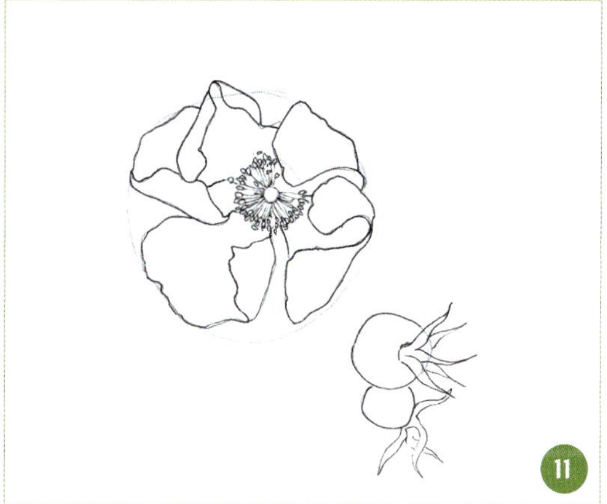

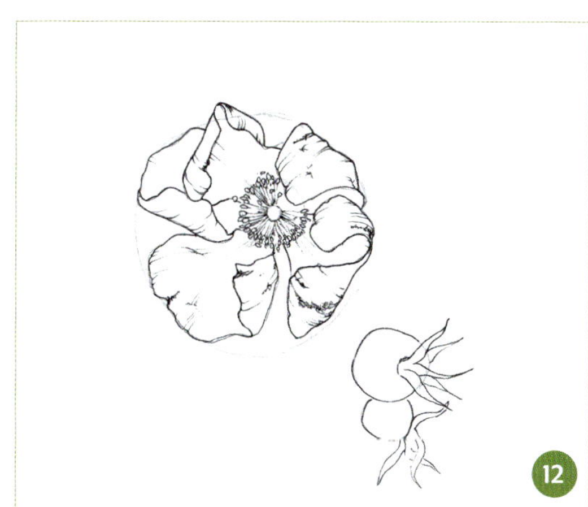

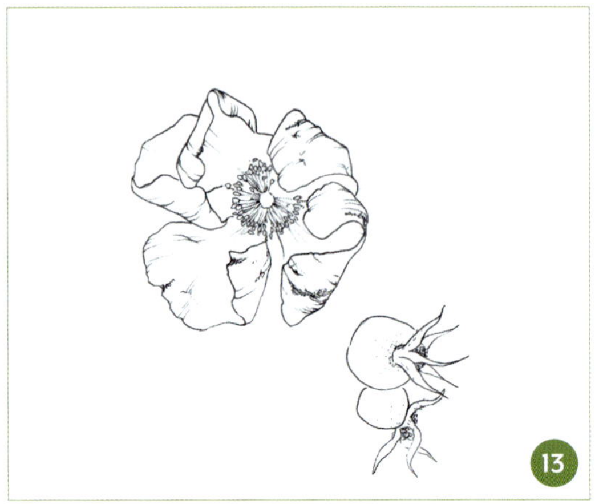

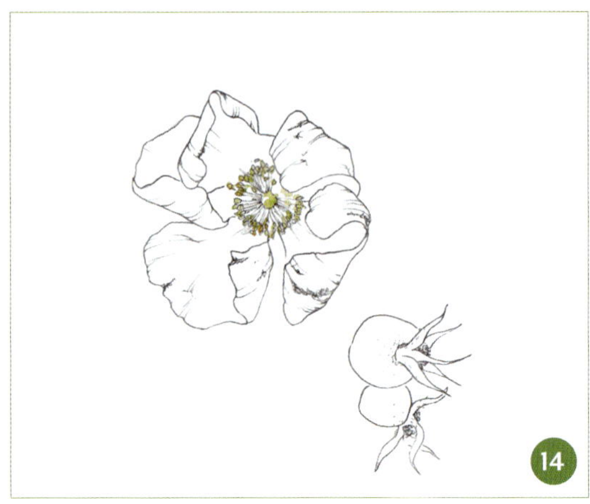

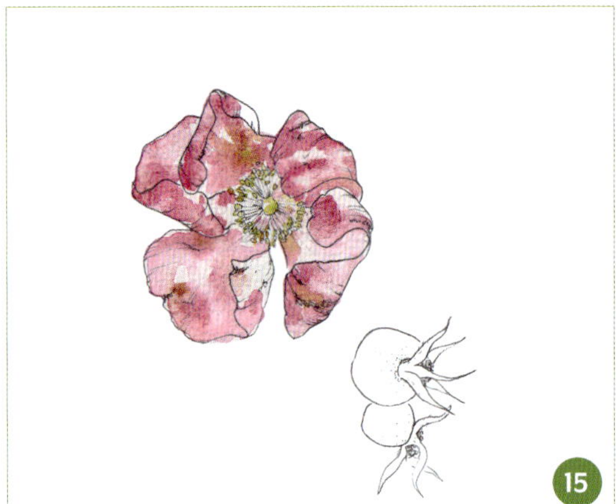

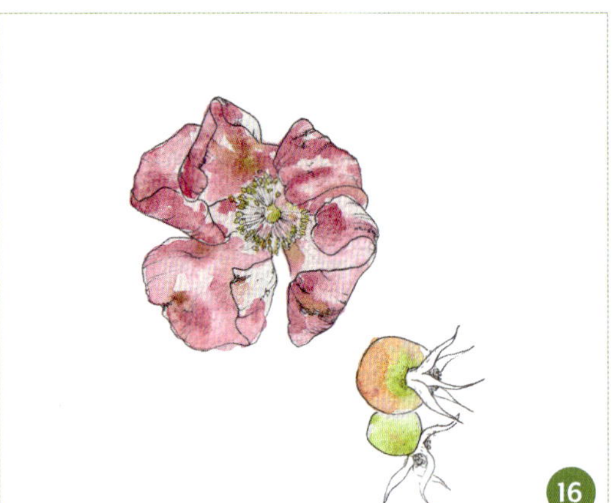

Step 13: Add small details on the rosehips with 005 fineliner like small dots on the fruit, hairs on the sepals and doodles in the center of the sepals. Send your pencil guides a bit of grateful love before you get out your eraser and remove them.

Step 14: Create a mix of green gold and new gamboge on a palette. Paint the seeds and center of the rose with your new color and size 4 brush. Drip in a bit of green gold in the bottom part of the center. Use a bit of vibrant new gamboge in the seeds as well to vary the colors.

Step 15: Now we paint the rose petals by taking one petal at a time. Wet most of the petal but leave a few spots dry. Then drip quinacridone rose into the water. While it's wet, mix a bit of quinacridone rose with green gold. Drip this mix into the wet paint in a few places where you want variations in color and in areas with over-lapping petals or doodles and wrinkles. Take a second to enjoy how the colors interact. It's truly magical. Let dry and then repeat with the remaining petals.

Step 16: Paint the rosehips wet-on-wet as well. Remember the rosehips are in an early stage so they are closer to green than red. Wet the biggest one with clean water. Drip green gold close to the top, then new gamboge and the mix of quin-acridone rose and new gamboge. While it dries, drip in a single droplet of vibrant quinacridone rose. Once dry, paint the small rosehip in green gold with a single droplet of new gamboge.

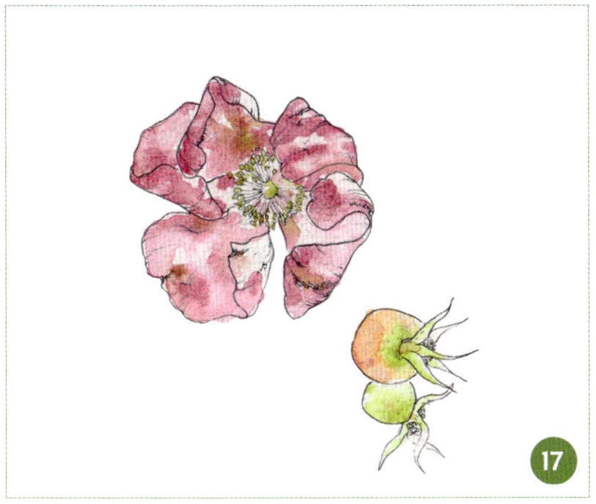

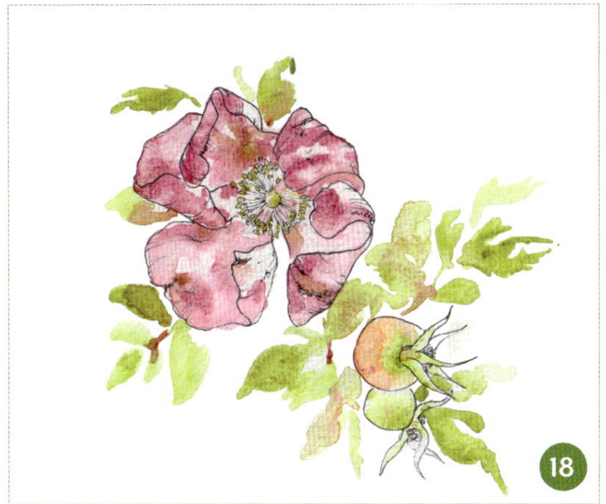

Step 17: Paint the sepals wet-on-dry in a green gold with a small droplet of new gamboge at the bottom where they attach to the rosehip.

Step 18: Now switch to a bigger size 8 brush. Paint loose leaves on stems behind the flower and rosehips in green gold, dripping in a bit of quinacridone rose at the stems. The leaves are roughly teardrop-shaped, getting smaller at the tip and the base near the stem. Be loose and fast about it so the leaves don't outshine the flower.

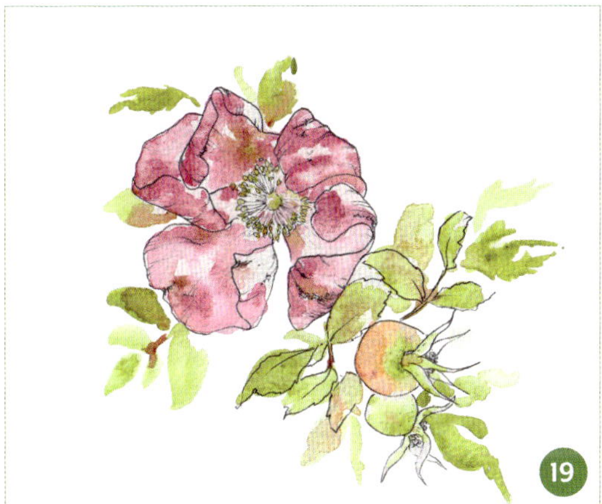

Step 19: Once dry, with the 01 fineliner, draw outlines on a few of the leaves in the area between the rosehips and the rose. This will tie the elements together. Keep the rest of the leaves painted with just watercolor to get a clear focal point.

Step 20: Add the final details in the rose with the 005 fineliner. Draw dots at the bottom of the very center for a bit of shadow. Repeat to add a bit of shadow on the seeds and a few shadows below some of the bending petals.

This was a long one and you did it! Please take a moment to congratulate yourself! You are incredible! Step back and enjoy the sketch that you did all by yourself.

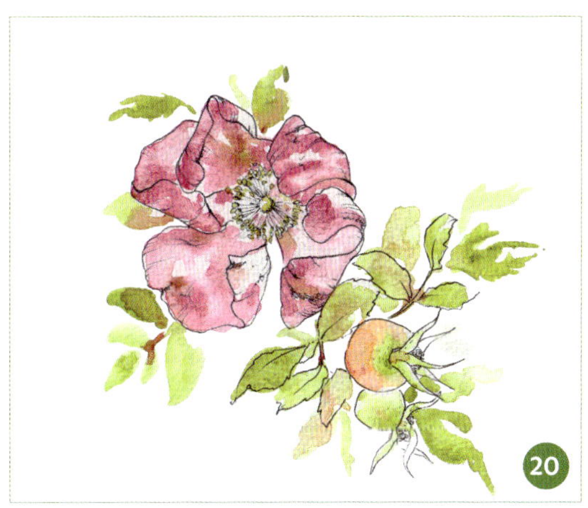

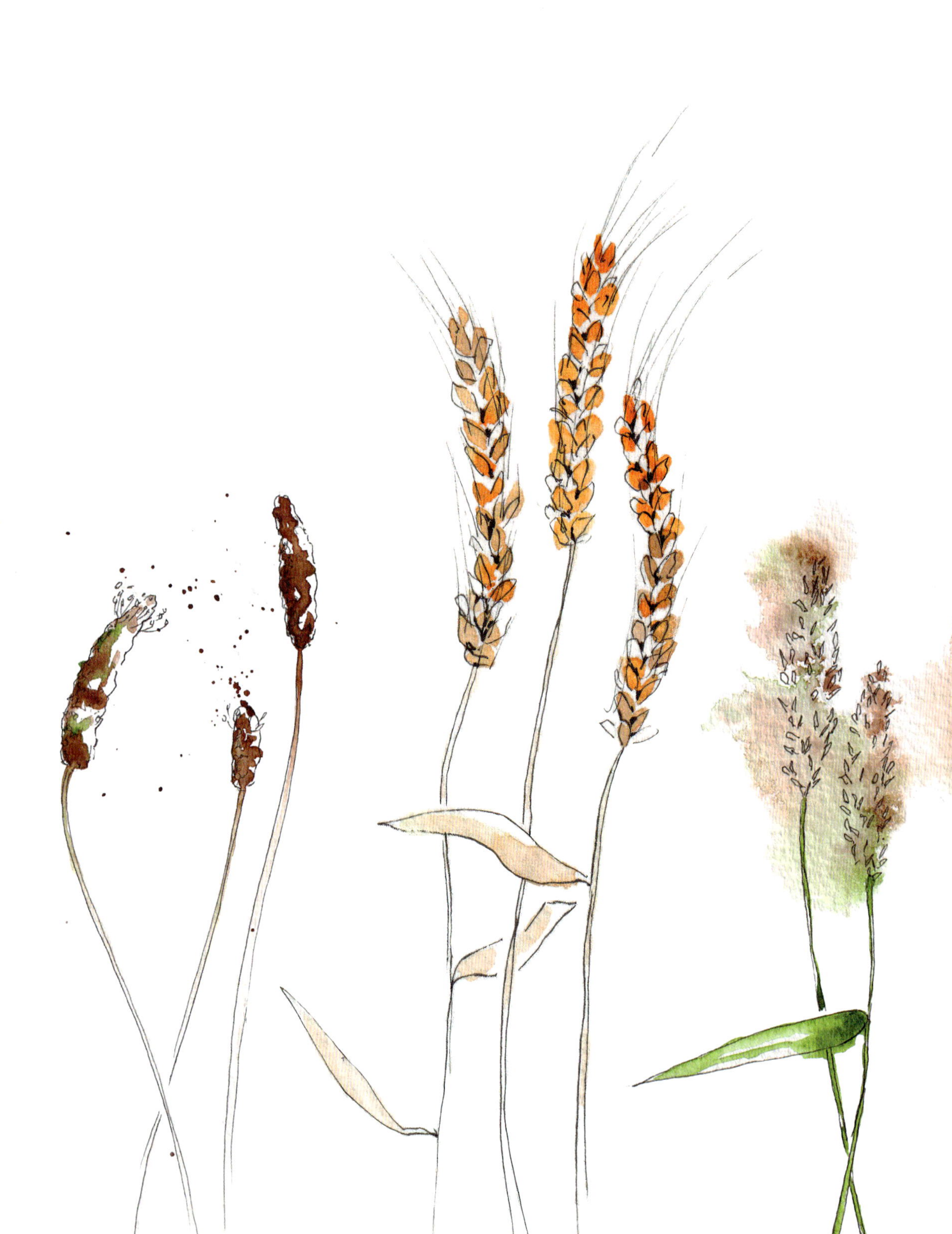

part III
five dancing grasses

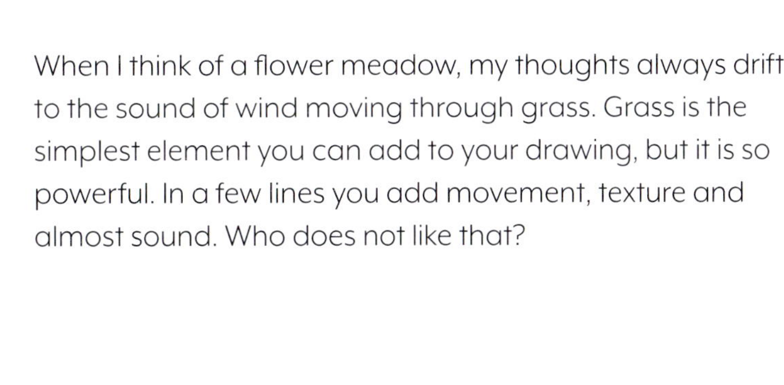

When I think of a flower meadow, my thoughts always drift to the sound of wind moving through grass. Grass is the simplest element you can add to your drawing, but it is so powerful. In a few lines you add movement, texture and almost sound. Who does not like that?

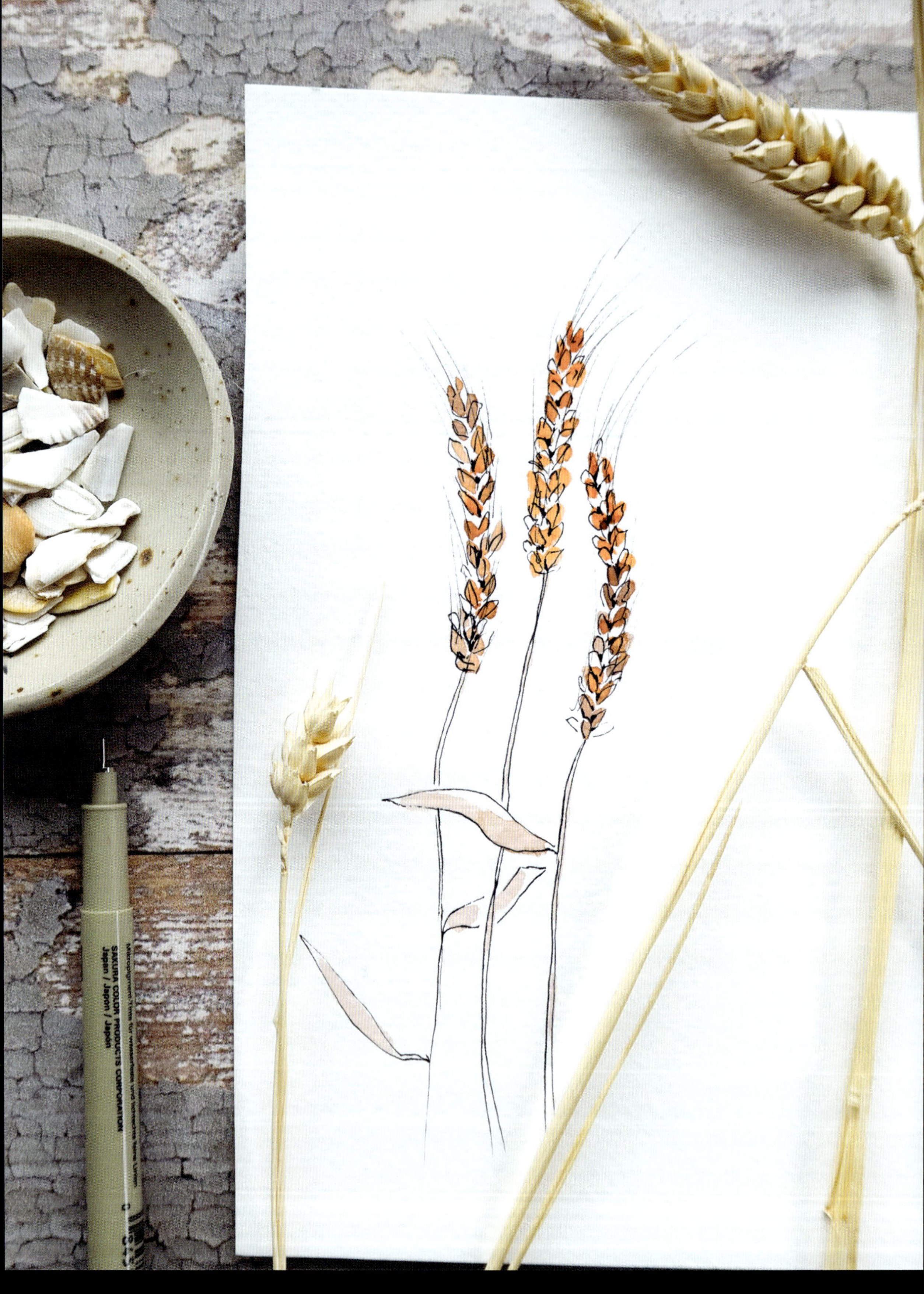

wheat
a grass of substance

Here in Denmark, the fields are filled with wheat and it often spreads
to the fields of wildflowers . . . like two separate parties that
turn into one colorful bash.

Materials

Paper: Canson Montval 300gsm (140lb) cold press

Watercolor brush size: 4

Water and cloth

Palette

Fineliner sizes: 01 and 005

Colors

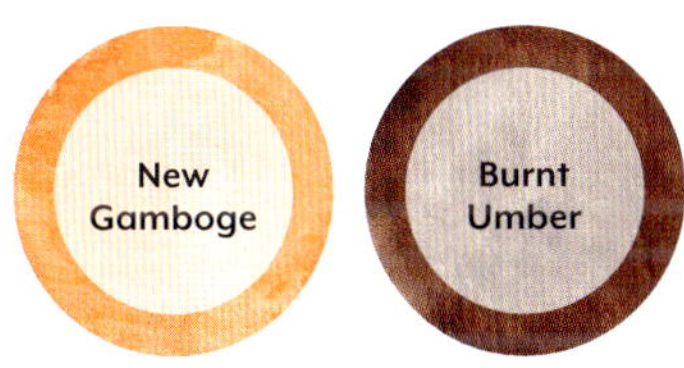

Mix

Create a mix of 50% new gamboge and 50% burnt umber on a palette, but keep some of the color unmixed so you have a palette with yellow, brown and a mix of both.

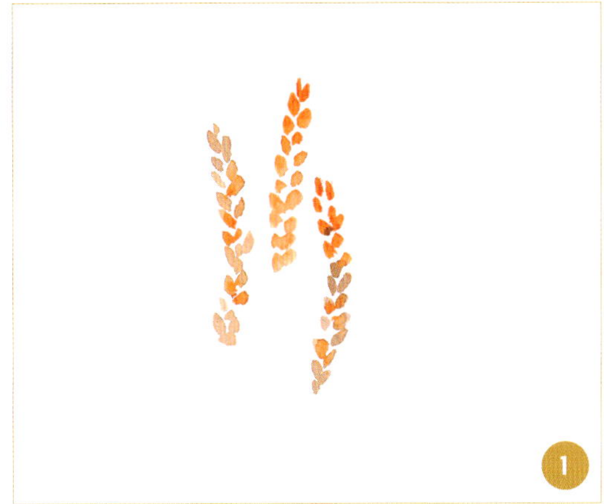

Step 1: Start by creating the mix of new gamboge and burnt umber on a palette and getting out your size 4 brush. Paint three tall, dancing strands of wheat consisting of small teardrop shapes. Use the tip of your brush to make these marks. Switch the color often so you use all of the yellow variations you have on your palette.

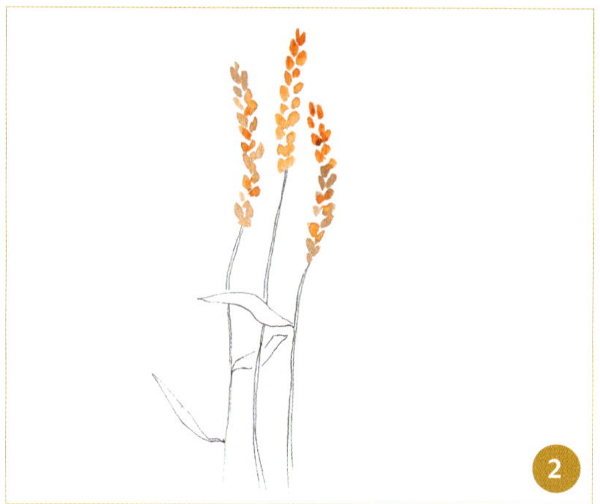

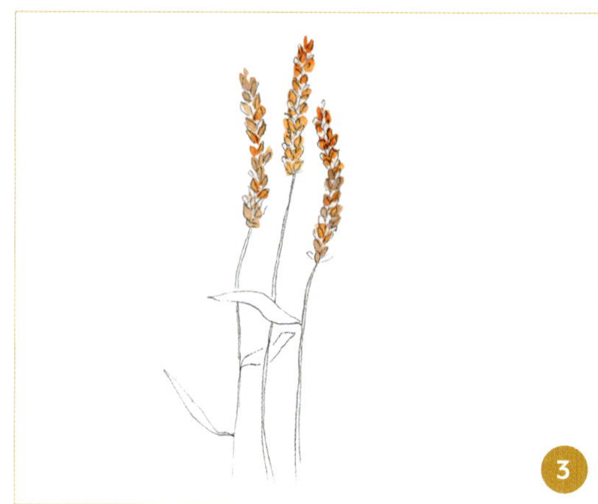

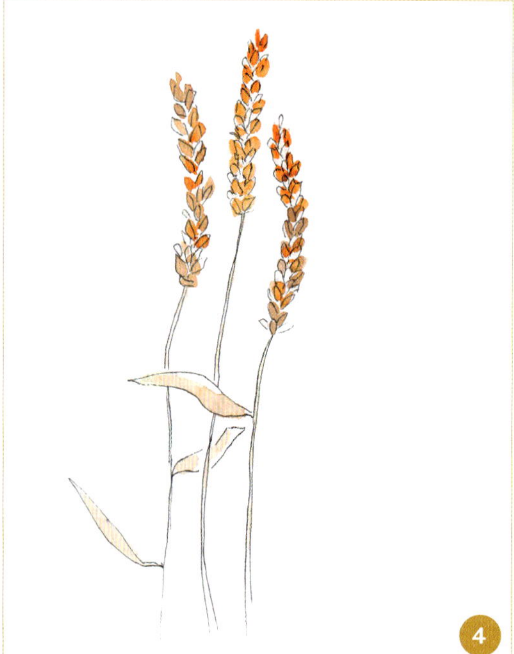

Step 2: Using the 01 fineliner, draw the stems and a few long, pointy leaves on them. Let them overlap each other to create depth. As long as your lines do not touch the paint, you don't need to wait for the wheat heads to dry.

Step 3: Using the 005 fineliner, draw small teardrop shapes on top of the brush marks. Draw some in the areas where there is no paint to create interest.

Step 4: Put extra water in the paint mix and paint the stems and leaves with it.

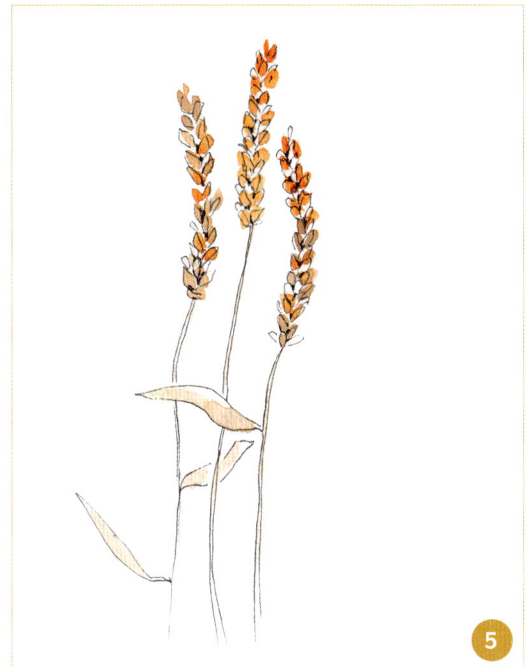

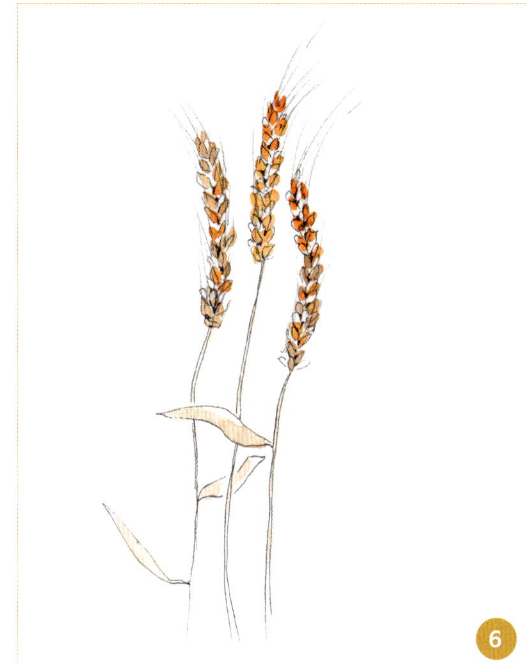

Step 5: Using the 01 fineliner, add some dark shadow areas in between the single seeds on the stem.

Step 6: Finally, get out your 005 fineliner and add some hair at the top of the wheat. Imagine how it would look if the wheat were dancing in the wind.

Perfect! I can almost feel the warm summer breeze in the fields of wheat now.

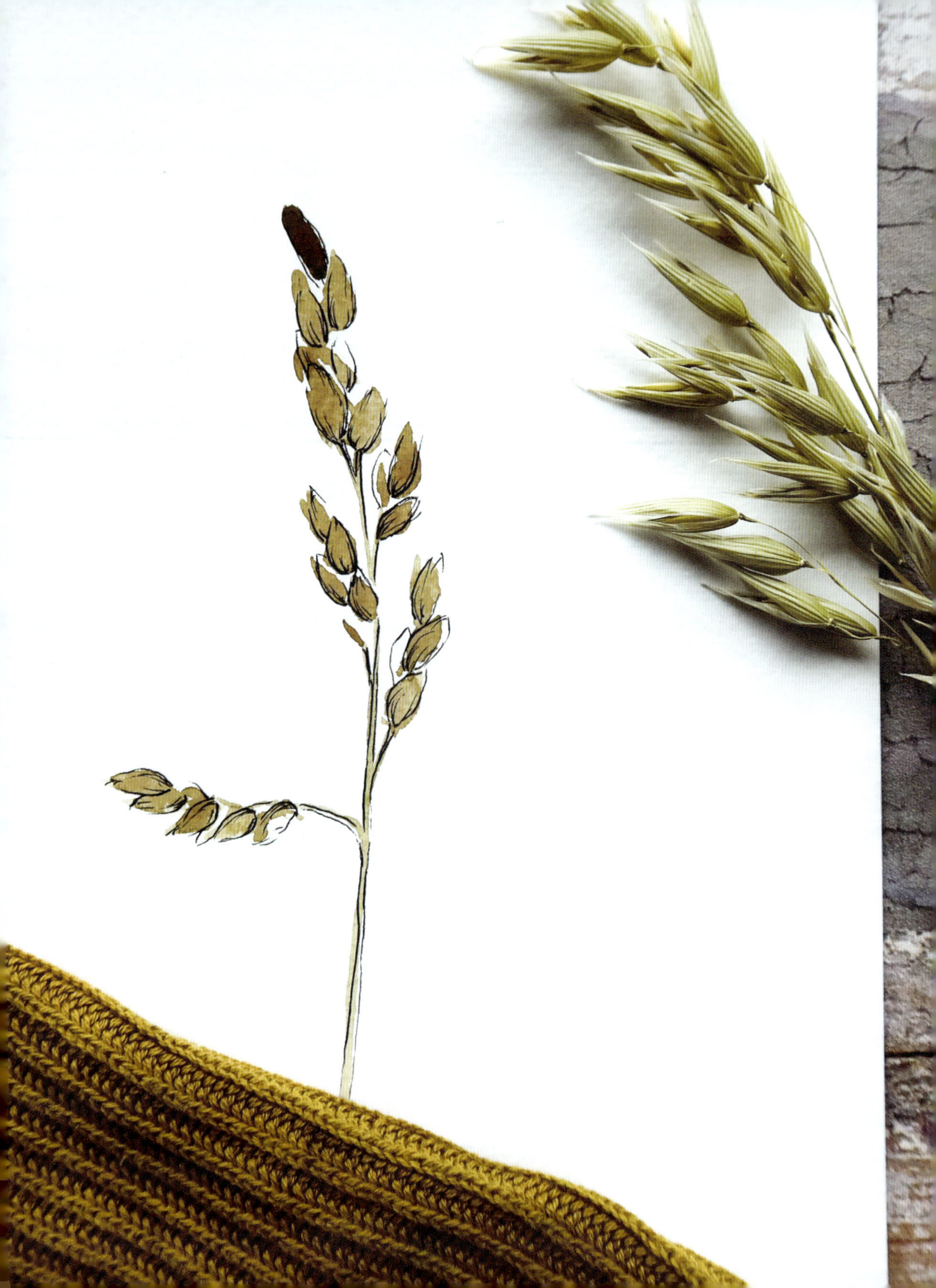

cock's-foot
a grass with many names

This is one of the more confusing grasses. Known by many names, some call it cock's-foot because it looks like a bird's foot. Others call it dog grass, or even cat grass, in some places. Maybe birds, cats and dogs have more in common than we think. Whatever you call it, this is a beautiful, sturdy grass with a nice, neutral color that will complement a lot of flowers perfectly.

Materials

Paper: Canson Montval 300gsm (140lb) cold press

Watercolor brush size: 4

Water and cloth

Palette

Fineliner sizes: 01 and 005

Colors

Mix

It's all in the mix with this grass. Take your palette and mix 45% sap green, 45% burnt umber and 10% new gamboge. Don't mix it completely, leaving a few bits of each clean color.

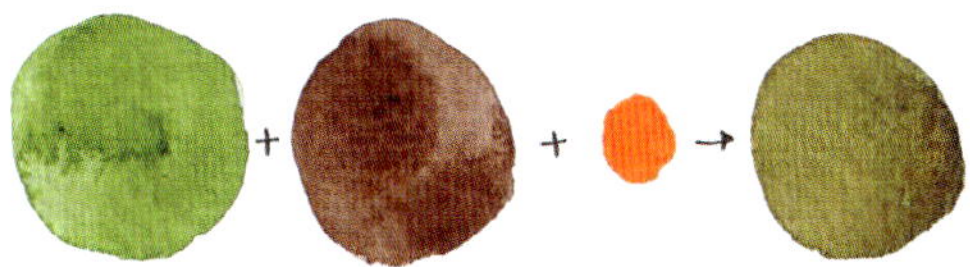

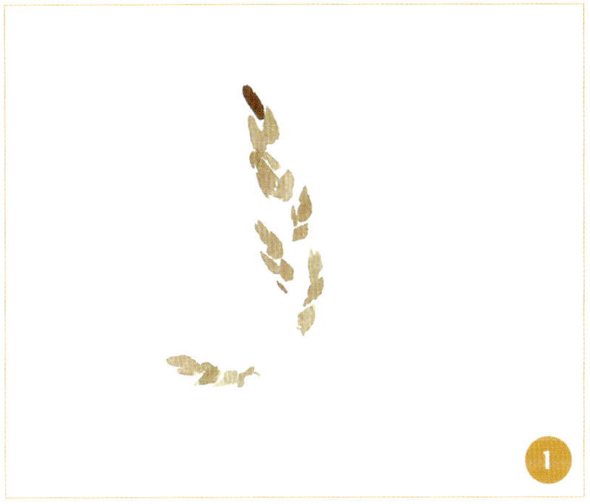

Step 1: Create the mix and paint the florets of the grass with the size 4 brush. A floret is almost like a flower on a stem, and the name itself just sounds so poetic. Create the florets by making simple brush marks in a few clusters. Imagine that there is a main stem and a few side stems. Finally, add a cluster of marks that are leaning drastically to the left, creating a side branch that is broken.

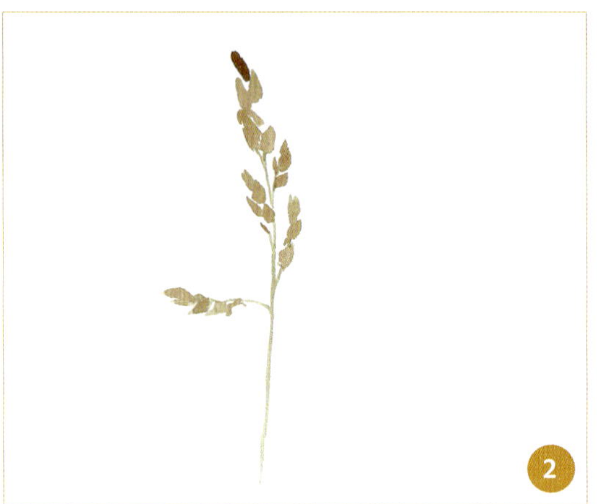

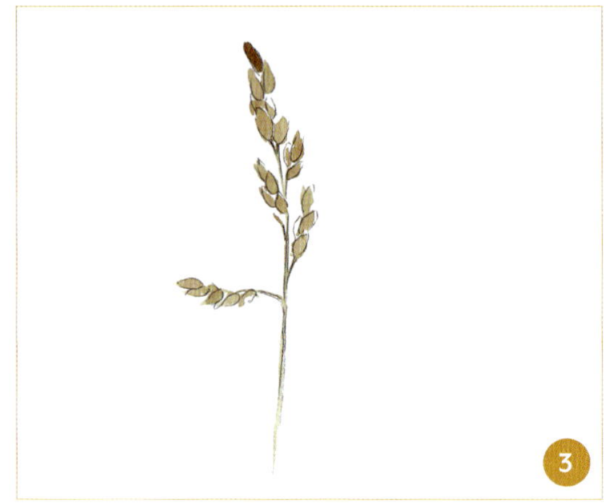

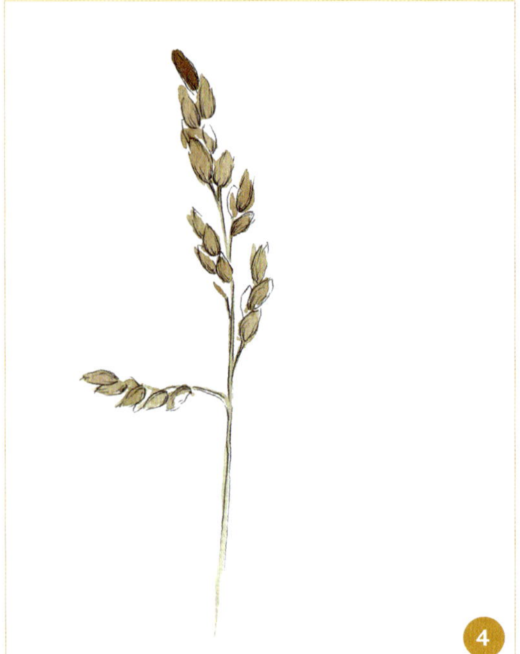

Step 2: Paint the stem with the same mix and brush. Let the stem branch out to make all the clusters come together at one main stem.

Step 3: Once dry, outline the separate parts of the grass clusters with a 01 fineliner. Keep it loose so the shapes don't close up or become too heavy. Draw a loose outline down the stems.

Step 4: To finish, you can get your 005 fineliner and draw a few direction lines in the florets.

Now you have the most wonderful grass to pair with your blooms.

english plantain
a dancing grass
with healing power

When my kids accidentally touch stinging nettle, we always look for an English plantain. If you take one of the English plantain leaves and rub it onto the affected area, it helps right away. In this tutorial, we will create a beautiful, dancing version of this grass so you can use it as the perfect, elegant filler between the wild blooms in your meadow illustrations . . . and this will make it easy for you to spot if you accidently touch stinging nettle.

Materials

Paper: Canson Montval 300gsm (140lb) cold press
Pencil and eraser
Fineliner sizes: 01 and 005
Watercolor brush size: 1
Water and cloth

Colors

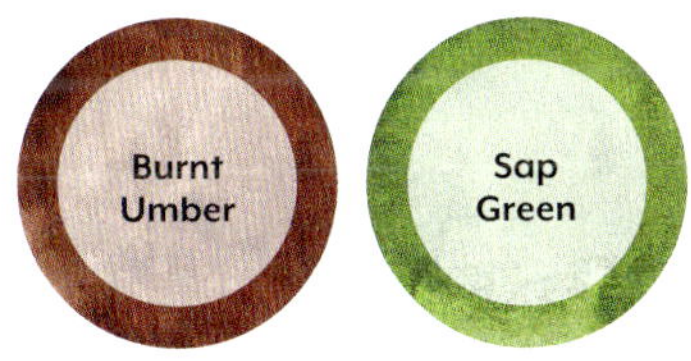

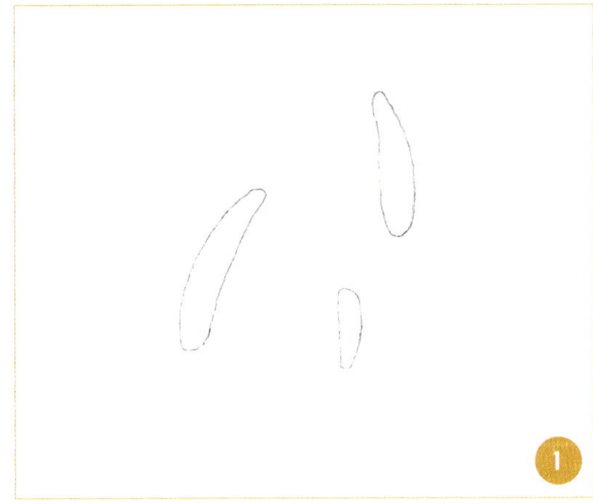

Step 1: Draw three bent bean shapes in pencil. Let two of them be big and one small.

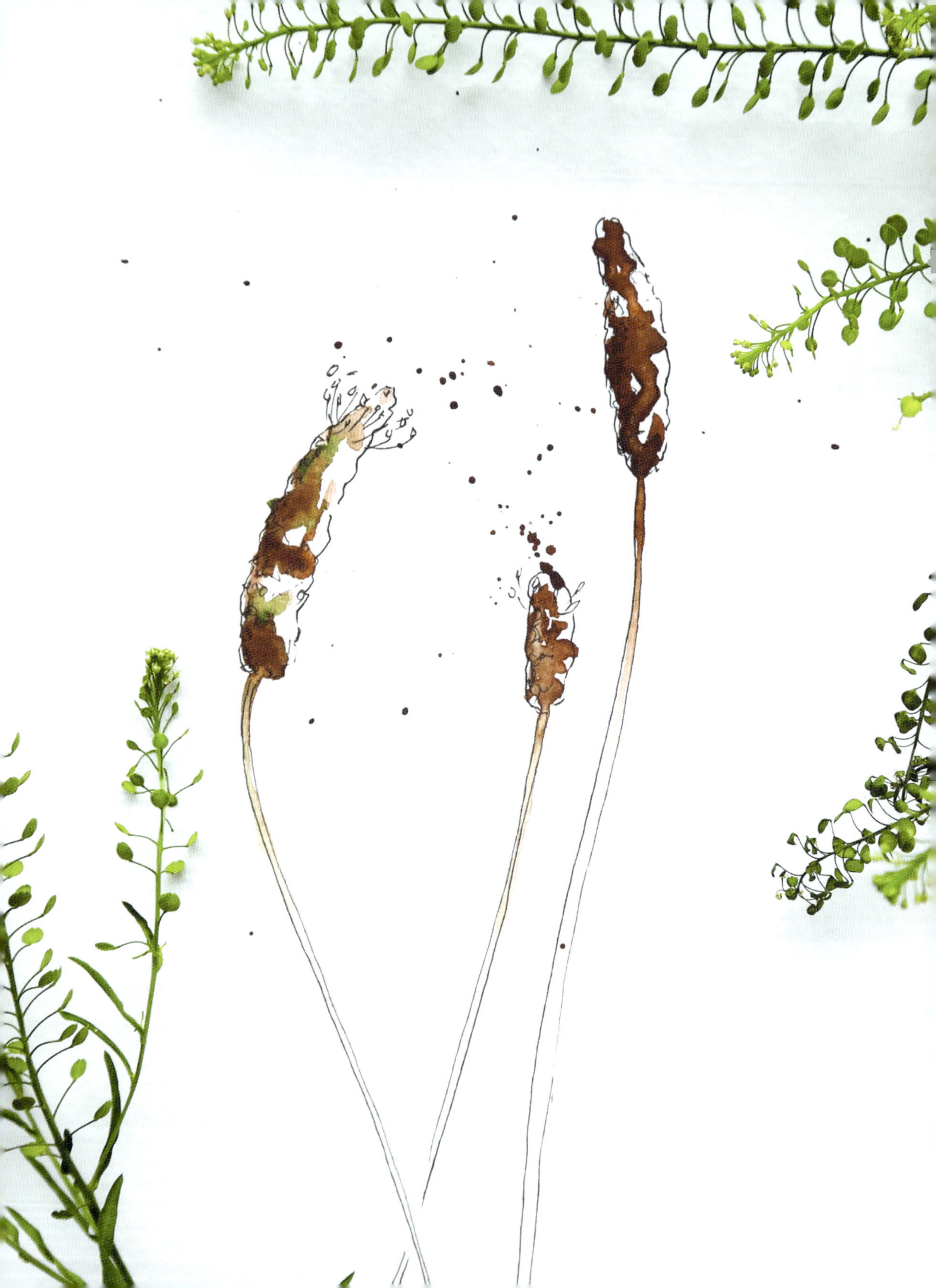

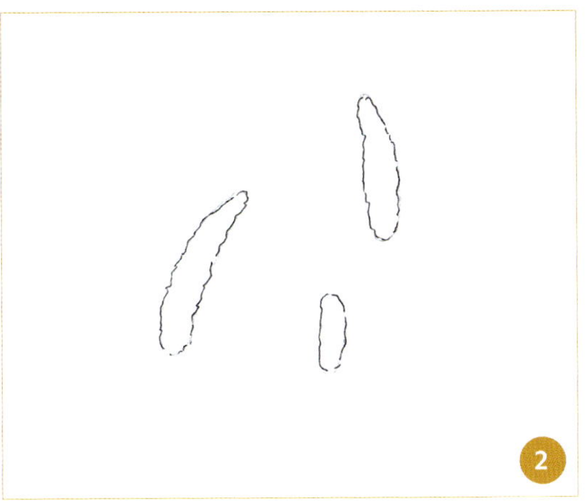

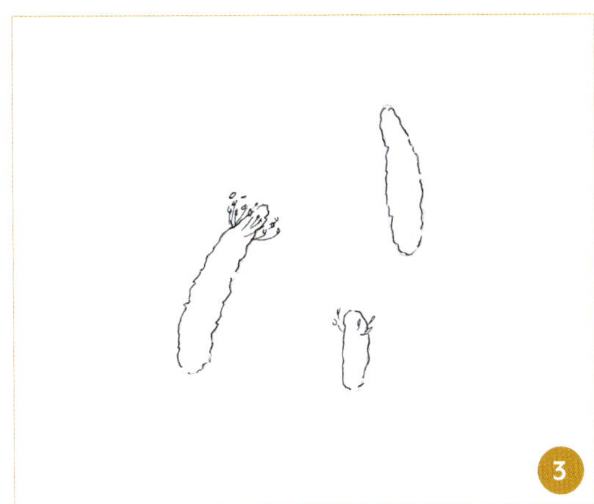

Step 2: Draw an outline with the 01 fineliner. Keep it super rough and unfinished so it has a texture.

Step 3: Grab the 005 fineliner to add details. Draw the small seeds at the top of the left grass. Attach them with small, C-shaped lines. Add a few to the small one in the middle as well.

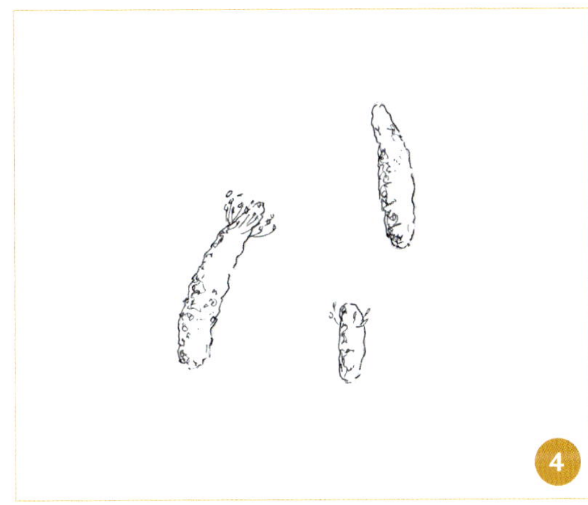

Step 4: Doodle on the left side of the grasses to add texture and the feeling of a shadow.

Step 5: Draw the dancing stems with the 005 fineliner. See if you can get some of them to overlap for depth. When you are happy with your fineliner sketch, erase the pencil lines.

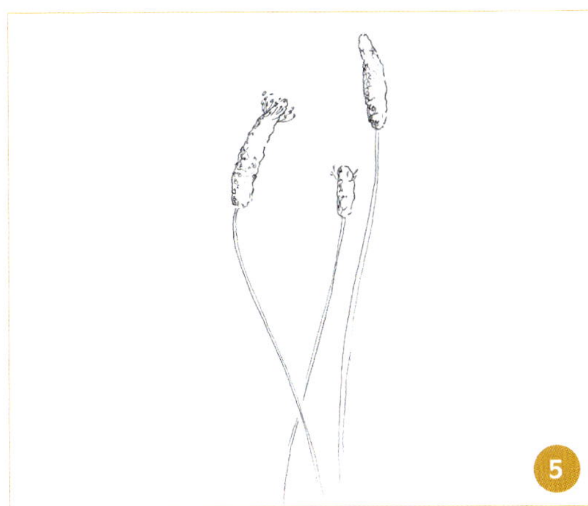

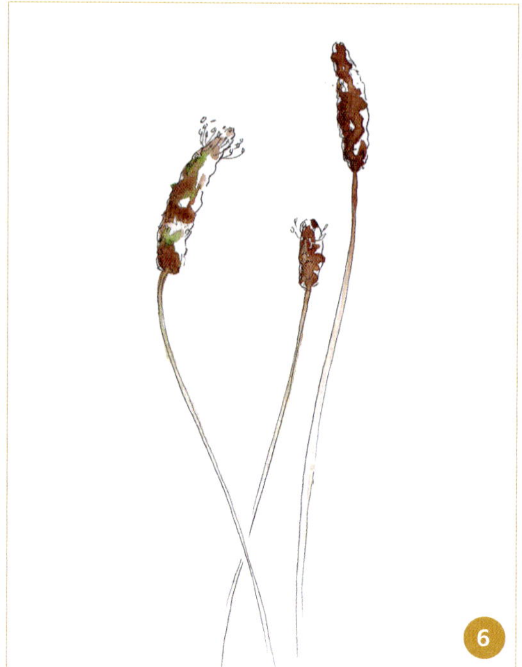

Step 6: Paint wet-on-dry with the size 1 brush. The English plantain is burnt umber with a drip of sap green in a few places.

Step 7: Add a few splatters in burnt umber to emphasize this grass's happy dance.

Now all you need to do is find floral dancing partners for this joyful grass.

meadow foxtail
a grass of joy

Imagine a soft, happy tail on a fox. That is exactly what the foxtail grass looks like! So beautiful! In this tutorial, we are going to play around with that unique, fluffy joyfulness. Get your mist spray bottles out of your supply stash and let's have some fun.

Materials

Paper: Canson Montval 300gsm (140lb) cold press
Pencil and eraser
Fineliner sizes: 005 and 01
Mist spray bottle
Watercolor brush size: 4
Water and cloth

Colors

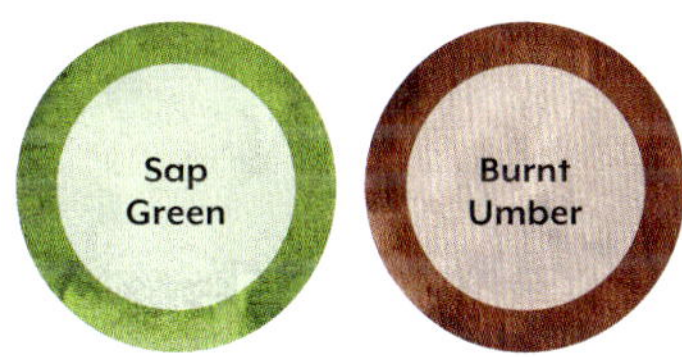

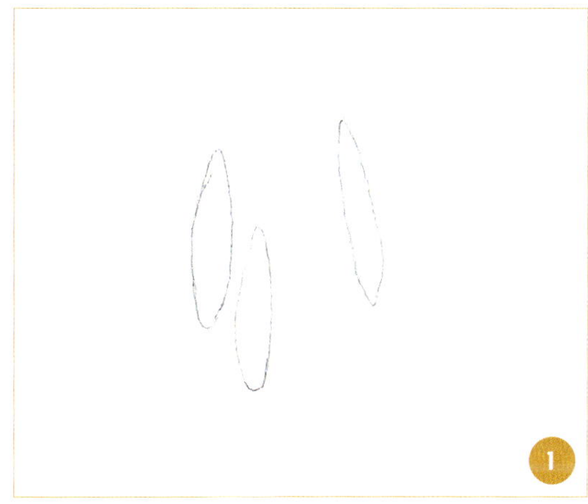

Step 1: Draw a guide for three grass heads in pencil by creating long ovals with soft tips at the top, just like the flame of a candle.

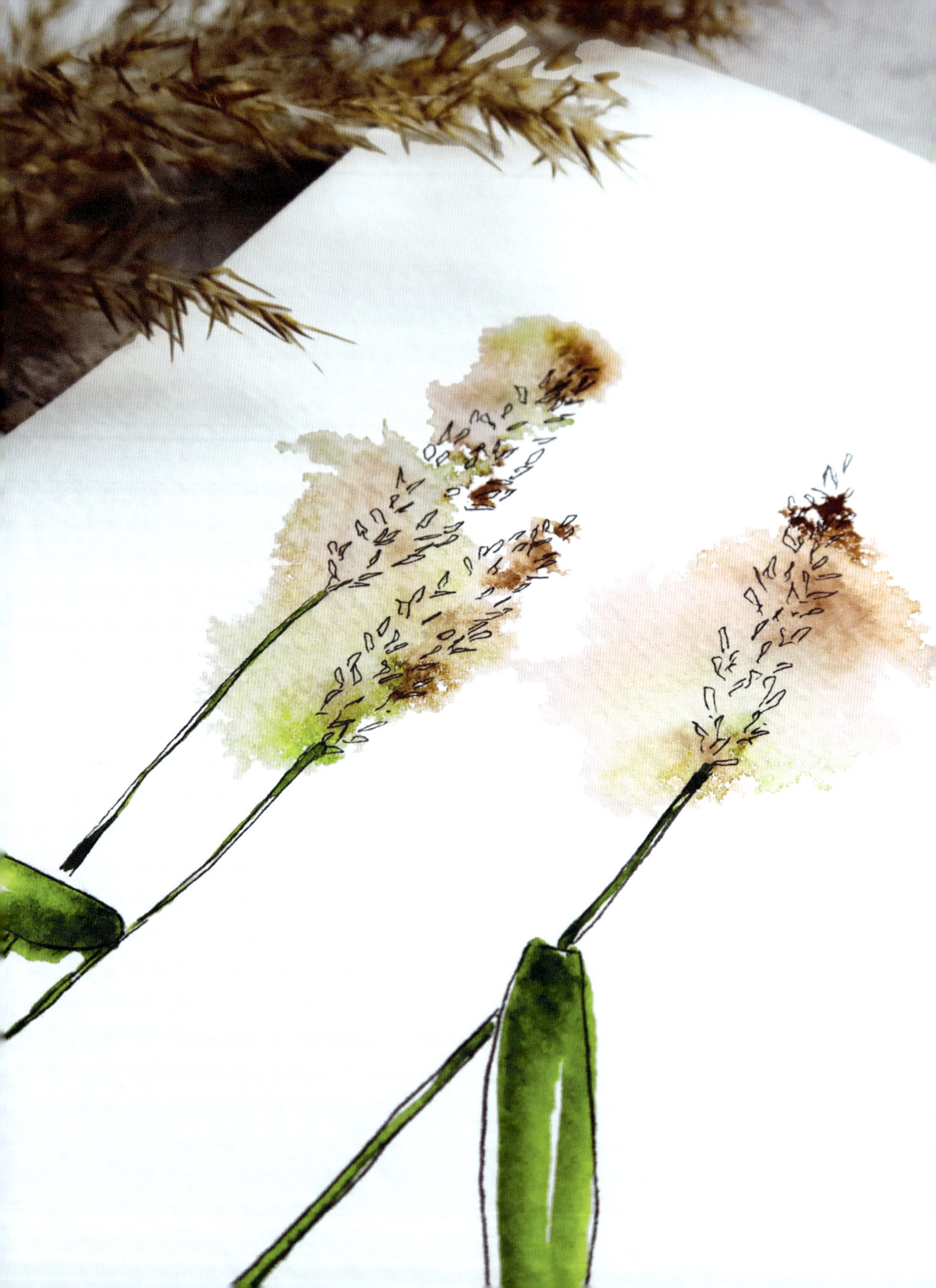

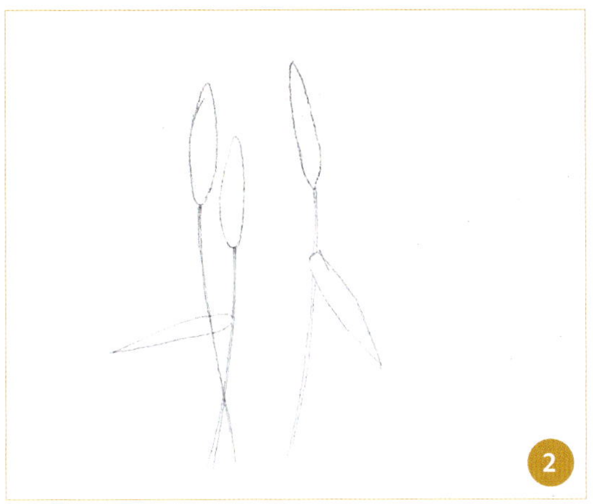

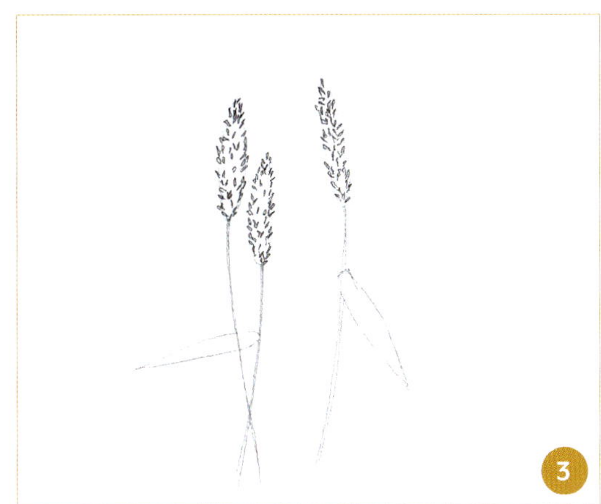

Step 2: Continue with the pencil by drawing stems and very sleek, pointed leaves.

Step 3: Put down the pencil and grab your 005 fineliner to draw the foxtail hairs. You don't need to fill out everything, but just enough to create the shape of the grass.

Step 4: Outline the stem and leaves with the 01 fineliner. Before we add the paint, make sure to erase the pencil lines.

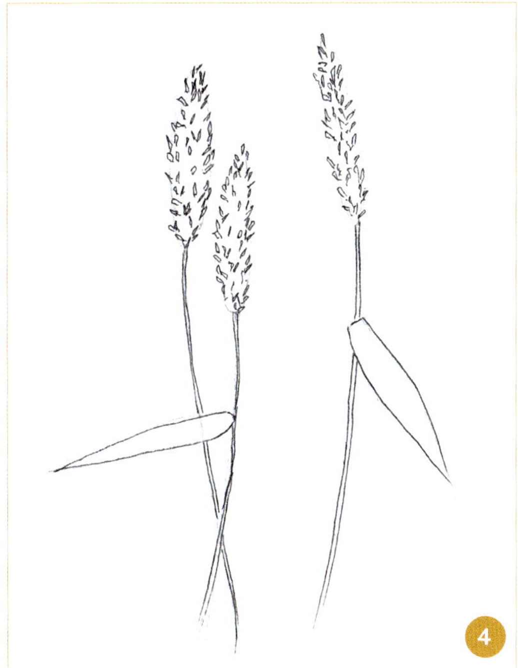

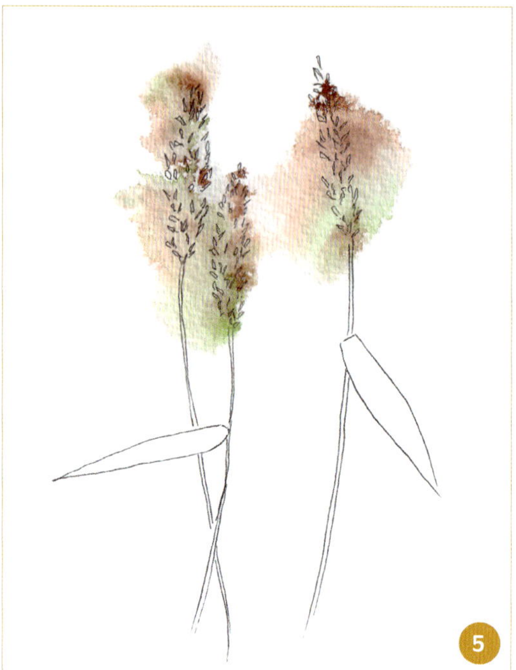

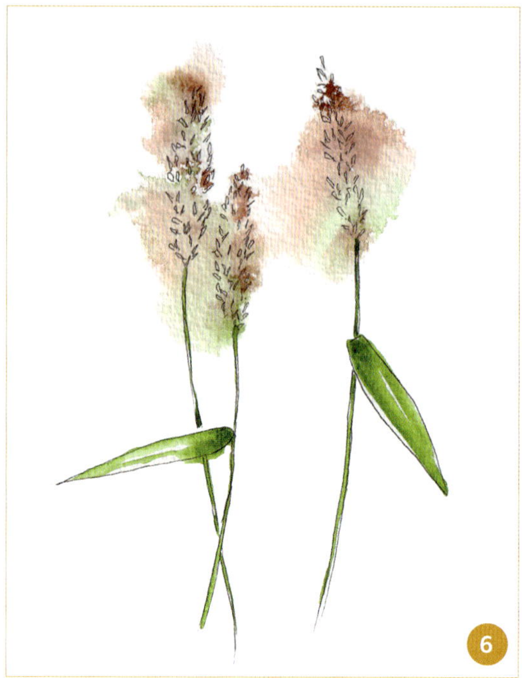

Step 5: Holding it about 8 inches (20 cm) away from your paper, use a mist spray bottle on the grass heads to create a fluffy feeling. Drip in sap green and burnt umber with your size 4 brush and let the paint spread by itself without touching it.

Step 6: Paint the stems and leaves with sap green when the heads are completely dry. When you paint the leaves, leave a white line in the center.

Oh, that was some delightful mist spray fun! Just don't do it too much—it can get addictive (now you've been warned!) and you don't want the entire top half of your paper to become one giant foxtail plume.

feather grass
a perfect grass for broadway

Imagine a beautiful diva getting ready for the stage on Broadway. She is wearing a stunning hat filled with feathers. That is exactly the feeling I get when I see flowing feather grass. This grass is very special and can be used in compositions to create movement and texture. With feather grass, it is not about the single stems but much more about the feeling of the entire grass tuft. That is why we are going to play around with the fan brush for this one.

Materials

Paper: Canson Montval 300gsm (140lb) cold press

Fan brush size: 2

Water and cloth

Palette

Fineliner size: 005

Colors

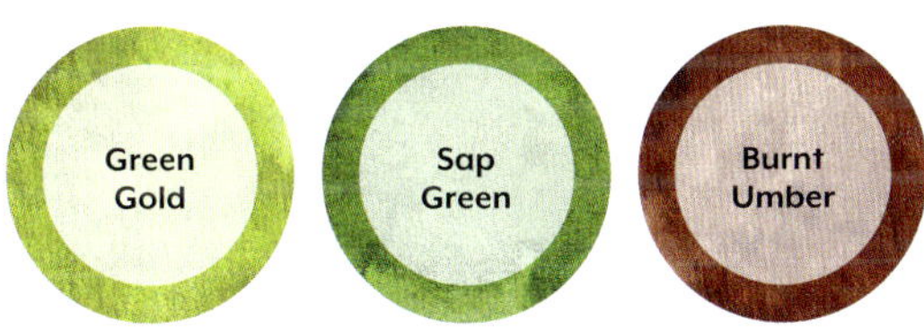

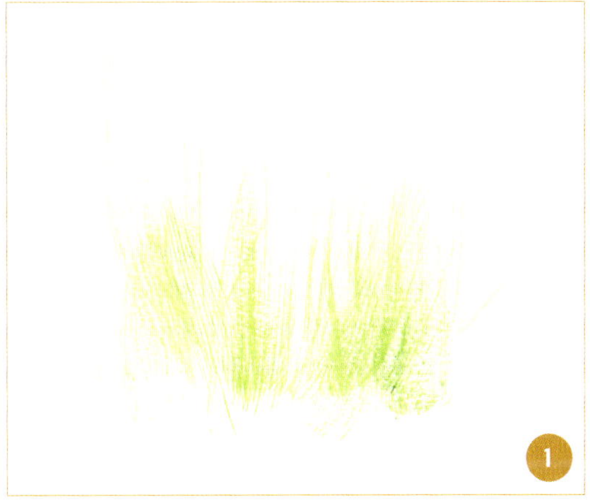

Step 1: Start by putting green gold on your palette. Wet your size 2 fan brush a little and dip it into the paint. If you don't have a fan brush yet, don't worry . . . just use the tip of your size 1 brush. Swoop it across the paper, painting the first layer of the grass tuft. Leave plenty of white space and then let it dry completely.

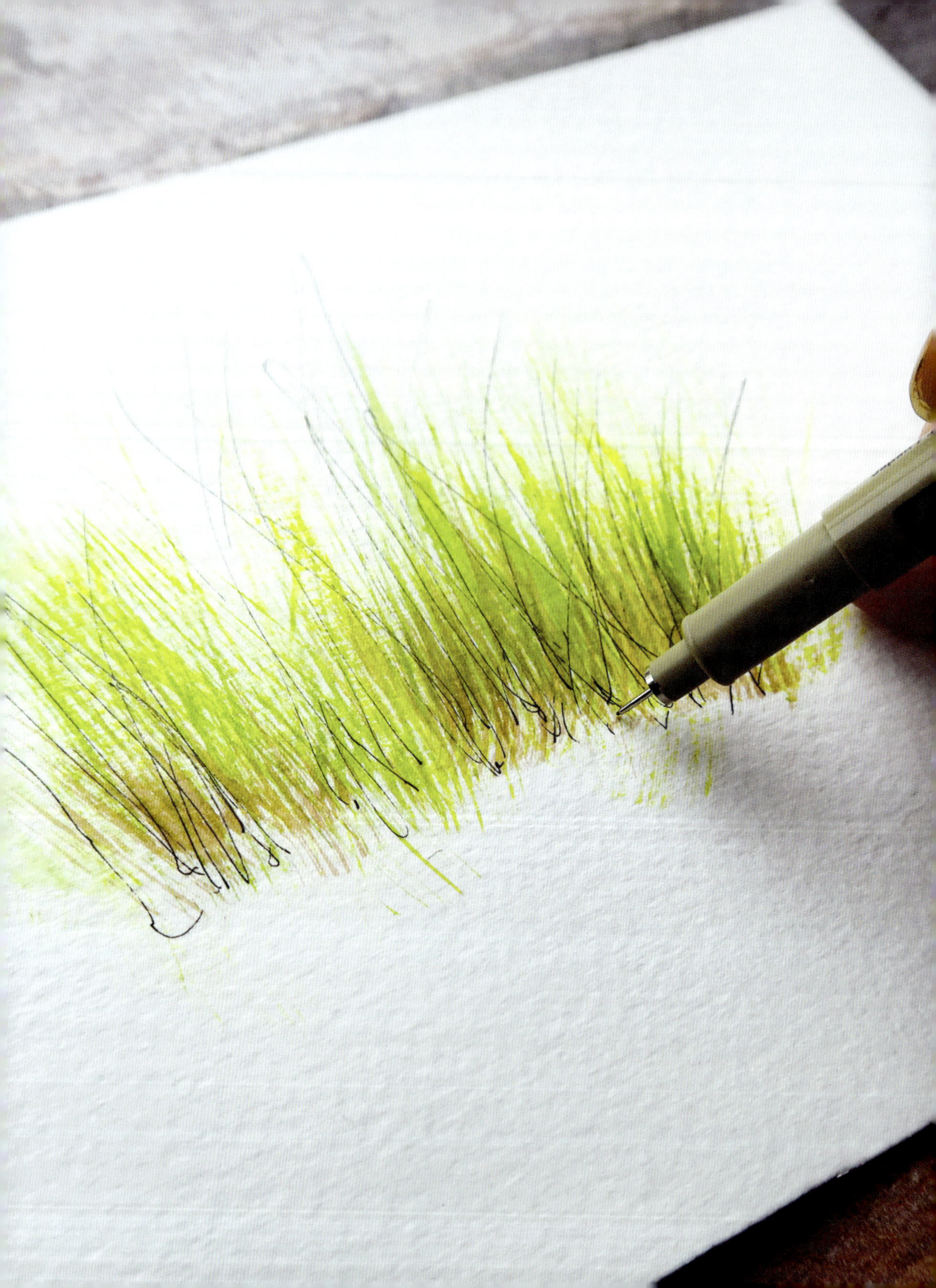

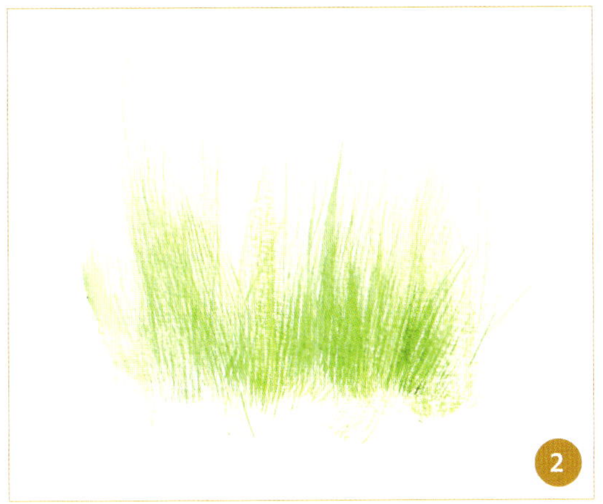

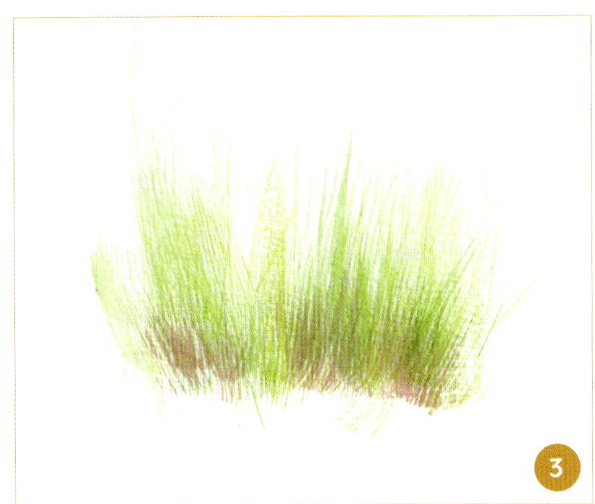

Step 2: Repeat the first step, but use sap green this time. Don't paint all over—let the green gold shine through. Give this some time to dry.

Step 3: Finally, do it again but with burnt umber. This time, only paint at the bottom of the tuft.

Step 4: Once dry, finish off the sketch with long lines with the 005 fineliner. This will give your tuft a bit more texture and definition. Your feather grass is now ready to take the stage.

Well done! That was your final grass! Now you can get a cup of tea and enjoy your progress before turning the page.

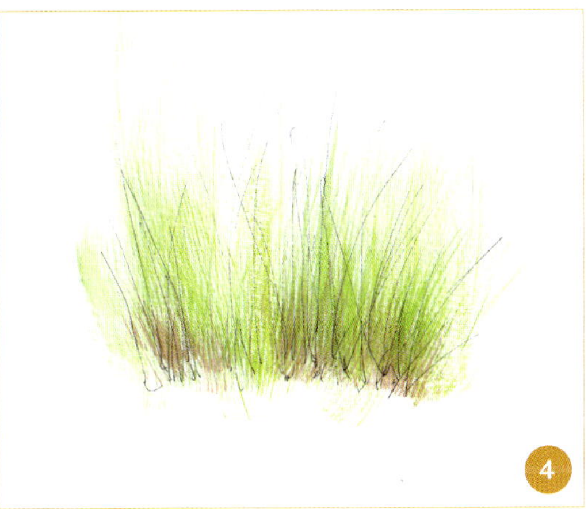

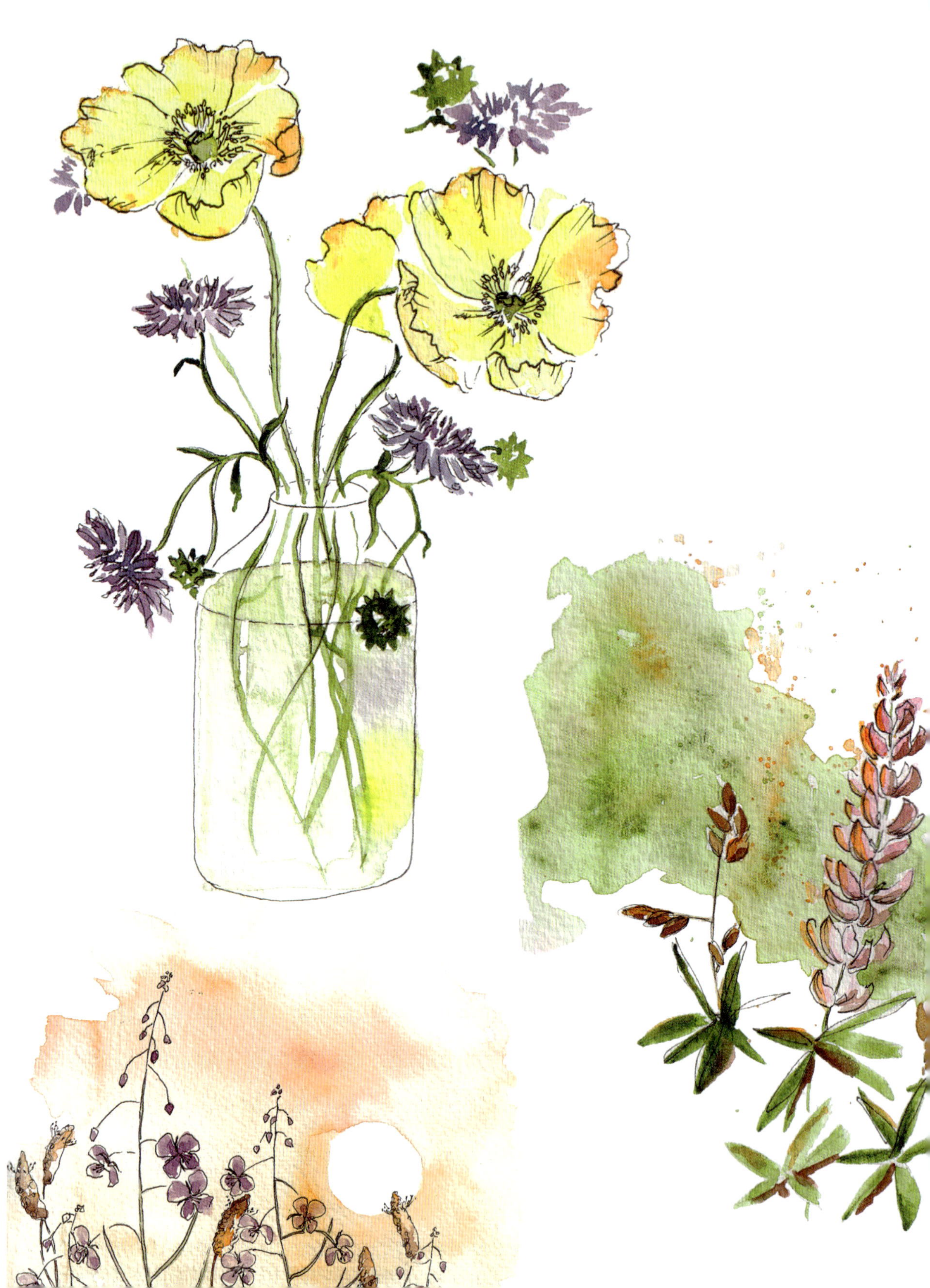

part IV
four dreamy meadow compositions

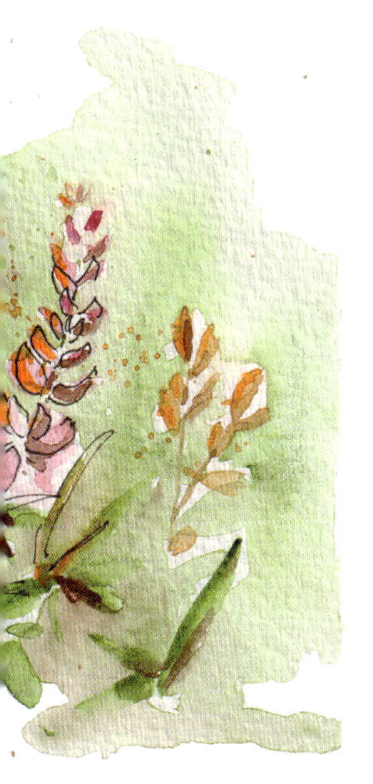

Wow, you are amazing! You just finished sixteen blooms and five grasses! And I hope you feel ready to put it all together in beautiful compositions. As mentioned earlier, you want to start thinking now about how to build your compositions before you even begin to paint. What will be in the foreground, background and middle ground? Where do you want the focal point to be? What mood do you want this painting to radiate? Of course, I will help you here in the book. I can't wait to walk you through four wonderful compositions filled with wildflower magic. Let's get to it.

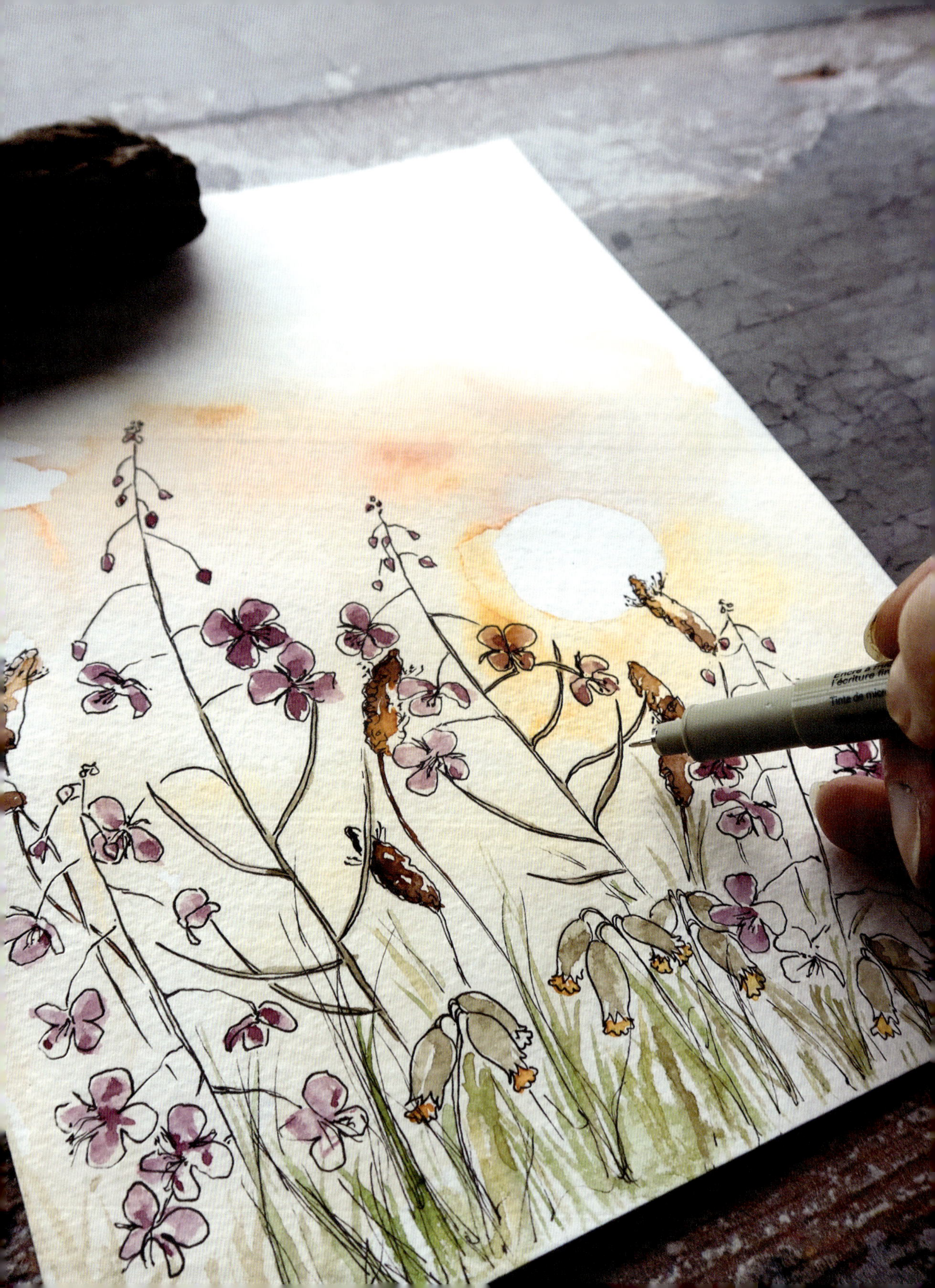

a meadow at the brink of day

Imagine you just woke up; you made your first cup of morning coffee and you're still in your robe as you step out into your garden. The birds are awake and are singing all around. You see the sun rising behind the trees. It greets you with rays of light that paint the entire garden in warm yellow tones, like everything has got a fancy Instagram filter . . . but this is real.

We are going to create this stunning golden hour with the underpainting technique that I talked about on page 14. And then we will fill the meadow with fireweeds, cowslips and some English plantains dancing in the rising sun.

Materials

Paper: Canson Montval 300gsm (140lb) cold press
Pencil and eraser
Watercolor brush sizes: 8 and 4
Water and cloth
Palette
Fineliner sizes: 01 and 005

Colors

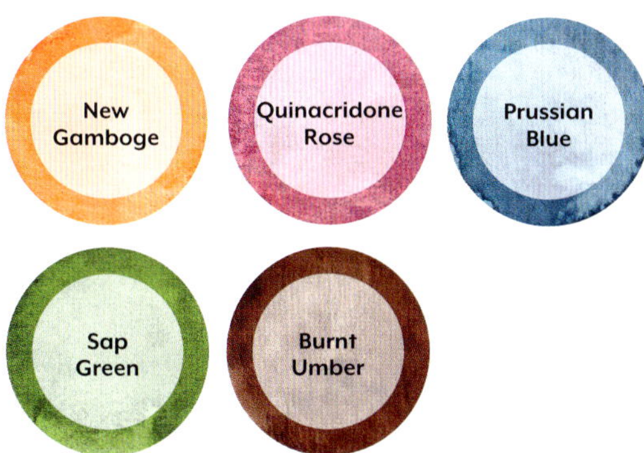

Mixes

For the sunrise mood, mix 50% new gamboge and 50% quinacridone rose.

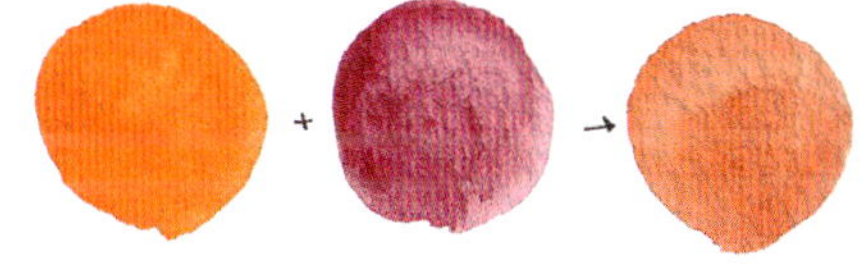

The flowers on the fireweed are painted in a mix of 90% quinacridone rose and just 10% Prussian blue.

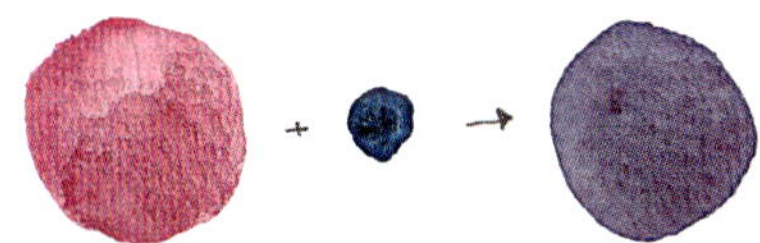

Grasses are painted in two 50/50 mixes: A mix of sap green with a watered-down version of the purple mix from the fireweed flowers and then a mix of sap green with new gamboge.

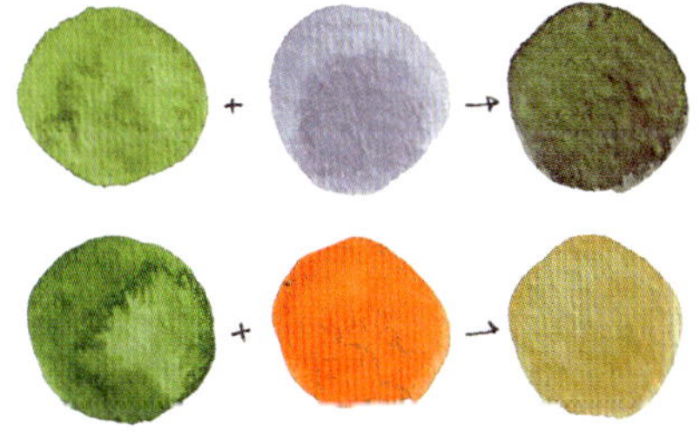

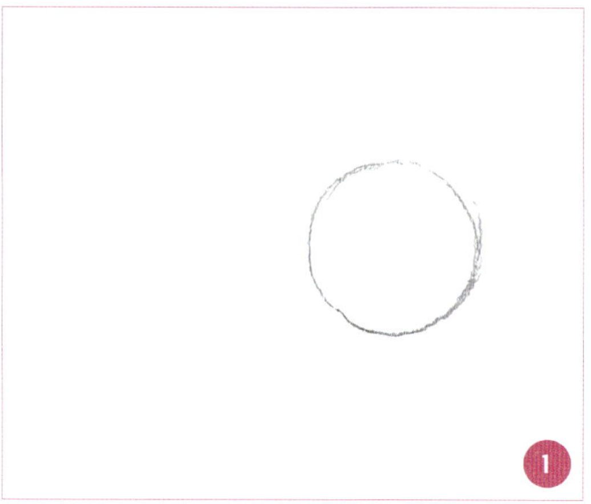

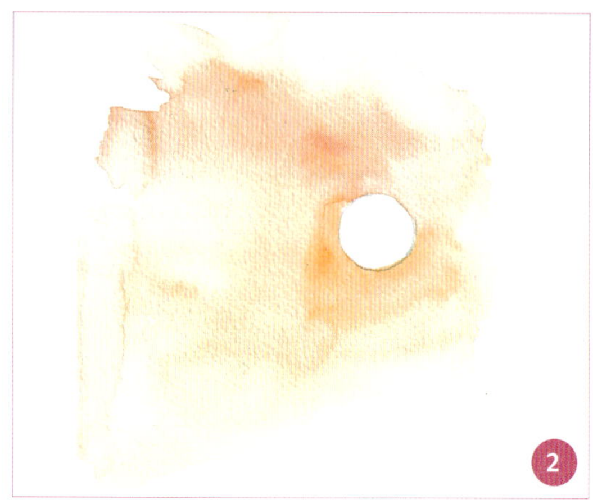

Step 1: Start by drawing a circle in pencil on the right side of the paper.

Step 2: We are going to create a sunrise mood by using the underpainting technique I talked about on page 14. So, grab a palette and get a mix of new gamboge and quinacridone rose ready. Wet the paper with a big size 8 brush, but leave the pencil circle clear of water so you still have a space for the sun. Paint the wet paper with new gamboge using the wet-on-wet technique. To get a nice sunrise glow, dip the brush into the paint mix you created before and use this on the area above the sun.

Step 3: When the paint is completely dry, carefully erase the pencil line around the sun.

Step 4: Now we are ready to plant some flowers in our sunrise meadow and we are going to start with fireweeds. A great tip is to locate pages 57, 33 and 113 where you learned how to sketch fireweeds, cowslips and English plantains and put bookmarks there so they are easy to find. Use a pencil to draw curved lines where you want to place your fireweeds. Let the longest stem be opposite the sun and draw one on the right side of the sun for a nice balance.

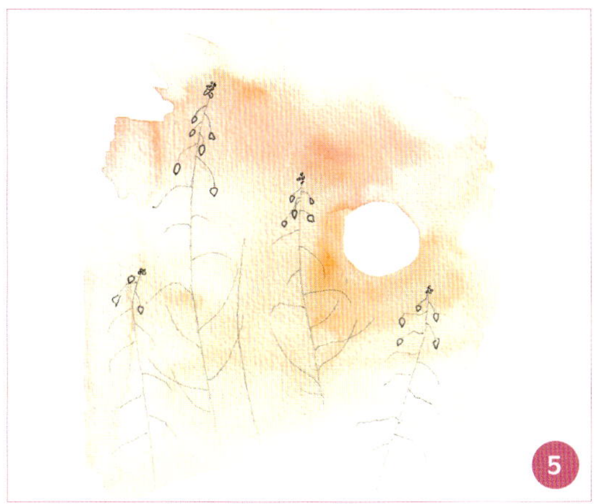

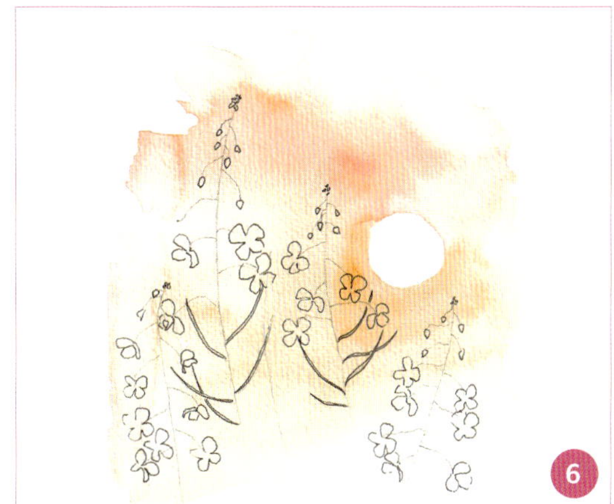

Step 5: Draw extra guides for smaller stems on the fireweeds with your pencil and then grab your 01 fineliner. Draw all the small buds at the top of the stems.

Step 6: Continue with the fireweeds by drawing flowers and seedpods with the 01 fineliner.

Step 7: Finish the flowers by drawing the stems, still using the 01 fineliner. At the bottom of the page, let the stems stop at different heights so you have room for cowslips. When you are done, you can erase the pencil guides. Don't put your eraser too far away.

Step 8: Draw the pencil guides for the cowslips at the bottom of the page.

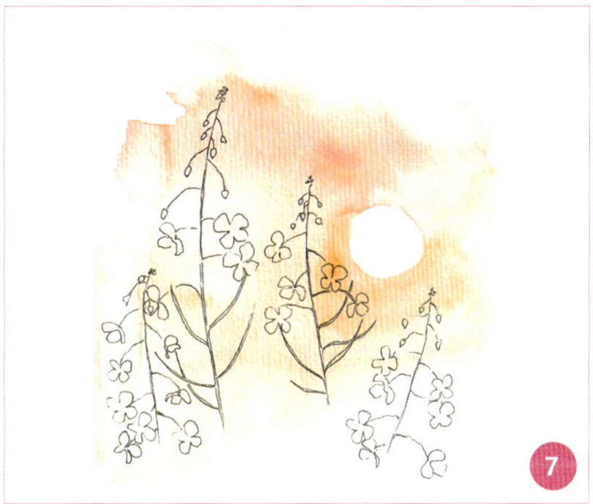

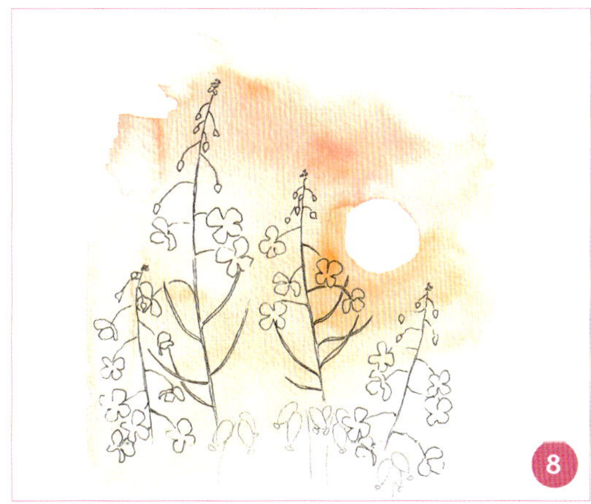

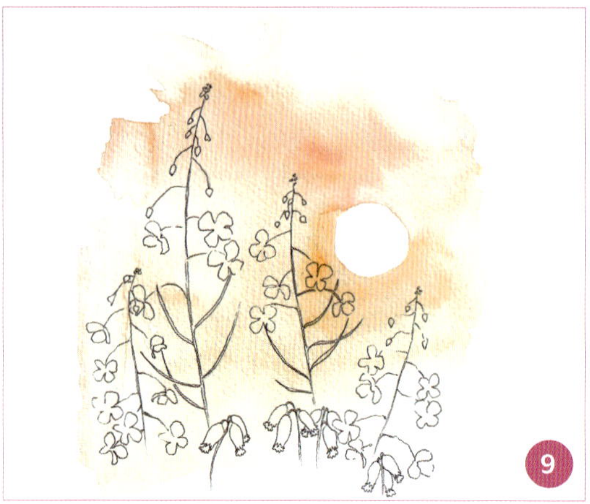

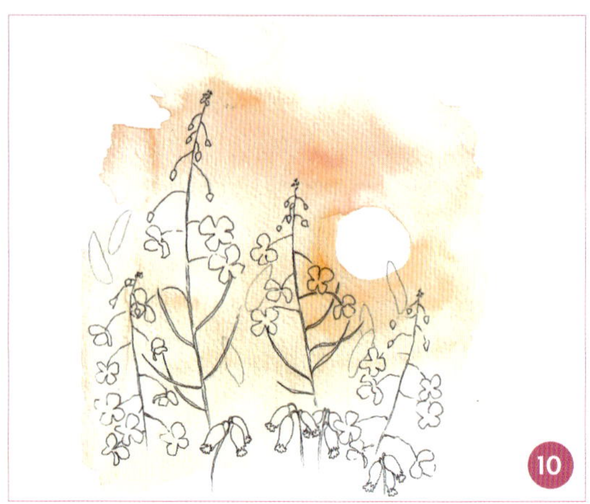

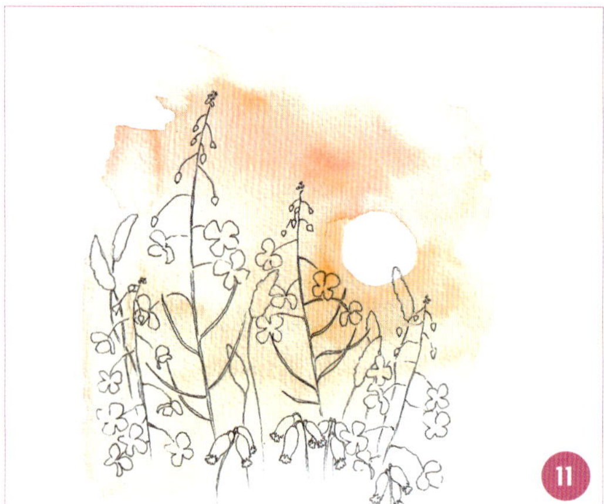

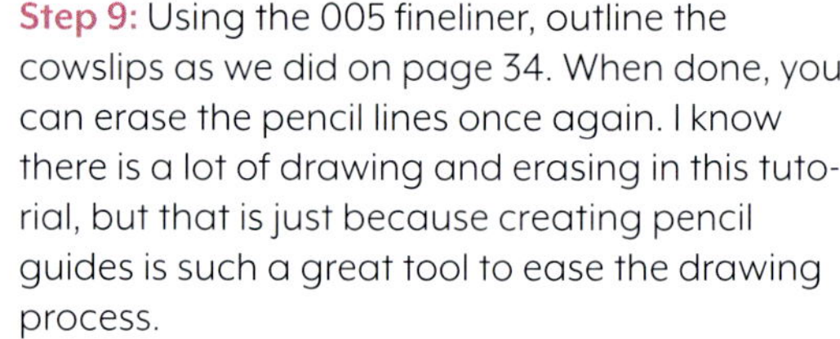

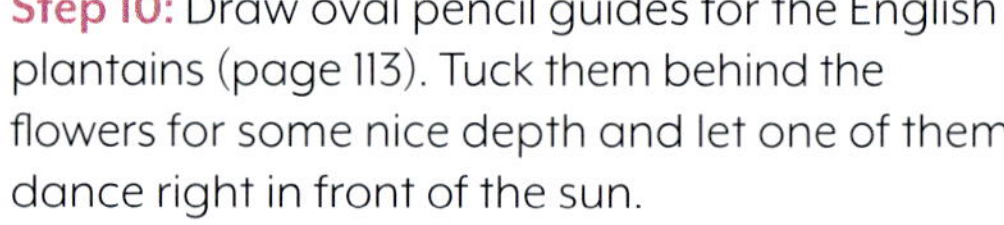

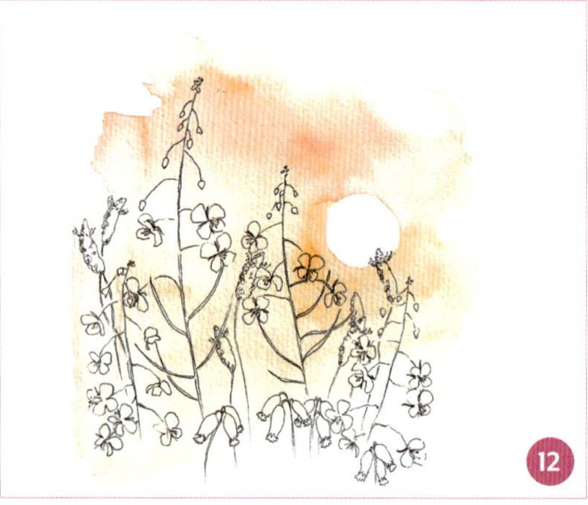

Step 9: Using the 005 fineliner, outline the cowslips as we did on page 34. When done, you can erase the pencil lines once again. I know there is a lot of drawing and erasing in this tutorial, but that is just because creating pencil guides is such a great tool to ease the drawing process.

Step 10: Draw oval pencil guides for the English plantains (page 113). Tuck them behind the flowers for some nice depth and let one of them dance right in front of the sun.

Step 11: With the 01 fineliner, create a rough outline for the English plantains like we did on page 115. Give each a long, curved stem. Be careful to keep them behind the other elements in the drawing. Erase the pencil guides.

Step 12: With the 005 fineliner, add details like seeds and texture on the plantains (page 115) and details on the fireweeds (page 58).

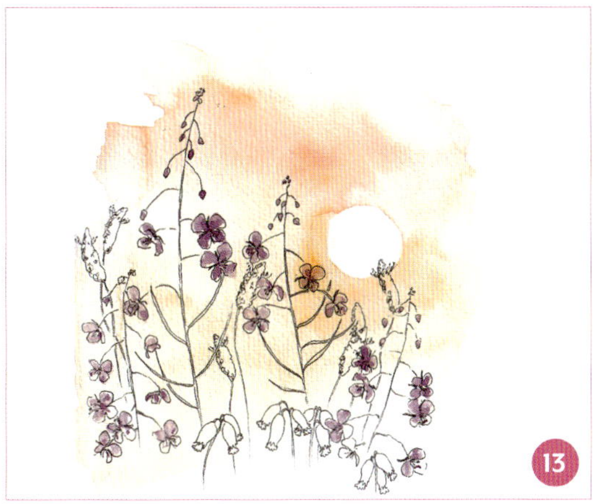

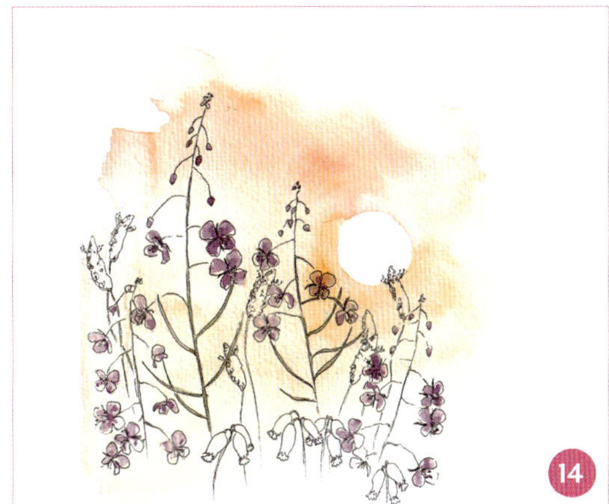

Step 13: Mix quinacridone rose with a bit of Prussian blue. With your size 4 brush, paint the flowers and buds on the fireweeds.

Step 14: Add a bit of water and sap green to the flower mix from Step 13 and paint the seedpods on the fireweeds.

Step 15: Load your brush with burnt umber and paint the English plantains with lots of white space. While it's still wet, drip in new gamboge on the side of the grass that is turning toward the sun for an even warmer glow.

Step 16: Paint the yellow part of the flower on the cowslips in new gamboge using the same brush.

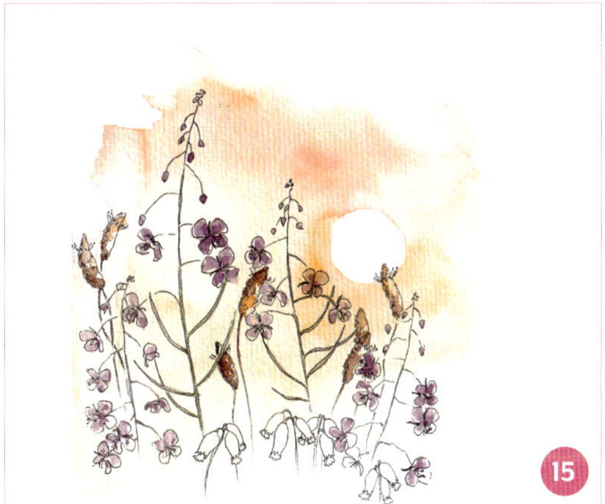

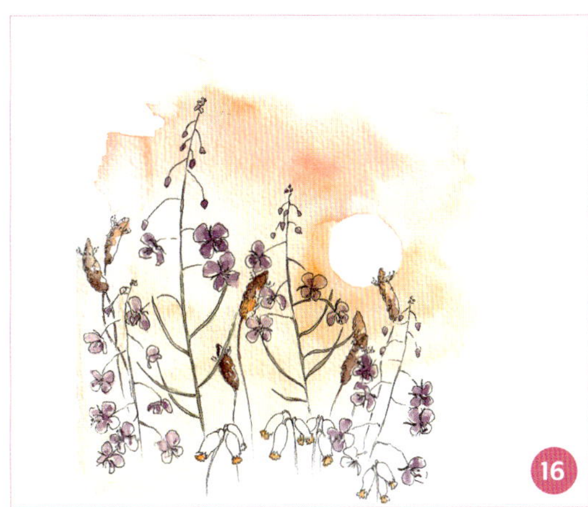

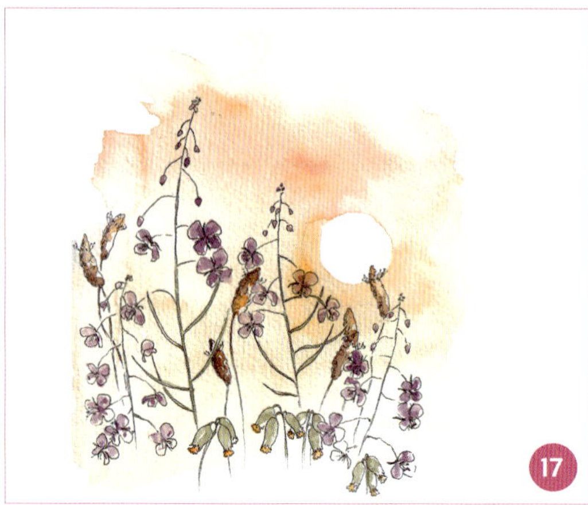

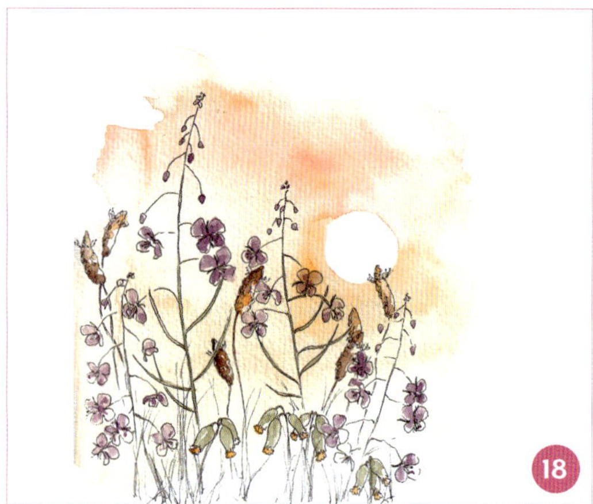

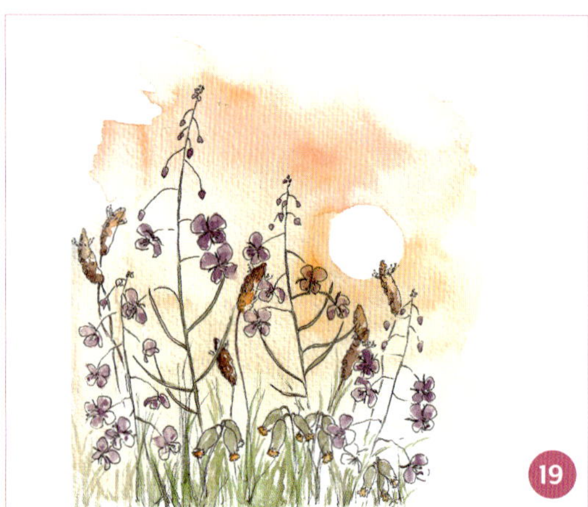

Step 17: Locate the mix you created previously for the fireweed seedpods and use it to paint the greens on the cowslips. This will create nice and cohesive colors, and we like that.

Step 18: Draw loose grass at the bottom of the page with your 01 fineliner and keep it super loose.

Step 19: Prepare the last two mixes of paint now. First, a new mix of sap green with new gamboge and then the fireweed seedpod mix from Steps 14 and 17. Paint grass loosely at the bottom with the size 4 brush, switching among the two mixes and a vibrant sap green. Let some of the grass dance in front of the flowers, and some behind. Continue the grass all the way to the edge of the left side of the paper.

You are done! Breathe in deeply. Take in the feeling of a warm morning where everything is new, and you have all the time in the world. You can almost taste that first cup of coffee. It's the best.

a sunlit flower field

I am the biggest sun girl you can imagine. I just love to stand facing the sun, soaking it all up (with sunscreen, of course). And flowers are just the same. They get so much important nutrition from the sun, so in this tutorial we are going to show beautiful, life-giving sunlight. In the warm sun, we experience very clear, dark shadows and vibrant colors. We are going to do this by diving into a magical flower field of lupins and cock's-foot grass.

Materials

Paper: Canson Montval 300gsm (140lb) cold press

Pencil and eraser

Watercolor brush sizes: 4 and 8

Water and cloth

Palette

Fineliner sizes: 01 and 005

Colors

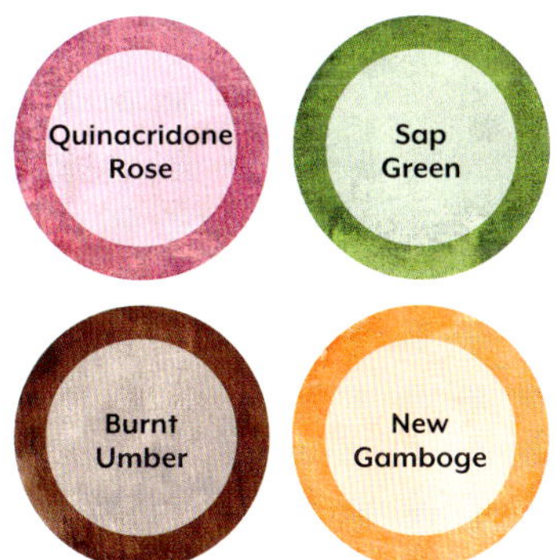

Mix

For the grasses, make a mix of an even amount of sap green, burnt umber and new gamboge.

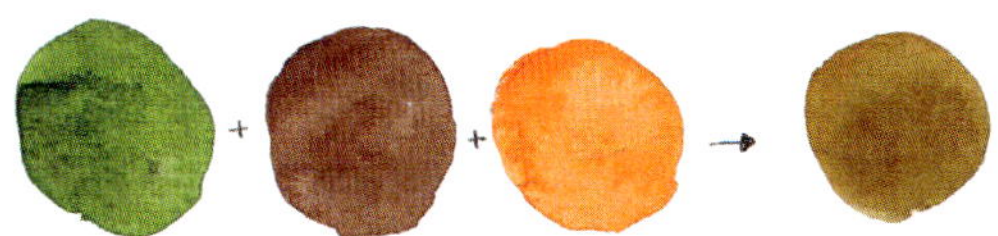

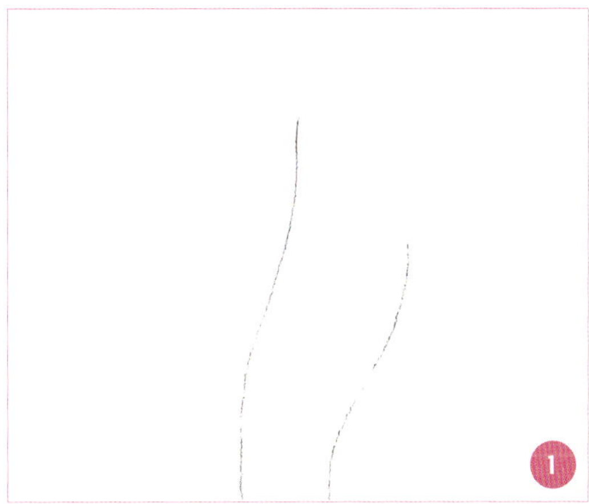

Step 1: First, put two pretty bookmarks on pages 79 and 111 so you can follow the process of drawing the lupins and cock's-foot as we go into this composition. Draw the two main flower stems of our lupins in pencil. Let the left stem be taller than the right, and have them bending a bit for movement. They are swaying toward the sun that we imagine is on the left side.

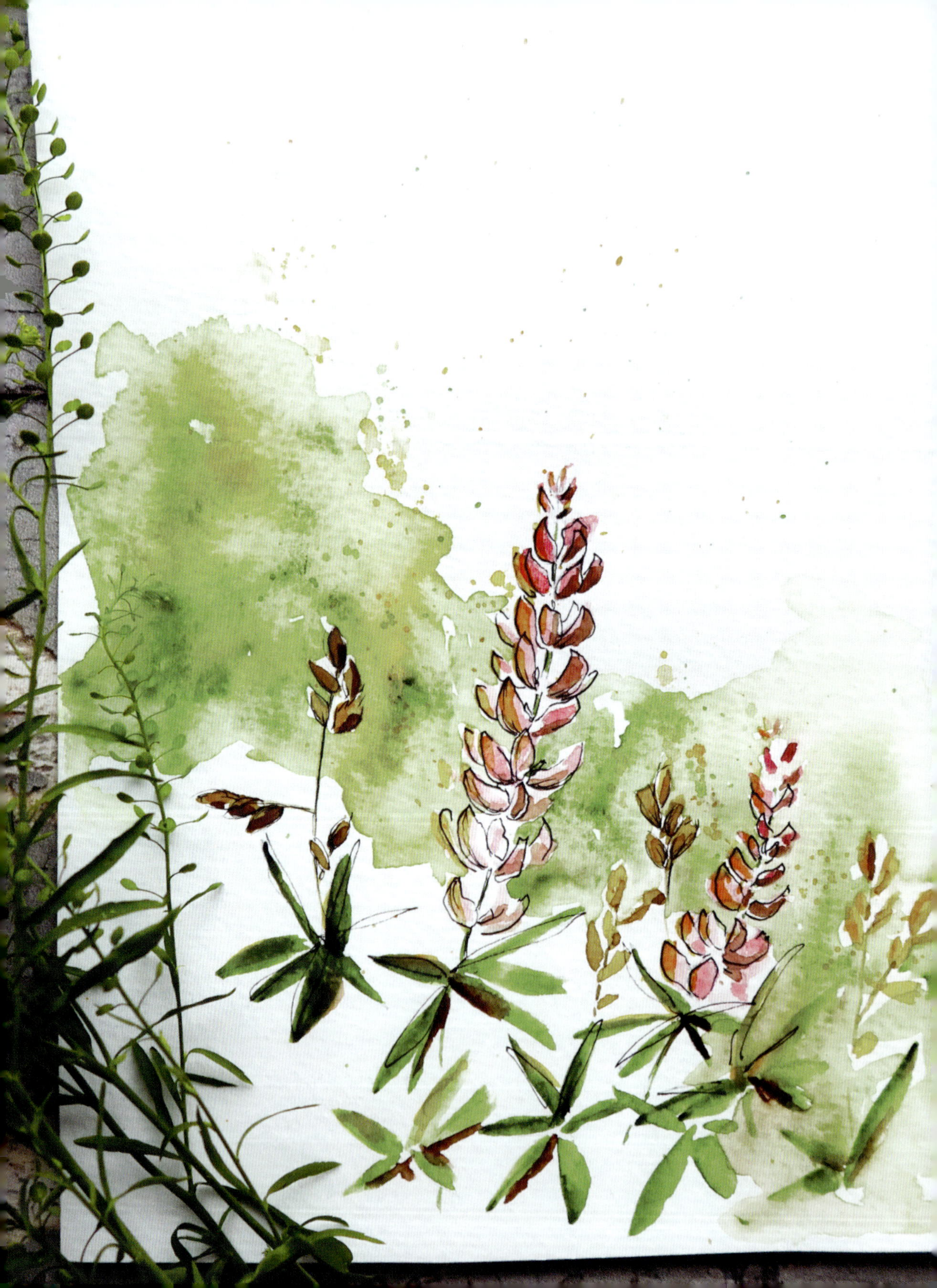

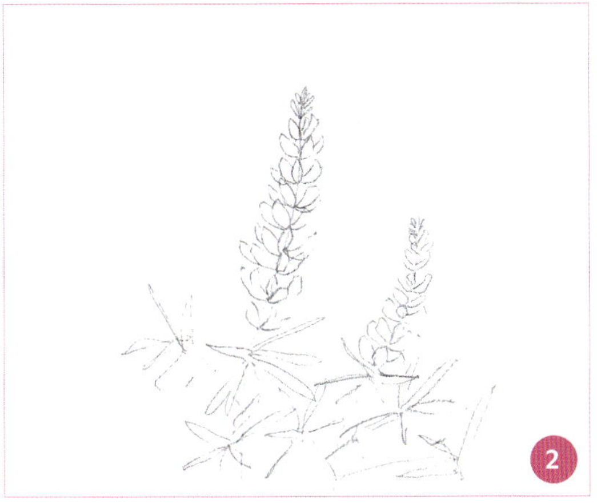

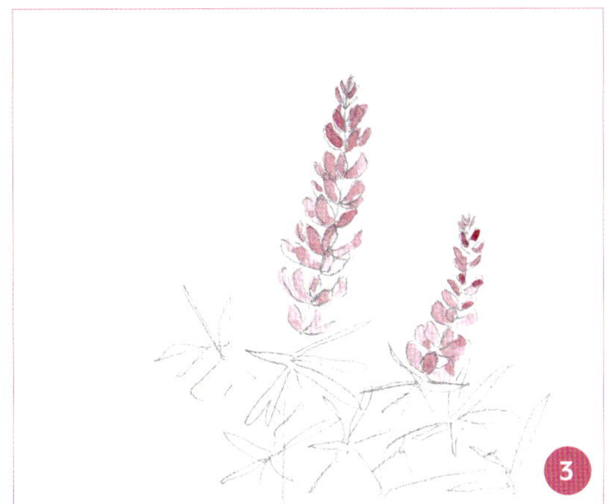

Step 2: Following the tutorial from page 79 you just bookmarked, continue the pencil guide by drawing petals and leaves on the two lupins.

Step 3: When you are happy with your guide, grab your size 4 brush and let's get some color in there. Paint the flower petals in a watery quinacridone rose.

Step 4: While it dries, draw a few lines with side branches in pencil as guides for the grass behind the lupins.

Step 5: Get your palette out and mix sap green, burnt umber and new gamboge on it. Create the brush marks on the grass florets, again using the size 4 brush.

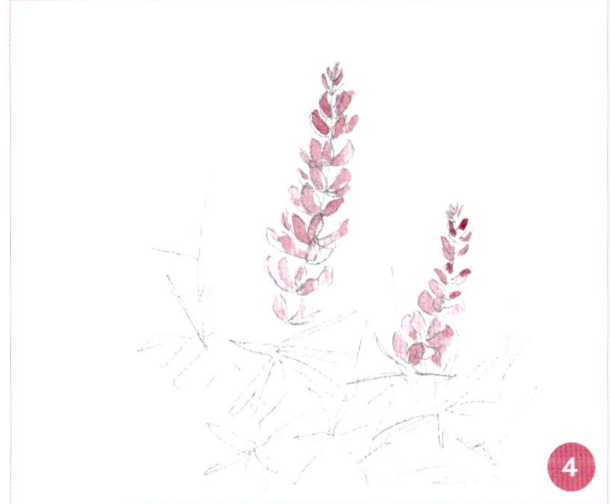

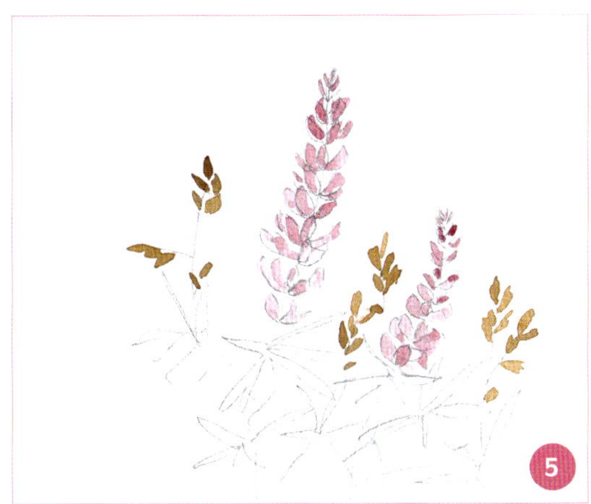

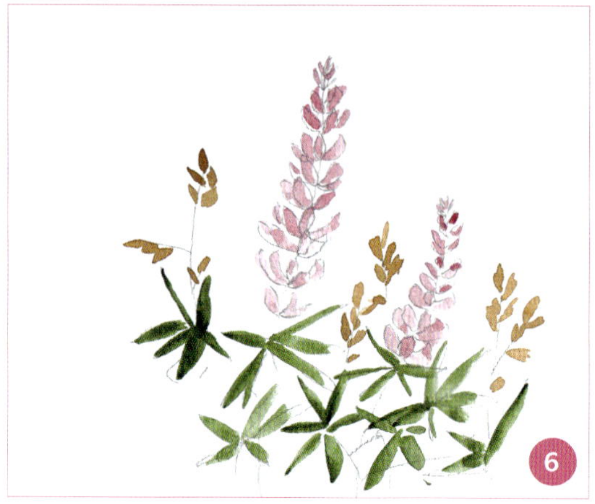

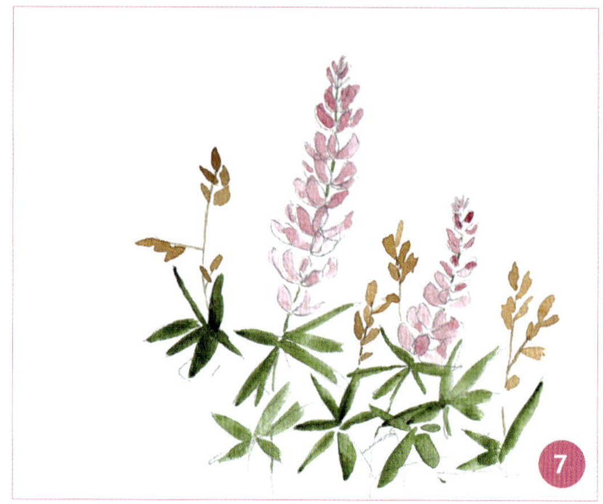

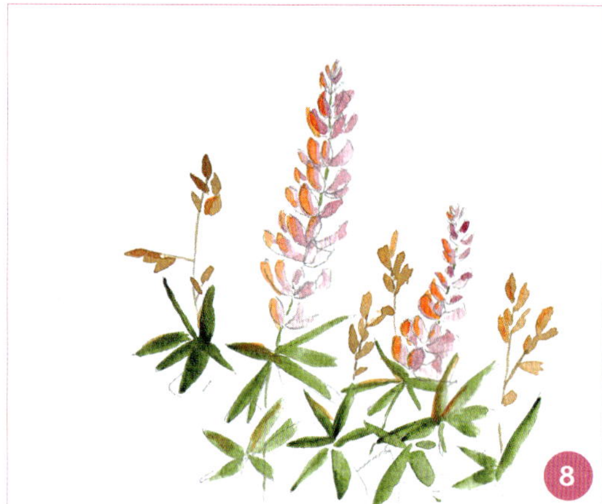

Step 6: Load your size 4 brush with sap green and loosely paint the leaves on the lupins.

Step 7: Paint the stems. On the grass, use the brown mix from Step 5 and on the lupins, the sap green.

Step 8: Now it's time to add some sunshine to this sketch. First imagine that the sun is on the left side of the flowers, just outside of the paper. Paint the left side of all the flower petals and grass florets in new gamboge as a second layer.

Step 9: To create a dark shadow, paint the right side in burnt umber. Give some of the leaves this color as well so they appear to be hiding in a few places in the shade. Notice how we are using a warm color as the shadow in this sketch. That is because we are in bright warm sun, and there is no cool shade in this scene. When the flowers and grass are completely dry, erase the pencil lines.

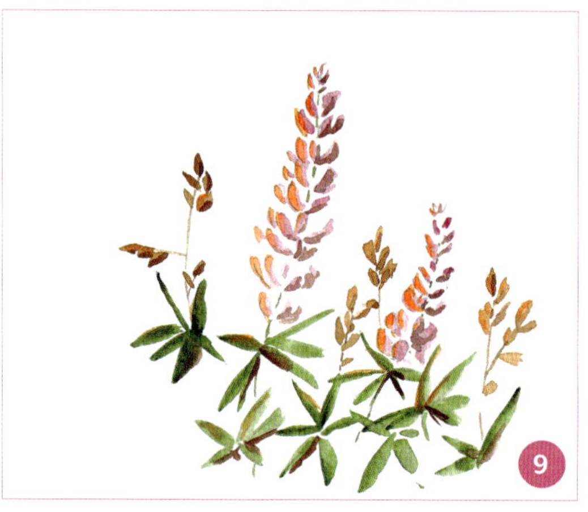

    Ink & Wash Wildflowers

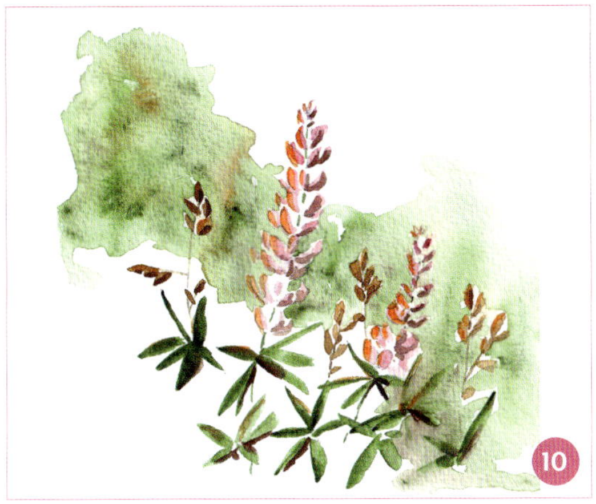

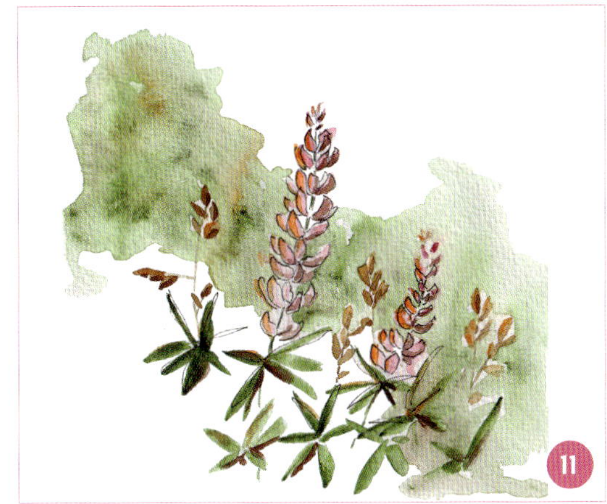

Step 10: Creating a dynamic background like this is similar to creating music, so putting on some jazz would not hurt the process. Wet the paper behind the flowers with clean water and with the big size 8 brush, drip in sap green. At the left side of the wash closest to the sun, drip in new gamboge. Add some burnt umber in a few places to vary the mix. This can take a while to dry, so this might be a good time to go out for a walk and soak up some of sunshine—or maybe take a dance break to the music.

Step 11: When you come back to your painting, get your 01 fineliner and draw the outline of the flower petals on the two lupins. Draw very loosely on the leaves as well. Outline some of them and add a few extra ones that will stand without paint.

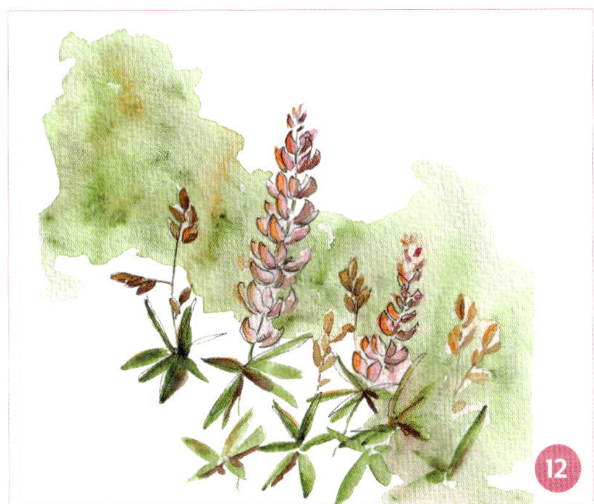

Step 12: Take your 005 fineliner and draw details on the grass like we did on page 112 and direction lines on the lupin petals like we did on page 83.

Step 13: Finally, load your size 4 brush with new gamboge. Splatter some paint on the top of the paper, all the way down to the flowers. Repeat this first with sap green and then with clean water. This technique will give you that feeling of a warm summer field, with insects buzzing happily around in the sun.

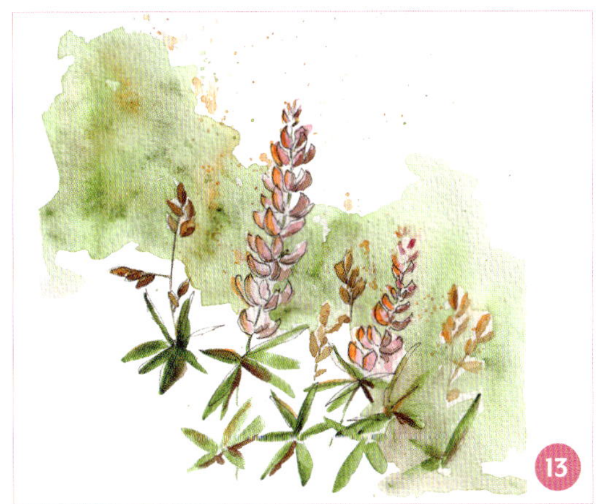

Incredible! Do you also just want to sit and enjoy a flower field and the sun's warmth on your cheeks right now? I am so with you on that!

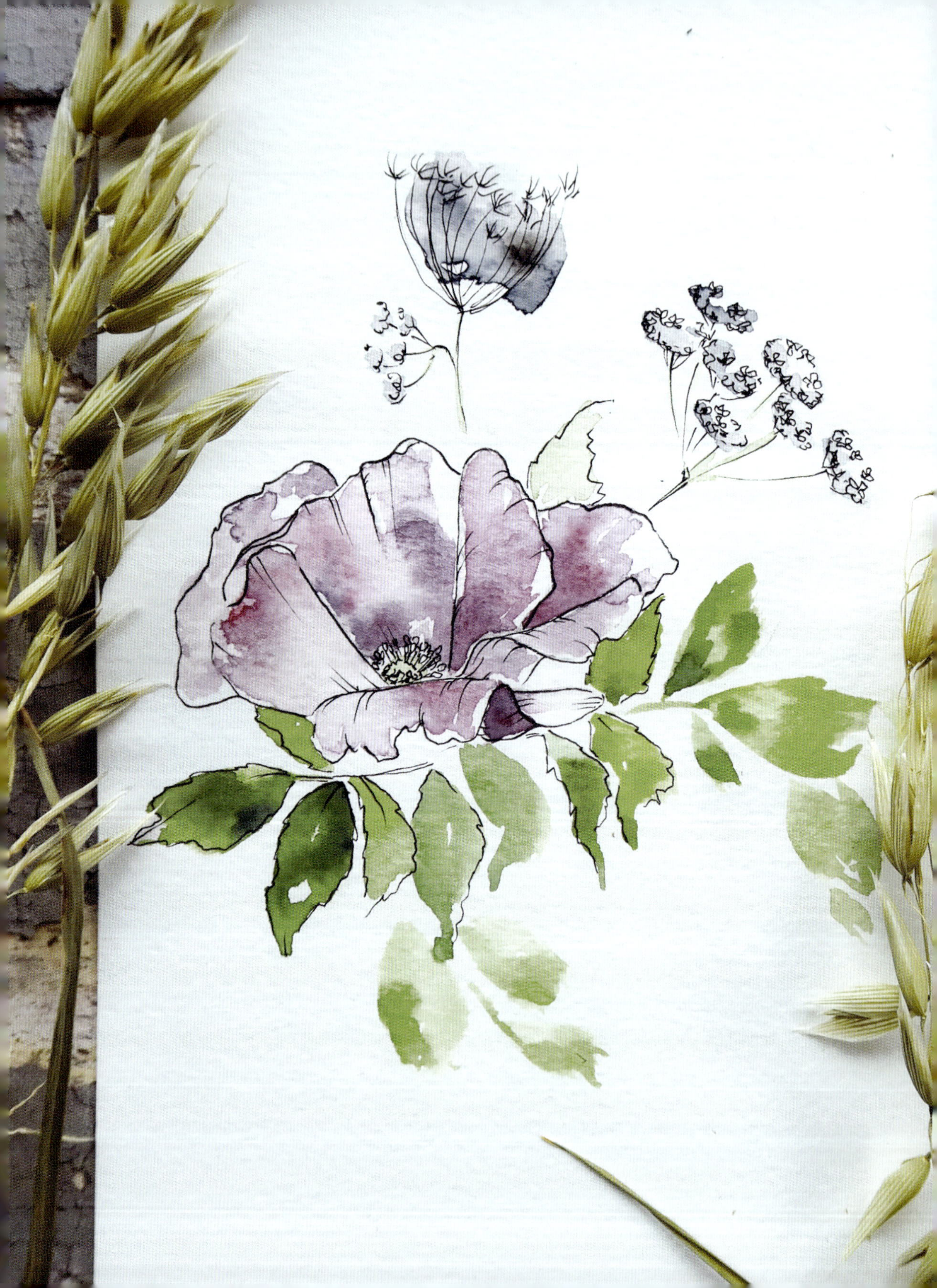

relaxing in the shade

After spending time in the sun, there is nothing as refreshing as relaxing in the shade. Just imagine: You are sitting with your back against an old oak tree, sipping on a cold lemonade, looking at the flowers while the birds are chirping. I would take that break any day over Netflix and fries. (And I love Netflix and fries!) In this tutorial, we are going to be joined in the shade by a few of my favorites: Wild roses and Queen Anne's lace. I am going to show you a super easy way to create a shadow color that works on flowers as well as greens. It's a lot easier than you think, so let's get started!

Materials

Paper: Canson Montval 300gsm (140lb) cold press

Pencil and eraser

Watercolor brush size: 4

Water and cloth

Palette

Fineliner sizes: 01 and 005

Colors

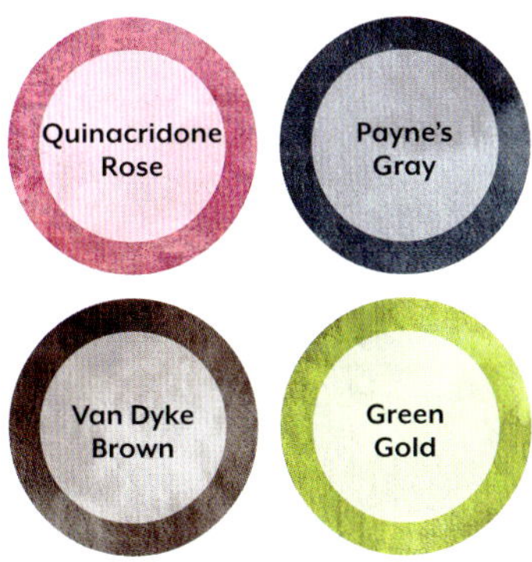

Mixes

For the rose petals, mix 50% quinacridone rose and 50% Payne's gray.

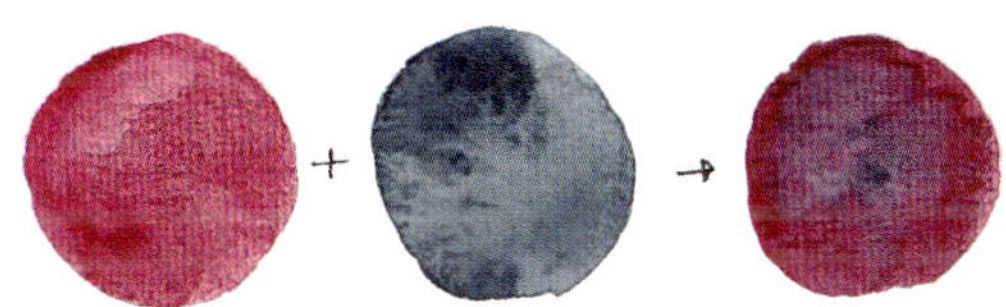

For the leaves on the rose, mix 50% green gold and 50% Payne's gray. Don't mix the colors completely—let some parts be more green and some parts more gray.

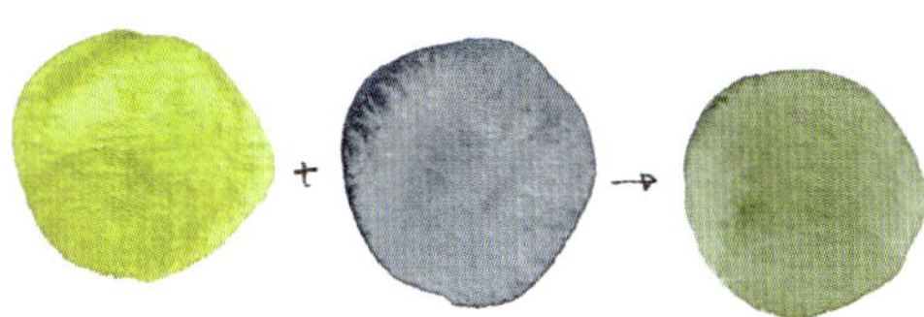

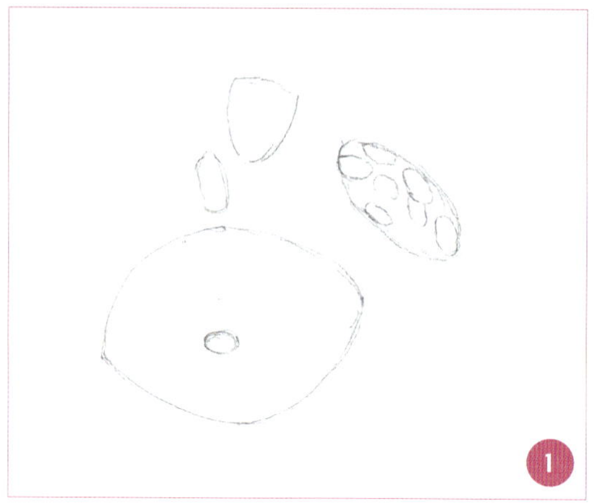

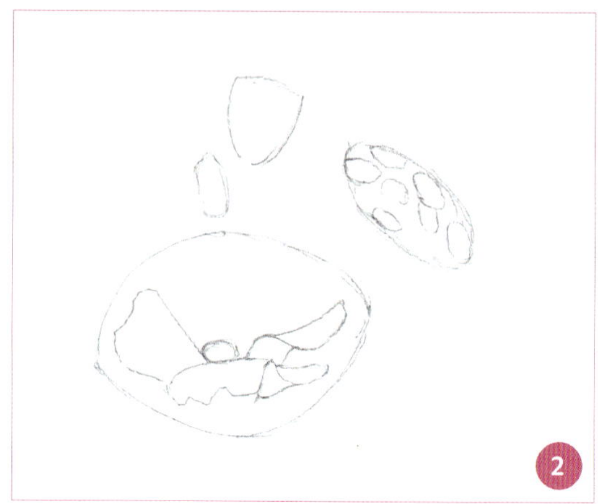

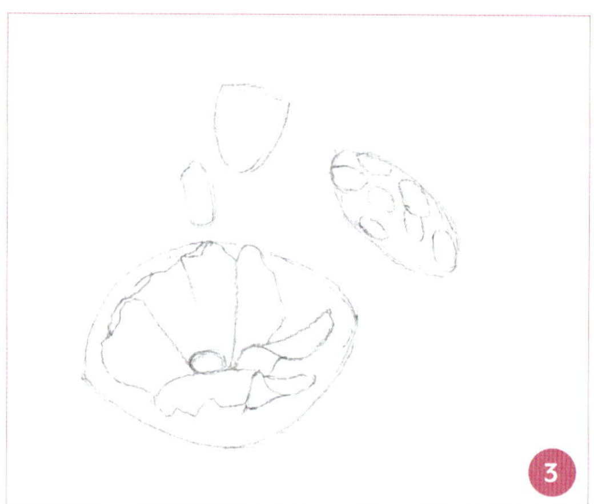

Step 1: Place your bookmarks on pages 97 and 87 so you are all set to sketch wild roses and Queen Anne's lace. Draw the guides for the rose and Queen Anne's lace in pencil. In the tutorial on page 97, we looked at the rose from the front. To shake it up, we'll see it from the side this time. That means the rose guide is shaped like an oval with a small oval center instead of a circle.

The Queen Anne's lace is shown in three growth stages: A full bloom, a wilted one and a young bud. The full bloom is shown with an oval guide with smaller oval shapes inside, the wilted beauty is an oval cut in half and the bud is an oval standing on its own.

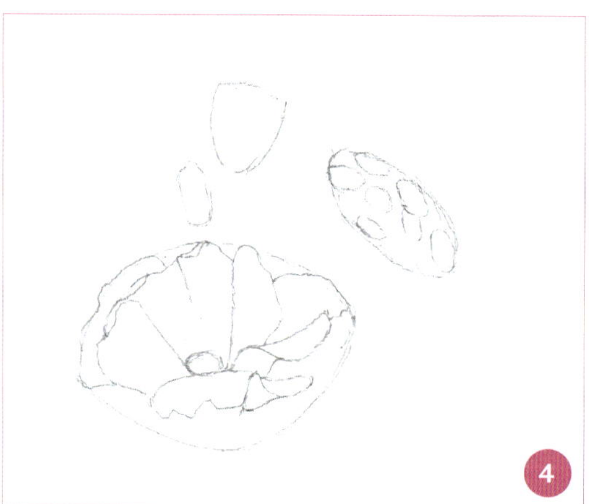

Step 2: The rose is a bit complicated, so I will walk you through the pencil sketch here. Start by drawing the front petals for the rose. These petals are foreshortened and bend downward, as explained on page 18.

Step 3: Draw petals behind the center of the rose.

Step 4: Finish the rose guide by drawing petals hiding at the back.

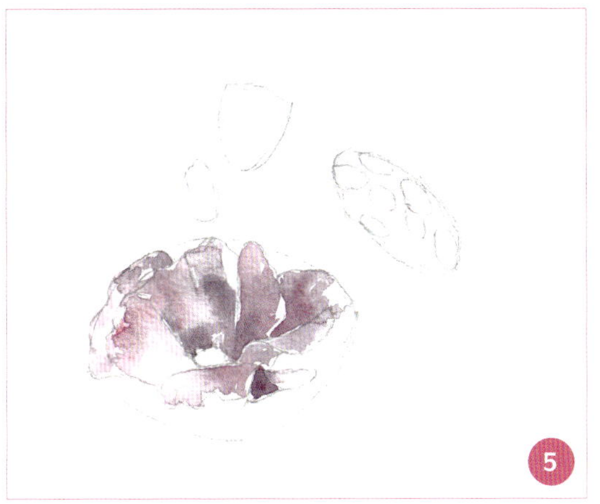

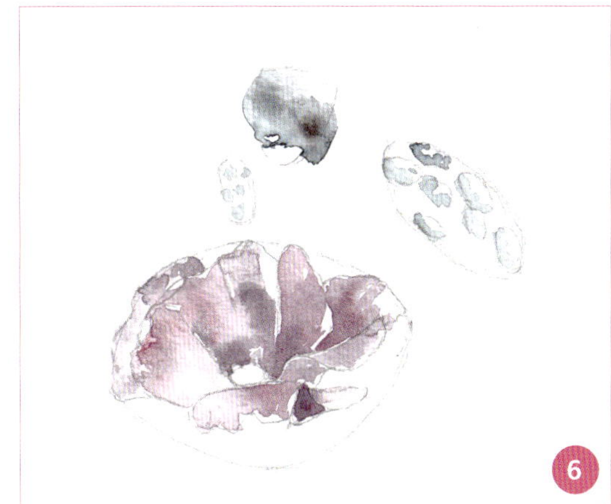

Step 5: Create a mix of quinacridone rose and Payne's gray and paint the rose petals in this mix. Payne's gray is the magical ingredient to create this cool shade. You can almost taste the cold lemonade at this point.

Step 6: Then we continue to the Queen Anne's lace blooms. Wet the inside of the wilted flower and drip in Payne's gray and Van Dyke brown. While that mingles in the water, paint the bottom part of each of the circles in the full bloom. Paint small dots in the oval guide that will become the bud.

Step 7: When everything is dry, draw the outline on the rose petals with the 01 fineliner.

Step 8: Grab your 005 fineliner and add details to the Queen Anne's lace like we did on page 89. It's important to use the smaller fineliner here so the lines don't take away from the focal point, which in this case is the rose.

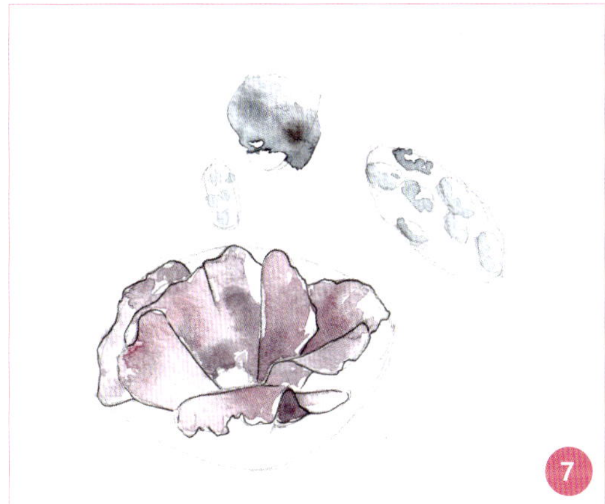

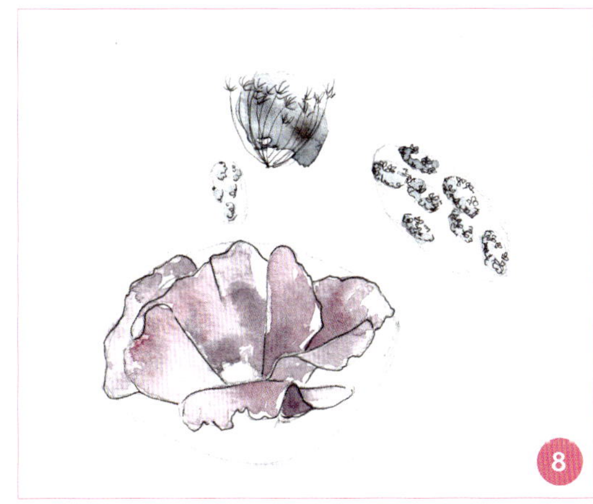

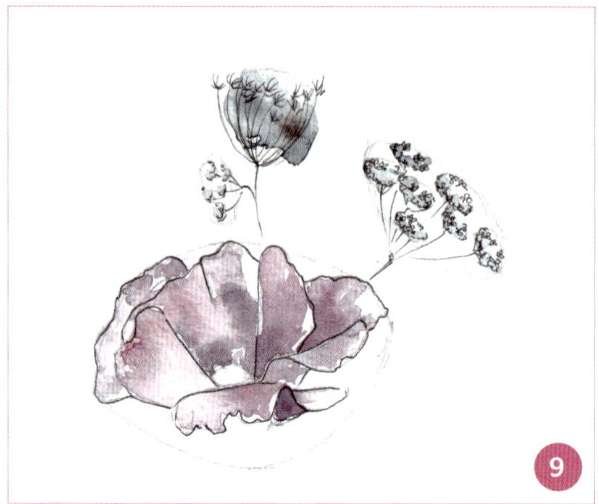 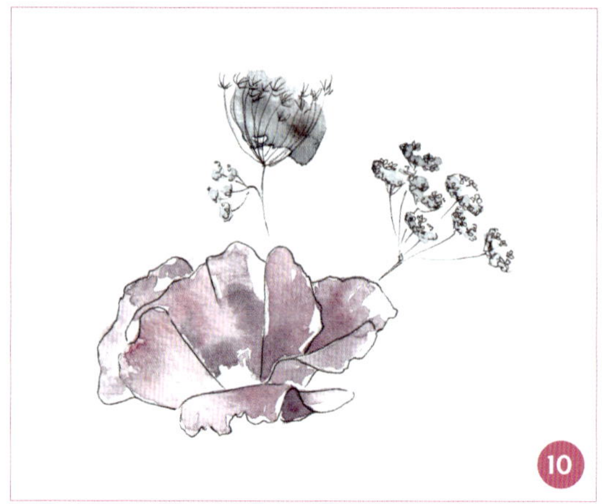

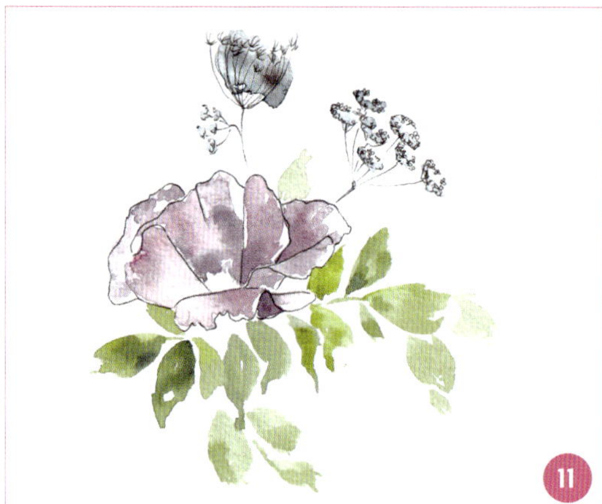

Step 9: Still using the 005 fineliner, draw the stems on the Queen Anne's lace.

Step 10: Are you happy with your sketch? Perfect! Erase the pencil lines.

Step 11: Create a loose mix of green gold with Payne's gray; don't mix the colors completely. Let some parts be more green and some more gray. Then, load your size 4 brush with this mix. Paint the rose leaves below the rose. Let some of the leaves hide behind the rose and have one peek up behind the rose as well for some nice depth and whimsy.

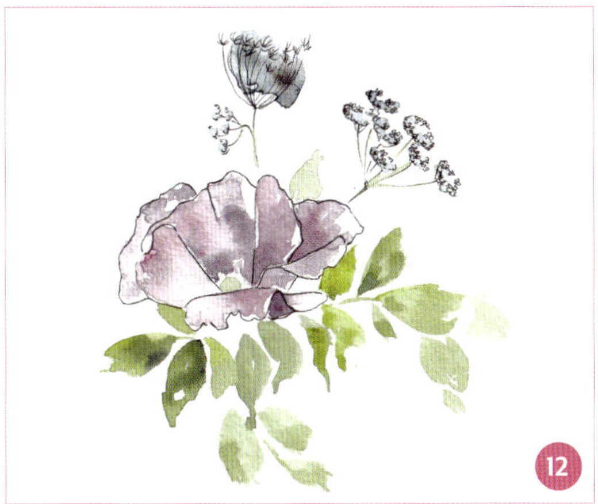

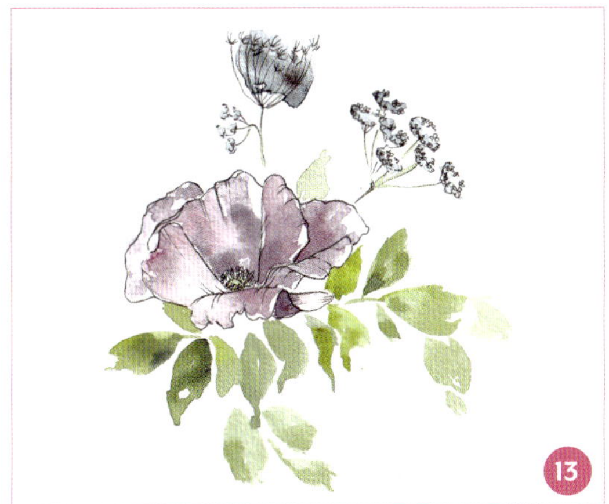

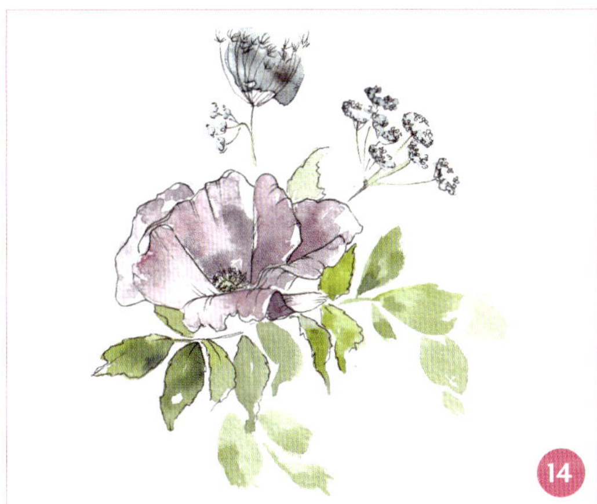

Step 12: Use the same mix from Step 11 to paint a small oval in the center of the rose and use it to give the stems on the Queen Anne's lace some color as well.

Step 13: Using the 005 fineliner, draw the details on the rose like we did on page 102. Draw seeds in the center and direction lines on the petals to show their beautiful curves.

Step 14: With the same fineliner, add details to the leaves closest to the rose. Give a few of them a curved line in the middle of the leaf as well.

And that is it! Do you see the difference it made to use the Payne's gray in all parts of the flower? It worked just like magic to create a balanced, cool color scheme. Pretty cool and super simple.

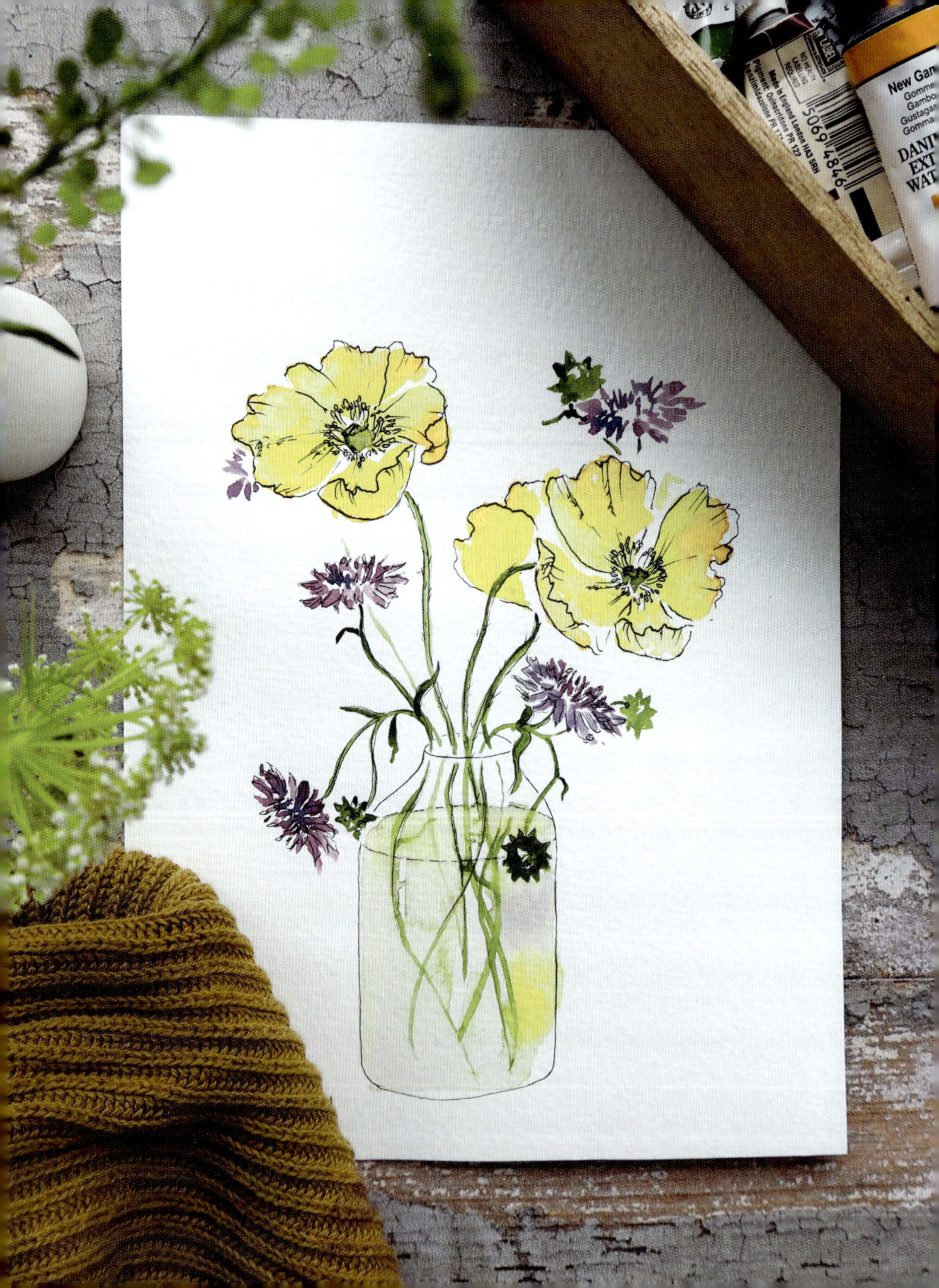

a dreamy summer posy

We are ending the book with a floral dance party. And this time, we are going to enjoy the freshly-cut Icelandic poppies with their pincushion flower backup dancers in a playful, summer posy filled with movement and energy.

We will make sure that the poppies get their Beyoncé moment by creating a hierarchy in the flowers, choosing big flower heads for a focal point and smaller dancing pincushion flowers for street-smart movement and texture. So put on some tunes and let's get started, because this will be a dance to remember.

Materials

Paper: Canson Montval 300gsm (140lb) cold press
Pencil and eraser
Watercolor brush sizes: 8 and 4
Water and cloth
Palette
Fineliner sizes: 005 and 01

Mix

For the pincushion flowers, mix 50% quinacridone rose and 50% Prussian blue.

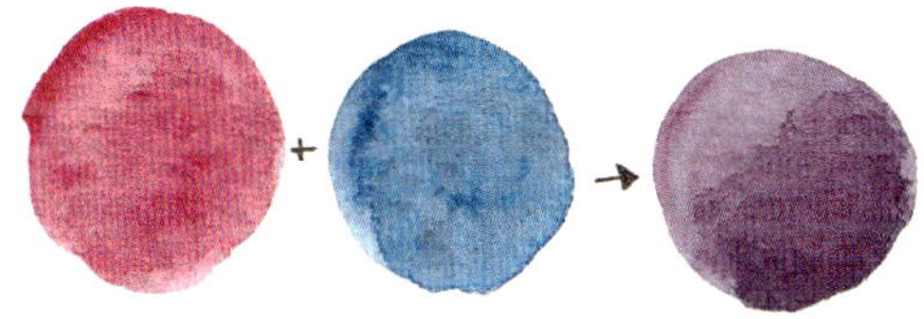

Colors

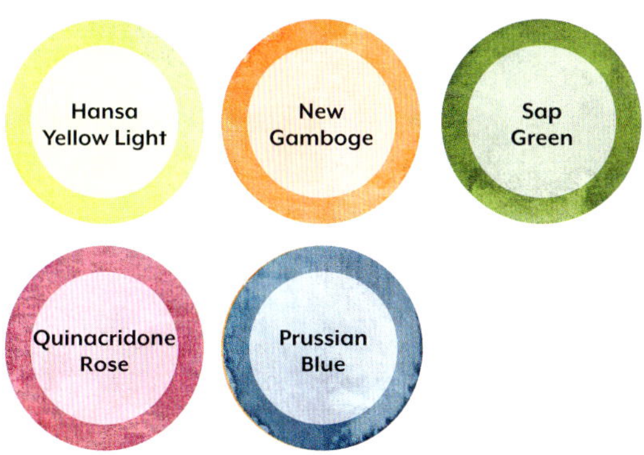

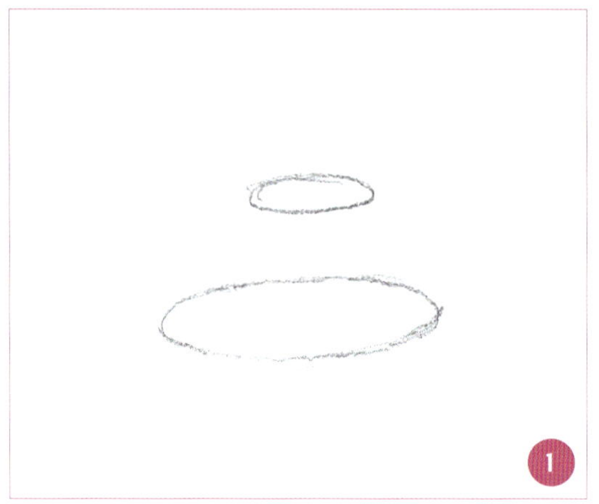

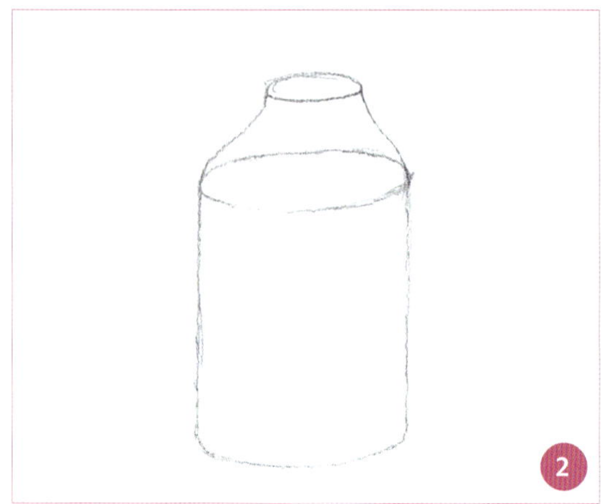

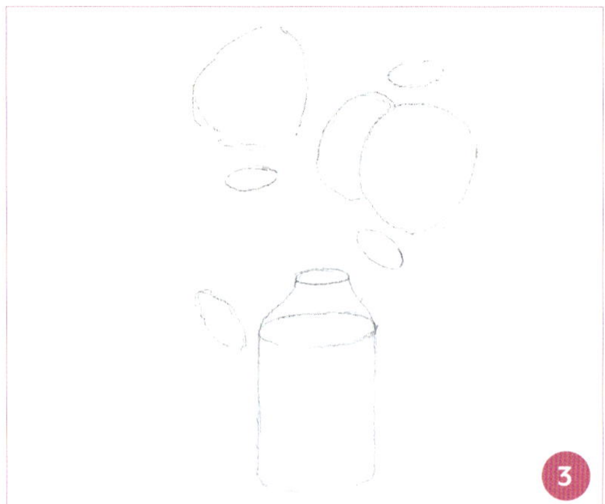

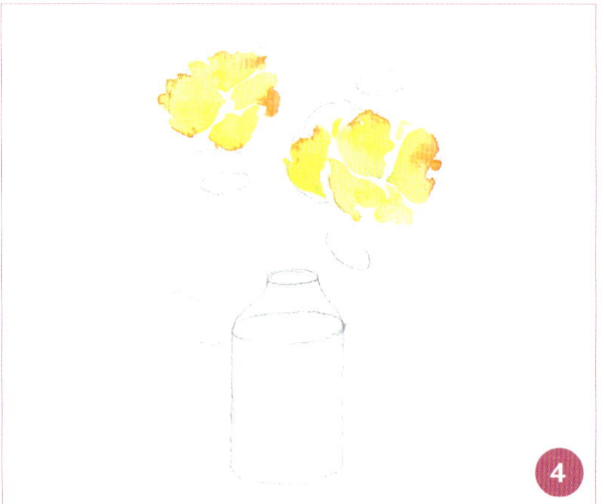

Step 1: Start by drawing two oval pencil guides, one above the other, to mark the top of the vase. The top oval should be small and the bottom one should be three times bigger.

Step 2: Still using the pencil, draw the vase by adding sides and a bottom that curves just like the oval above. Draw curved lines from the top oval to the bottom oval to give the vase a small neck.

Before drawing your blooms, find page 39 for the poppy and page 53 for the pincushion flower. Put your favorite bookmarks there and then you are ready to start sketching your flowers.

Step 3: It's time to place some blooms. Draw two big circles, still in pencil. One circle should be big but hiding behind the right circle. This area will hold our big poppies. Draw four smaller ovals dancing around in the rest of the space— these are our backup dancers.

Step 4: Grab your size 8 brush and paint the petals on the poppies in hansa yellow light as we did on page 39. Drip in a bit of new gamboge at the edge and a tiny bit of sap green in the center. Let dry.

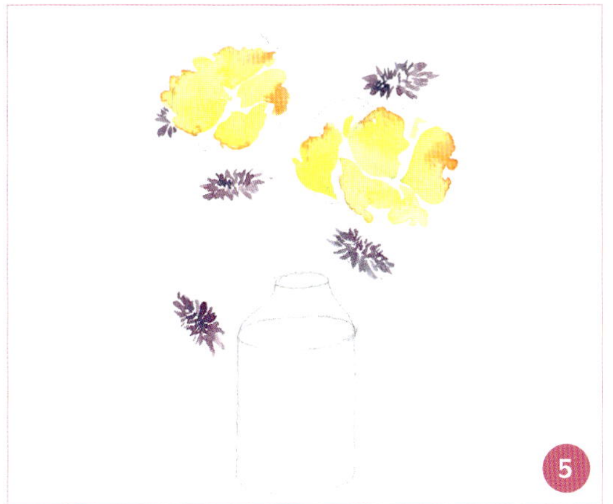

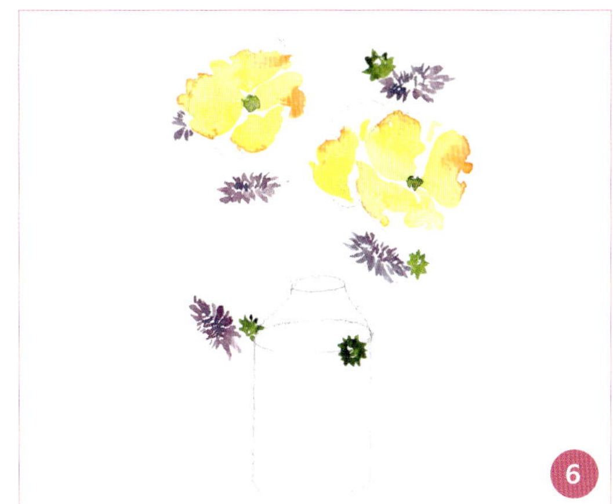

Step 5: Prepare the mix for the pincushion flowers. With the size 4 brush, paint the flowers like you learned on page 53. If you feel like you need more flowers, just paint them, too. I added an extra hiding behind the left poppy for some depth in the composition.

Step 6: Once everything is dry, load the size 4 brush with sap green. Paint an uneven circle in the center of the two poppies. Drip a bit of the mix you created for the pincushion flowers in the center as well. Paint round buds for the pincushion flowers. As you see on page 54, they are round with white space and have triangles around the edge like a small sun. Spread these buds around the composition. Place one in front of the vase for depth and one hiding behind a flower as well.

Step 7: Paint the dancing stems with the tip of the size 4 brush and sap green. Make sure some of these stems are placed close to the sides of the vase, like they are leaning on the edge.

Step 8: Using the size 4 brush, paint the leaves on the stems of the pincushion flowers, still using the sap green.

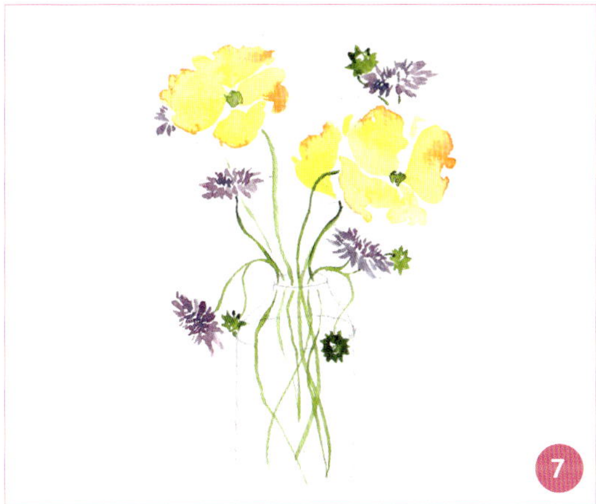

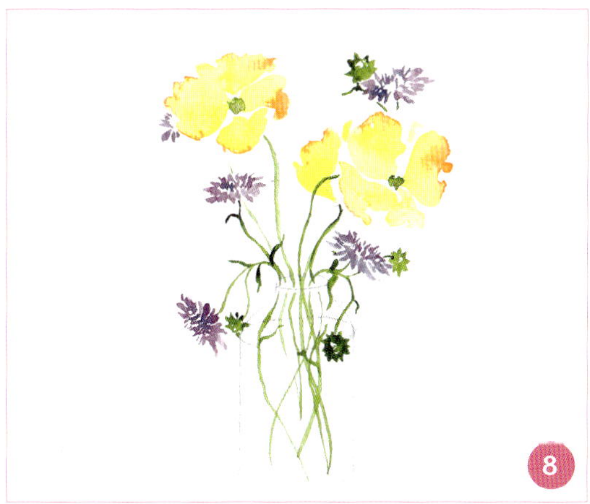

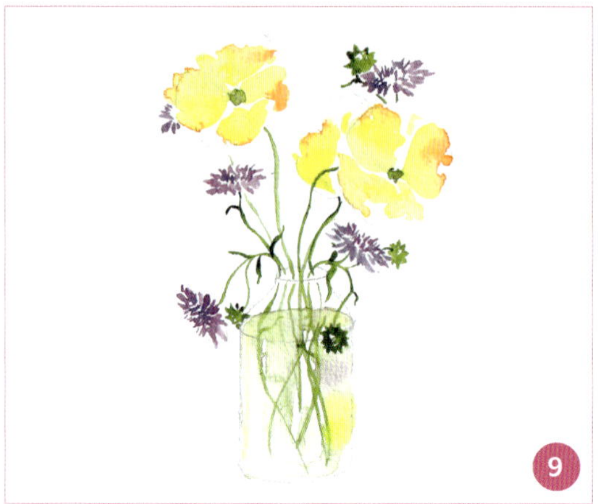

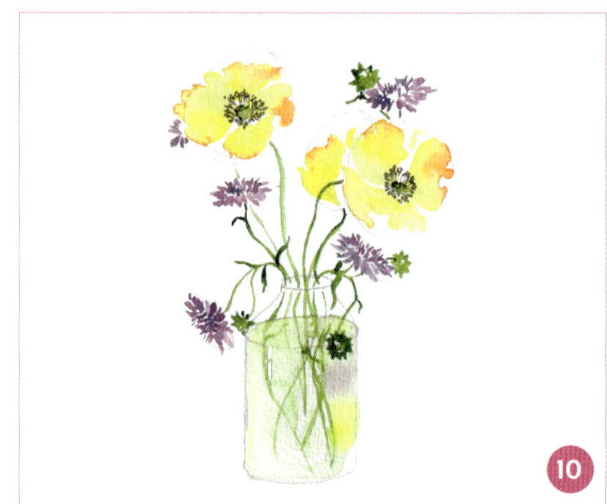

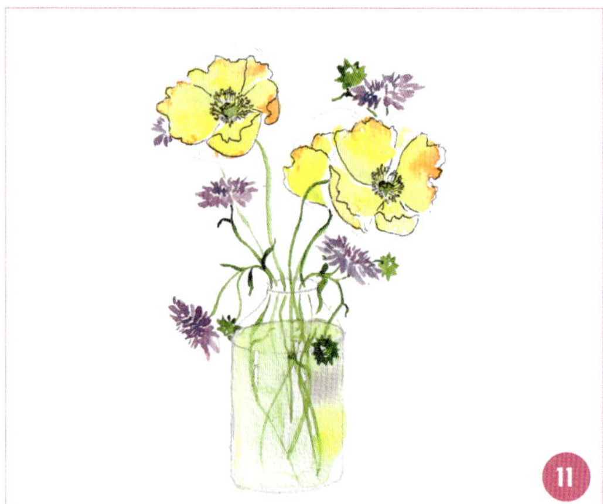

Step 9: The flowers look thirsty after all the dancing, so let's give them some water. Wet almost the entire area of the water in the vase, but keep a few spots dry for highlights. The water will instantly make the green stems run a bit but just let them, and enjoy how it looks when colors are set free.

Drip in some hansa yellow light in the water. Add a bit of the pincushion flower mix. Make sure you are not touching and mixing the paint in the water. It should be very watery and mix by itself.

This is the time when you go make yourself a cup of tea while you wait for the water to dry.

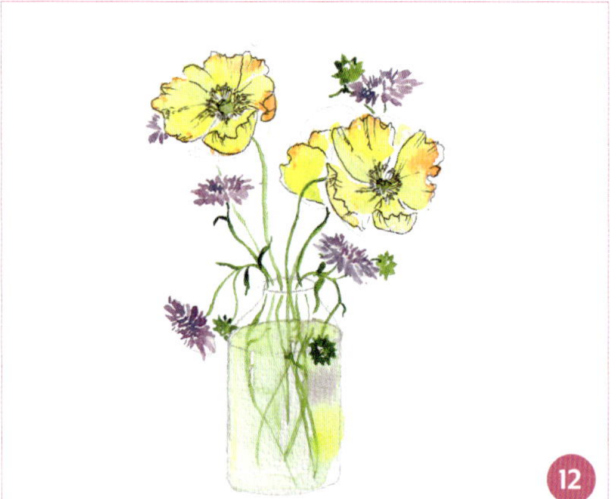

Step 10: When you finish your tea and your painting is dry, you can grab your 005 fineliner and draw the seeds in the center of the poppies like we did on page 41.

Step 11: Switch to the 01 fineliner and draw the outline of the poppy petals.

Step 12: Going back to the 005 fineliner, draw all the shaping lines for the poppies. Add some cute wrinkles for that crepe paper feel, like I showed you on page 42.

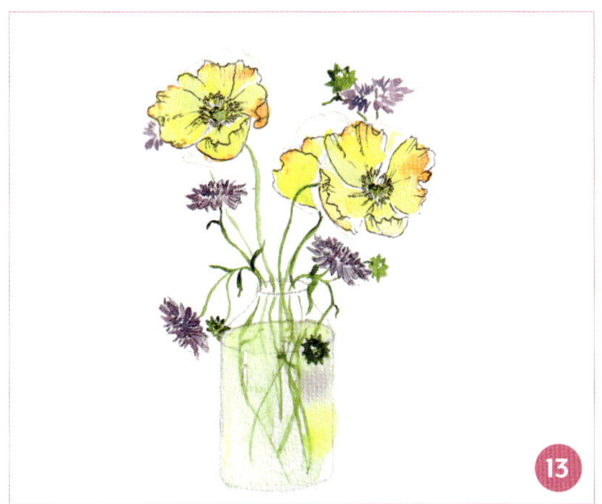

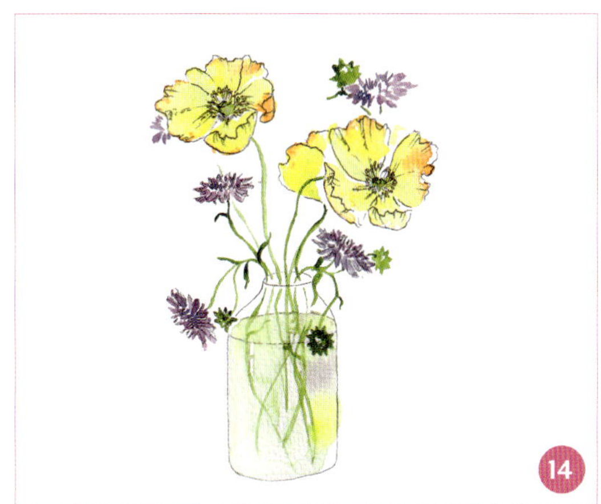

Step 13: Using the same fineliner, add details to a few of the pincushion flowers but also leave some without detail. Draw details on the buds closest to the vase. Remember that details attract attention, so we want to make sure the most detail goes to the poppies and the buds closest to them.

Step 14: Outline the vase with the same fineliner. When you outline the surface of the water, make sure to make an outline with a lot of holes, so it looks lighter than the edges of the vase. Erase the pencil now.

Step 15: It's down to the final details, so return to your 005 fineliner and draw on the stems. The poppies didn't shave this morning, so draw a few hairs on their stems as well.

And that is it . . . flowers in a perfectly balanced dance! This is just the beginning. You can create so many stunning posies just by following these few guidelines to build the composition.

While you sit back and enjoy the sketch you just created, I want to congratulate you on getting here! If you did all the sketches in this book one by one you have reached an incredible mile-stone! Wow!

Make sure to treat yourself to something nice. I would go for a piece of delicious chocolate and then put out all of the sketches next to each other. What a ride!

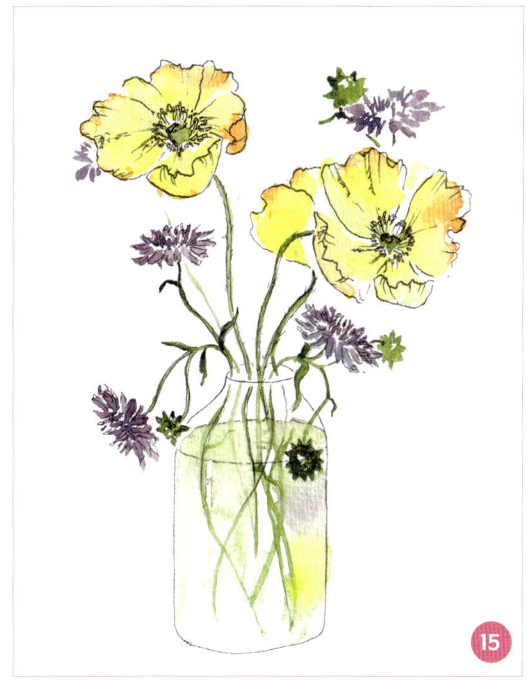

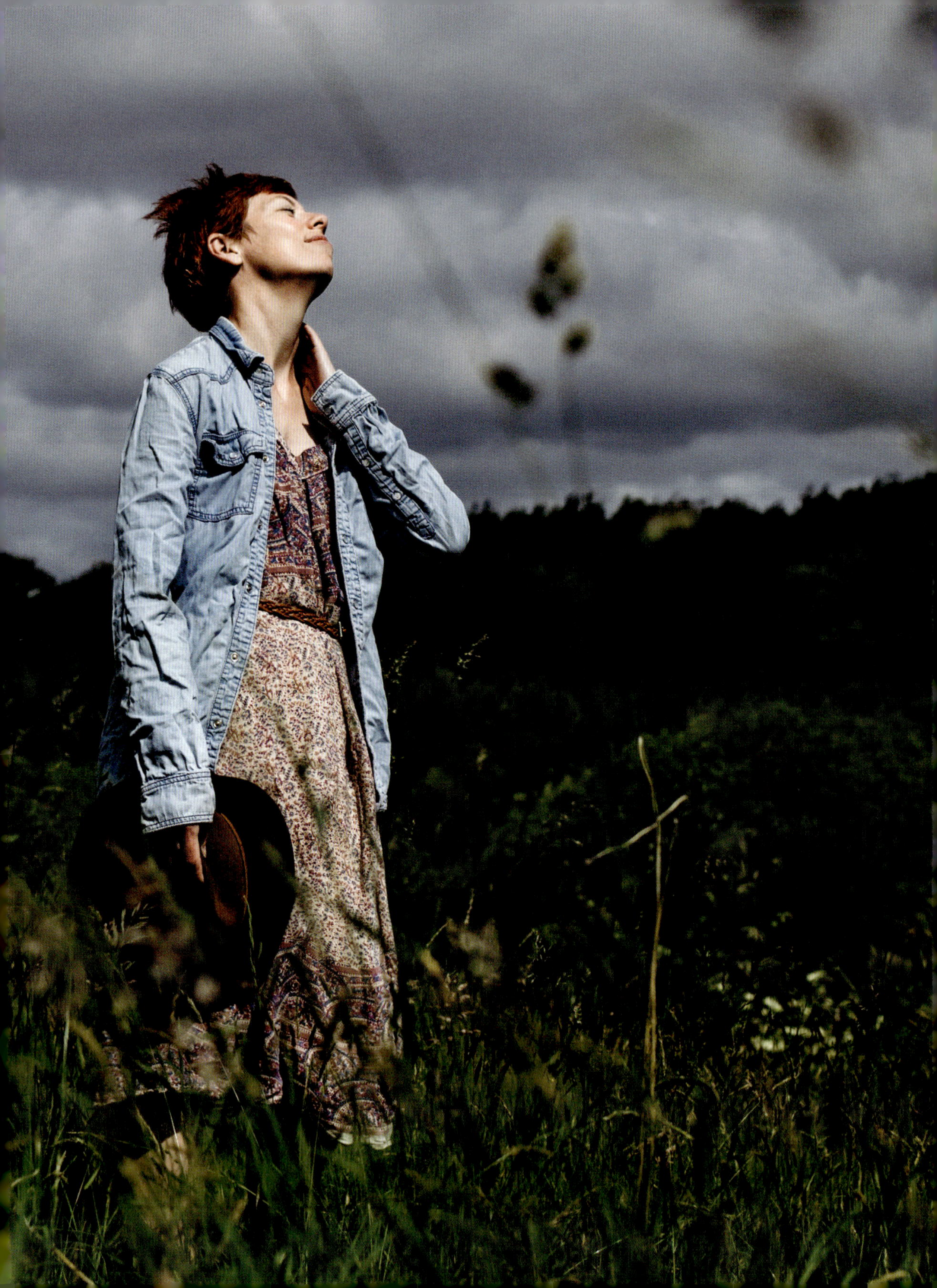

part V
wildflowers are a love story

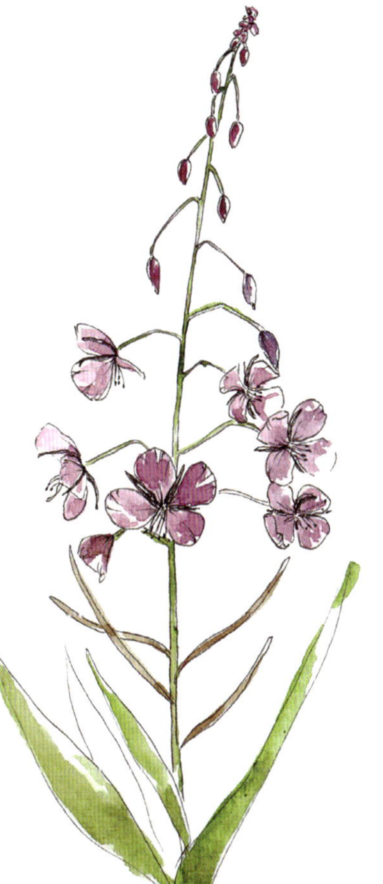

Once you get the basic floral shapes down, it is time for you to expand your knowledge. As I mentioned on page 16, there are at least nine different distinct floral shapes. All these shapes can be seen from many different angles, at different growth stages and in different lighting.

There is so much to explore. And I only covered a fraction of that in this book.

What you want to do now is close the book and go out there in the wild and fall in love. Take photos. Observe. Bring your sketchbook.

Sketching a flower is truly a love story. It makes you want to look beyond the beautiful makeup in bright sunlight. You want to start observing, maybe for an entire season. Get curious about your bloom. Learn how they look when they wake up in the morning and how they bloom in the day. See how they grow up and how they fade beautifully over a season. I know this can seem like a lot when you just want to do a sketch, but who says you can only do one sketch? There are hundreds of possibilities when sketching even just one bloom. All you need to do is be there, observe and draw.

always bring your floral artist goggles

There is a saying that artists see the world in a different way than others. They notice details and constantly make mental notes of things they want to sketch or paint. I think there is a truth to this. I once heard someone say, "Drawing is seeing," and that is so right. When you start to sketch the world, you also start to notice it.

You will see a color and start to think about how to mix it. Or you will see a shape and begin to think about how to place the lines in a drawing to get the right texture or curve.

This is incredible!

At times it can be overwhelming, because you suddenly get a lot of input every time you see a new flower, tree or branch. You will see something that sparks your inspiration every time. I personally get this feeling of overwhelm every summer when all the flowers are in full bloom. There is SO MUCH INSPIRATION! And this overwhelm can turn into a creative block. But that does not mean you have to leave your floral artist goggles at home.

Instead, my recommendation to you is to keep an ideas book. Every time you see something and get an idea, you can either just sketch it or photograph it and put a note of it in your book. This way, you won't risk overwhelm. You can keep fresh ideas in a safe place, ready to be sketched.

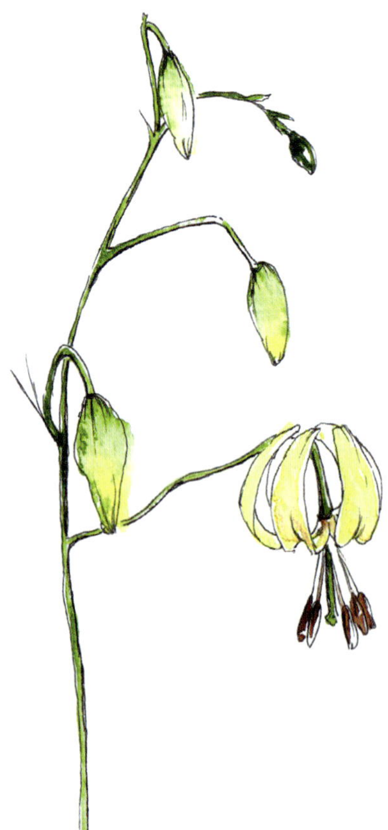

acknowledgments

As you may have noticed, I am very fascinated by and grateful to nature and all the quirky little things that make it so perfectly imperfect.

And gratitude is one of the most important lessons in this book, even more important than line and wash. I have wonderful people in my life that I am very grateful for . . . people I have seen throughout their lives, just like watching the flowers grow.

To my parents and grandparents that I have known all my life, you show me that every year is a new adventure with new colors. To my sister and brother who I have known for their entire lives, I am so grateful to have you as my cheerleaders and to see you both grow and bloom.

To old and new friends that have come into my life. A new friend is just like discovering a new flower to sketch. Old friends are like exploring the flowers on a deeper level. Both are incredible and make life such a fun ride.

Of course, to my two sweet little dandelion buds that will someday fly out into the world, but right now just ooze that fresh, green vibe like a bud in the spring. And to my hubby who is always looking out for me, even when I ramble on for hours about the changing colors in a tulip.

A big sun-filled, summer bouquet is sent out to all my wonderful students across the world. If you are following on Instagram, watching on YouTube or are a part of my wonderful community on Patreon—thank you! I can't begin to describe how much you mean to me.

And very importantly I am sending a big bouquet of wild roses to the incredible team at Page Street! Thank you so much for trusting me with a third book. This is beyond my wildest dreams.

Finally, I want to thank you. Thank you for reading and inviting me on your creative journey. It is such an honor.

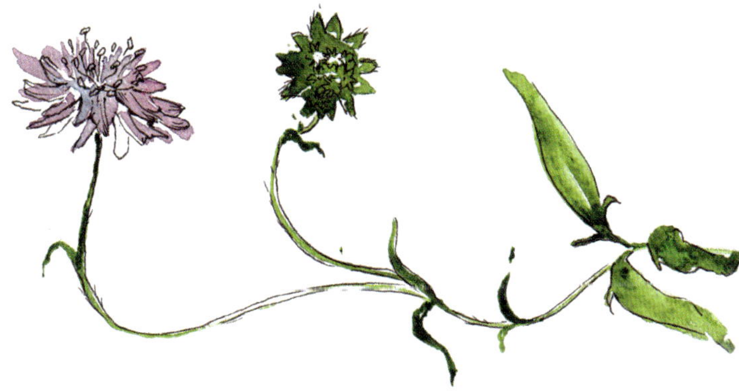

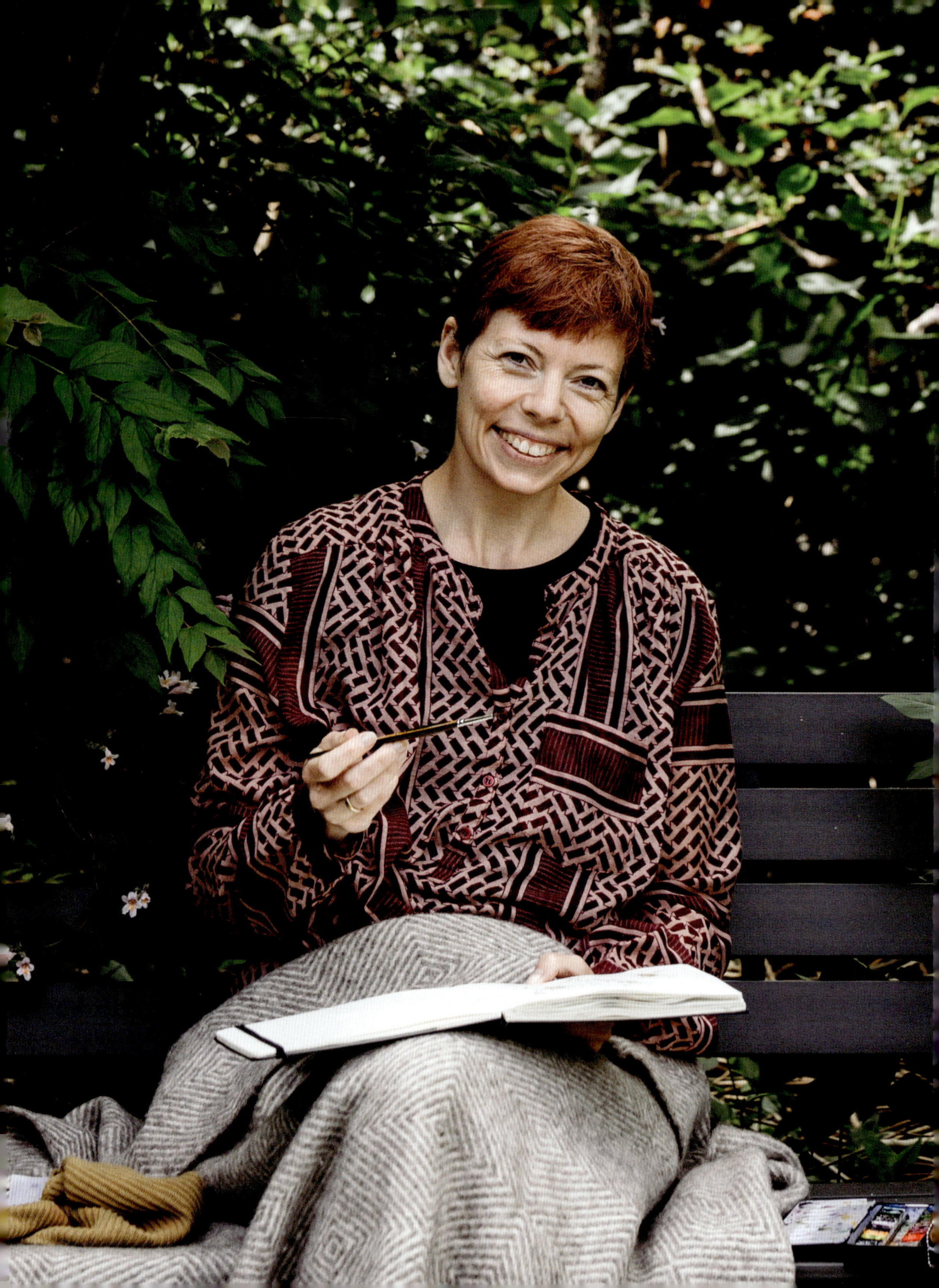

about the author

Camilla is the hand and heart behind the floral sketches you find here in this book. She is a mom, wife, flower lover, nature enthusiast, watercolor teacher, author and crazy cat lady all wrapped up in one passionate artist.

She lives in a small red house in rural Denmark that's surrounded by wildflowers from January to November. When she is not writing her bestselling books or teaching line and wash online, she goes for long walks in nature and often brings along her sketchbooks to capture the seasons changing.

You can dive even deeper into her fascination with the beauty of nature in her first two books, *Ink & Wash Florals* and *Ink & Wash in the Garden*, as well as on YouTube, Instagram, Patreon and in her online courses available on her website, camilladamsboart.com.

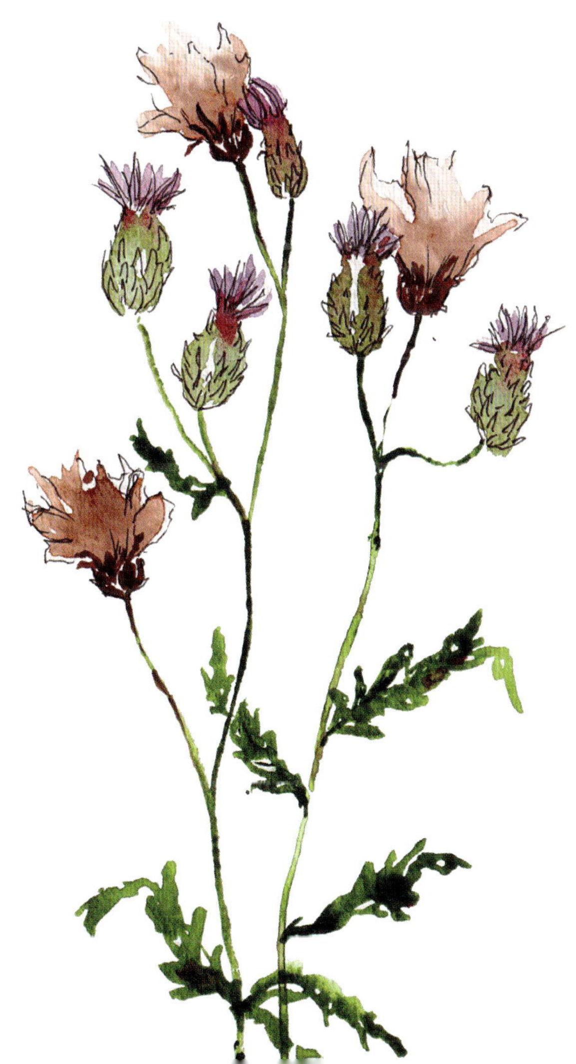

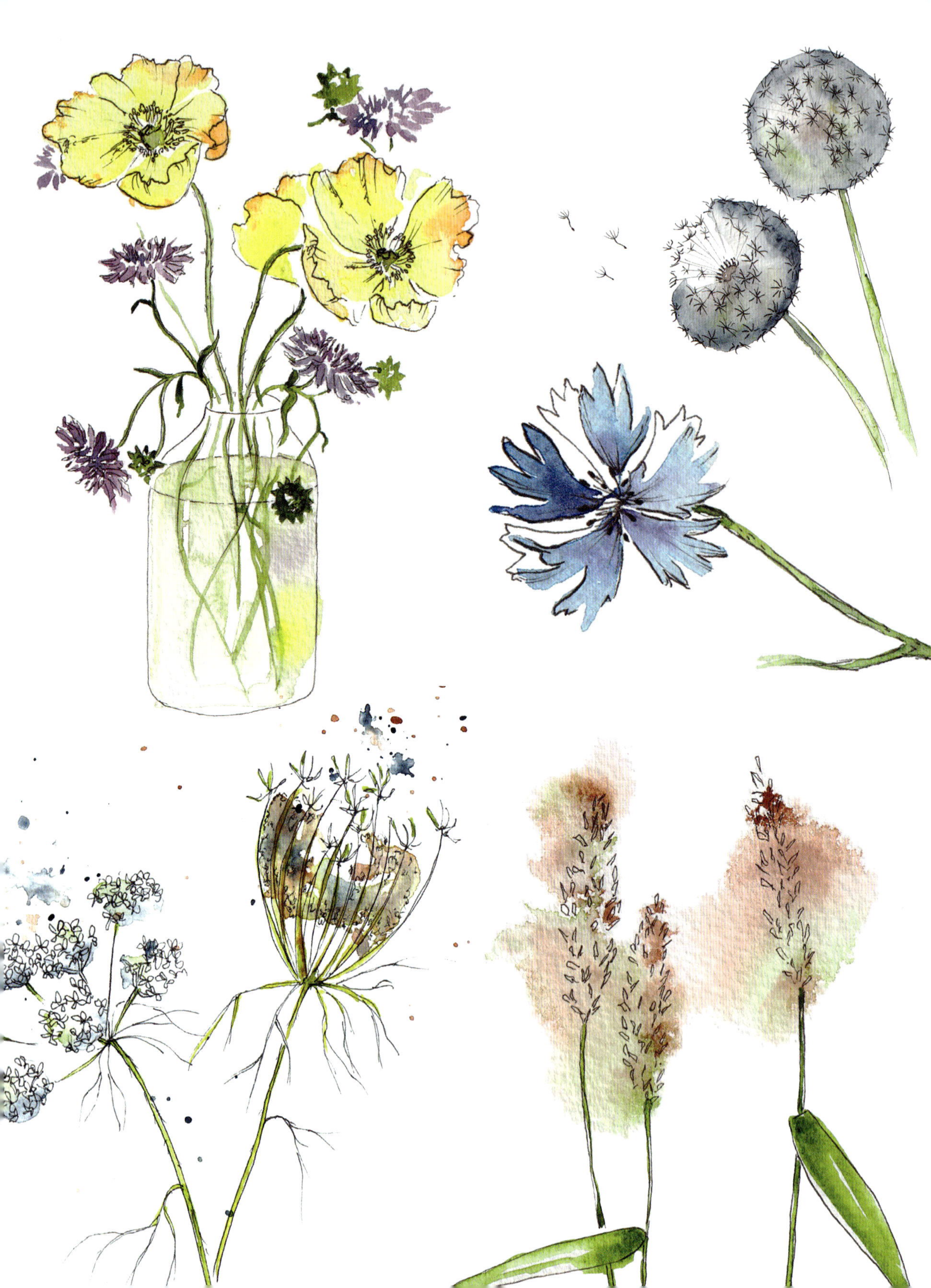

index

Page numbers in **boldface** indicate illustrations.